SOUTH

The Story of Shackleton's Last Expedition 1914-17

SOUTH

The Story of Shackleton's Last Expedition 1914-17

"For scientific discovery give me Scott; for speed
and efficiency of travel give me Amundsen; but when
disaster strikes and all hope is gone, get down on
your knees and pray for Shackleton"

SIR EDMUND HILLARY

by SIR ERNEST SHACKLETON

Edited by PETER KING

Trafalgar Square Publishing

NORTH POMFRET, VERMONT

INTRODUCTION

In a sense, *South* is one volume of Ernest Shackleton's autobiography or testament. Published in 1919 and rarely out of print since, it was his second book recording an expedition to the polar regions – the first being *The Heart of the Antarctic* of 1909. While purporting to be a factual record of the epic journey, *South* is in truth a highly selective account of what happened and why. Shackleton's choice of what to include and what to exclude tells us a great deal about the character of this extraordinary man.

Like his earlier book, *South* was not written solely by Shackleton. He was assisted by a New Zealand journalist whose contribution was so significant that the explorer wanted to put his name alongside his own on the title page. This was Edward Saunders, who had fallen under the spell of his hero's personality. He wrote, 'My work was complementary to his,' and while he clearly composed much of the text himself after listening to Shackleton's account, he added that the latter 'had a remarkable gift of literary suggestion . . . and when his interest was stirred . . . he had command of vivid and forceful English'. The book includes substantial quotations from the diaries kept by the other members of the expedition, whom Shackleton pledged to assign their copyright to him before departure. His own diaries were rather sketchy.

If *South* is in essence autobiographical, its text neglects aspects of its subject's character that biographers suggest are key to his life's story. For one thing (although the book virtually ignores the fact) Shackleton's polar life was inextricably bound up with the career of Robert Falcon Scott, the British explorer whom both the nation and the world at large believed for over seventy-five years to be a hero in the mould of Drake and Nelson. Unlike the undertakings of those earlier heroes, Scott's mission failed, but the British let this pass almost unnoticed. Recent research has since made it clear that – as Shackleton subconsciously suspected – the Scott myth was created by falsification of the record, and that whatever the extent of his bravery, the true nature of his expedition could not be described as heroic in any normal sense of the word.

The modern biographer of Shackleton is therefore presented with the difficulty of extracting the real man from the standards set by his contemporaries in the light of the comparison they could not avoid making between him and the kind of hero they (incorrectly) perceived Scott to be. This task is made more complex by the mutual antagonism between the two explorers. There is the irony that Scott is the more famous figure, yet the greater failure and, if a comparison has to be made, perhaps less imbued with heroic qualities.

Another problem facing the biographer is that the first two major published lives of Shackleton (by Mill in 1923 and the Fishers in 1957) do not paint a fully rounded picture of their subject.

The biographies principally referred to are *Shackleton* by Margery & James Fisher (Barrie 1957) alas no longer in print and *Shackleton* by Roland Huntford (Hodder & Stoughton 1985 and in paperback by Cardinal 1989).

(Opposite) A photograph of *Endurance*, which has all the classic Hurley qualities of contrast, composition and dramatic lighting. Hurley would sometimes make composite pictures to enhance his effects.

Both Fisher and Huntford give detail of the sources of information used and the latter had the benefit of being able to see records of his predecessor's interviews, 30 years earlier, with survivors.

A classic problem inevitably arises: is it necessary to know that a great achiever has faults common to many men? That he was a womaniser, could not manage his financial affairs, lived off his wife's money, had a brother who was a scoundrel, did not care overmuch for his parents in their declining years, and often lost his temper? These are after all not hanging matters. The present-day reader of biographies has come to accept that, perhaps to his surprise, certain of these same defects characterise many public men and women whom we have put on a pillar of hero-worship. The Fishers must have known some of the detail of Shackleton's defects when they wrote their biography, particularly as James Fisher had the benefit of interviewing many of Shackleton's contemporaries, but he did not feel it necessary to impart much of it to the reader – he may, indeed, have felt that much of it was not proved beyond a shadow of doubt. The Fishers give some information about Shackleton's financial difficulties but do not underline the difficulties that arose from the resultant unpreparedness of his expeditions.

Matters such as Shackleton's promiscuous behaviour with women, while again unlikely to have been totally unknown to the Fishers, are not only ignored but overpainted with a misleading suggestion that his marriage was a conventionally happy one. All such illusions were firmly shattered in 1985 by the publication of James Huntford's *Shackleton*, a best-selling biography which won two prize awards.

Therefore, whilst this edition of *South* reproduces the abridged text of 1922 without change, it seems wrong to force a reader who might have read Fisher or Huntford or both to accept Shackleton's version of events without the facility to cross-reference to the 'facts' of the case in the light of their studies.

The chosen solution has been to sideline the text with editorial notes which allow the reader to understand the background, whether or not he is familiar with the Fisher and Huntford biographies, and to caption the pictures in a way that draws attention to the later information now available.

(Below) **Henrietta Letitia Sophia (his mother), Dr Henry Shackleton (father) and Ernest Henry himself aged eleven.**

Ernest Shackleton was born on 15 February 1874, the second child and elder son of a family that eventually included two brothers and eight sisters. The family was of respectable Yorkshire stock – they had a coat of arms and a motto, *By Perseverence We Conquer* – and Shackleton's branch

had been settled in Ireland, where he was born, for four generations. The family had established a boarding school, which became known as the Eton of Ireland. Henry, Shackleton's father, had however been educated in England, at Wellington College, probably because it was his aim to enlist in the army. His health did not permit this and he returned to Ireland to finish his education at Trinity College, Dublin, where he became classical prizeman and graduated in Arts in 1868.

The Irish branch of the family must have been reasonably well-to-do. They had their own coat of arms and motto: *Fortitudine Vincimus (By Endurance We Conquer)*. Henry married in 1872 and had enough money to buy a farm in Kildare, some 30 miles from Dublin. The Fishers, who had the benefit of talking to her children and grandchildren, say of his wife, Letitia Gavan, that she was an energetic and charming woman who created an atmosphere of security and affection in the family home. A child was born in the first year of marriage, and Letitia was pregnant each year for the next ten years, not an unusual condition for those times.

The family's Irish coat of arms with its motto which translates as 'By Endurance We Conquer'.

The Irish farm did not prosper – this was the period of the Potato Famine – and Shackleton's father decided to cut his losses and change his way of life. He returned to Trinity College, Dublin, where he now qualified as a doctor. The family lived in a comfortable Dublin house for four years of his studies. These completed, he moved in 1884 to London, first setting up in practice in Croydon and, when that did not succeed, moving on to Sydenham, an affluent middle-class suburb in southeast London.

The Fishers describe the settled nature of Shackleton's early days. 'In the pleasant and peaceful setting of Victorian Sydenham the children grew and flourished. Stories of their games and jaunts remind one of the families in E. Nesbit's books. There is the same air of jollity and family affection, the same tolerance and mutual understanding, the same jokes.'

In contrast, Huntford paints a darker picture. He says that by the late 1880s 'the mother had by now become mysteriously an invalid' and was to remain one for the last forty years of her life. She spent her waking hours in her sick-room, scarcely noticed by her family. It was Dr Shackleton who brought up his children, helped by his mother-in-law and various female relatives who came over periodically from Ireland. So Shackleton was a rare male in a predominantly female household. Yet the father, not the mother, was the parent to whom he most closely related.

Until the age of eleven and a half, Ernest was educated at home by a governess. Then he went to a preparatory school nearby. He was friendly and good-natured but earnest by nature as well as name, joining the Band of Hope and persuading his sisters and others to sign the pledge against alcohol. His accent was markedly Irish and he remained quite clearly an Anglo-Irishman all his days. In 1887, Ernest went as a day boy to Dulwich College. This school has a somewhat special character in the class hierarchy of the British system of education. Founded by Edward Alleyn, Shakespeare's theatrical manager, it was not in the rank of the major London schools like Westminster or St Paul's. Yet it did not aspire to emulate and join them but merely to produce for its mainly middle-class pupils an education of equal excellence. A later well-known pupil was P. G. Wodehouse. The fees were comparatively low, only £15 a year.

Shackleton was early on a keen reader, of poetry as well as prose, although he did not find the Dulwich teachers inspiring. Later, when he was famous, he wrote in an article for the school magazine that the school had not taught him much, neither geography nor an understanding of literature. 'Teachers should be very careful not to spoil [the] taste for poetry for all time by making it a task and an imposition', he warned. He was usually towards the bottom of the class and he did not shine at team games.

According to Huntford, Shackleton's favourite reading at this time was the *Boys' Own Paper*, a weekly magazine that for nearly a century was a synonym for a certain kind of adventure story.

Dr Mills, Shackleton's earliest biographer, was told by masters at Dulwich that Shackleton suffered from lack of incentive rather than intelligence.

(Above) **Shackleton aged 16 in uniform of White Star Line (*left*), aged 27 as third officer of the *Carisbrooke Castle* (*centre*); and aged 30 in uniform of the Royal Naval Reserve (*right*).**

The Fisher biography has an appendix on Shackleton's creative writing which quotes this poem in full.

'*Boys' Own Paper* stuff' would have the same kind of ring about it as would, later, 'A John Wayne film'. Possibly because a fair proportion of its stories were about feats of derring-do at sea, Shackleton had already made up his mind that he would prefer not to follow his father into medicine, as the latter wished, but to go into the Royal Navy. The family's means were not sufficient, it was said, for him to go to Dartmouth College, the naval academy, and in any case he had passed the entry age. It would therefore have to be the Merchant Navy. A cousin of his father, an archdeacon who was Superintendent of the Mersey Mission to Seamen, secured him a place through a Liverpool owner. According to Shackleton, who later came to dislike and neglect both his parents, 'My father thought to cure me of my predilection for the sea by letting me go in the most primitive manner possible as a "boy" on board a sailing ship at a shilling a month.'

The life Shackleton had led at home and school up to the age of sixteen had not fitted him for a life on a sailing ship at sea. Although able to look after himself, he had characteristics that made him out of the ordinary, for example his teetotal convictions, which were much at variance with the norm of life at sea in those days, his bible reading and his enthusiasm for quoting poetry. His sisters recall his having a copy of Dante in his sea trunk at this time. It says a good deal for Shackleton's self-confidence and stubborn nature that he came through the experience without any obvious scars. The captain of his first ship liked him, although he told the archdeacon he was 'the most pig-headed obstinate boy I have ever come across'. In 1891, after his trial voyage, Shackleton was formally indentured by his father as an apprentice. He spent the next few years sailing the seas of the world, except for brief periods of leave at home with his adoring sisters and several weeks in 1894 when he was being coached at a nautical school in London for his examination for second mate. While he was qualifying for his master's certificate he followed the customary practice of filling in time on tramp steamers bound for the Far East. During this period, aged only twenty-one, he wrote a longish poem, 'A Tale of the Sea', dated February 1895, which is a thoughtful exercise, apparently influenced by Tennyson. He continued to be an avid reader, devouring the volumes of Motley and Prescott amongst others.

In April 1898, just twenty-four years old, Shackleton was certified as a master, theoretically able to command any British ship, sail or steam. He had conquered any fear of the sea (perhaps this

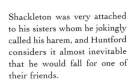

was some way of coming to terms with his relationship with his father) but already had his sights aimed at higher things. He told a shipmate, 'I think I can do something better. I would like to make a name for myself.' At this point he added 'and her' for he had already become attached to Emily Dorman, a friend of his sisters and six years older than he, and from a rather better-off background. Her father was a successful London solicitor. It was the first time that he had been in love; he seemed to have been able to avoid even the casual attachments common to the seafaring life. The two embarked on a vigorous correspondence, made more romantic by a mutual admiration for the poetry of Robert Browning.

In 1899 he moved to the Union Castle line, one of the élite of the Merchant Navy and the next best thing to the Royal Navy itself. He was soon promoted to third officer but, eager to marry Emily, he knew that he could not make enough money in his chosen profession to keep her in the style to which she was accustomed and that her family would expect. He was also bored with the naval 'monotony and method of routine'. With his fondness for quoting poetry and his ability to charm his audience when something fascinated him, he was already an unusual animal for a ship's officer, with much wider interests than most of his companions. For example, he persuaded a cousin to propose him for the Royal Geographical Society, of which he became a Fellow (a routine procedure, not requiring any particular qualifications). He also became a Freemason.

In March 1900, taking troops to South Africa, Shackleton met an army lieutenant, Cedric Longstaff, whose father Shackleton had heard was the principal benefactor of the proposed National Antarctic Expedition. Longstaff provided Shackleton with an introduction to his father, on whom he made an instant impression. The elder Longstaff promised to use his influence to secure Shackleton a place on the expedition, which would otherwise be difficult to obtain since it was to be primarily a Royal Navy affair, led by Scott, then a relatively unknown RN officer. Longstaff made a direct approach to Sir Clements Markham, president of the Royal Geographical Society, the organiser of the expedition. Markham, who would want more money from his patron in due course, was in no position to refuse. In any case, Markham made enquiries of Union Castle, who replied that Shackleton was more intelligent than the average officer and that his brother officers considered him to be a very good fellow.

Exploration of the Antarctic was a popular topic at this time, and not only in Britain. Shackleton later used to tell reporters that he had always been 'strangely drawn to the mysterious south' and that unexplored parts of the world 'held a strong fascination for me from my earliest recollections'. There is no other evidence for this, and it has to be noted that Shackleton was also writing to Emily's father to stress that he expected the expedition to allow him to return to England in a position to make money (he admitted that his present circumstances were 'not rosy'). He said, 'My fortune is all to make but I intend making it quickly.' Shackleton was not explicit about how this could be done, although there had been articles in the press suggesting that the Antarctic might be another Klondike with precious metals to be mined and fisheries to be exploited.

Shackleton now moved into a new social milieu, hobnobbing with the mighty in the expedition's headquarters in Bond Street and taking cabs to see Emily at her home in South Kensington. It was heady stuff for the young merchant sailor. So, too, was the royal inspection at Cowes before the *Discovery* set sail. In fact, this expedition, which got underway in the summer of 1901, was a badly-organised affair, lacking a scientific basis and probably aimed more at establishing British glory than anything else. A mark of its amateurism was that the selection of fancy dress for the crew's entertainment received more emphasis than did the selection of skis for their survival. Shackleton made himself popular with everyone on board, particularly with Dr H. R. Mill, a noted oceanographer and meteorologist, and Edward Wilson, another of the scientists

Shackleton was very attached to his sisters whom he jokingly called his harem, and Huntford considers it almost inevitable that he would fall for one of their friends.

Mill only sailed as far as Madeira but by the time he left the ship, he and Shackleton were firm friends.

(Above) His messmates on the 1902 expedition caricatured Shackleton whom they described as 'The Parsenger'.

(Above) Another member of the expedition, E. A. Wilson, was responsible for the more dignified silhouette.

and the ship's junior surgeon. The common bond with the latter was poetry. Shackleton's specific job, an exacting one, was the supervision of stores.

Mill, who was to become Shackleton's friend and biographer, wrote later, 'To Shackleton the National Antarctic Expedition was an opportunity and nothing more. He would have tried to join just as eagerly a ship bound to seek buried treasure on the Spanish Main.' To understand how Shackleton became an explorer of international fame and wrote *South*, the story of his most famous exploits, it is necessary to follow this first voyage in some detail.

First, one must dwell a little on the relationship between Scott and Shackleton, because their failure to like one another may have been at the base of Shackleton's future determination to make his own mark in the Antarctic. Scott had considerable shortcomings as a leader: for example, when they first encountered the ice, he ordered everyone else out on to a floe to learn to ski, while he himself remained aloof. Wilson described Scott as 'strangely reticent about letting a soul on the ship know what his immediate plans are'. He also lost his head several times and appeared to Shackleton to be in panic when the ship was virtually trapped in the ice. Shackleton, in contrast, was self-possessed, made a point of getting on with the other crew members whatever their rank, and gave an impression 'of immense physical power'. Although he was only five feet ten in height, most people thought of him as being very tall. His shoulders were 'immensely broad', and his firm mouth and square chin enhanced the image of determination. Scott, whose first command this was, appeared to the others in contrast to be something of a martinet whose response to any situation was to follow the naval rule book. According to Huntford, Shackleton, although the junior officer, rapidly assumed 'psychological leadership' over Scott.

The amateurism that characterised this expedition is now becoming general knowledge. Many of the men had never put up, or slept in, a tent. Most could not ski, sledge or use dog teams. Their clothes were inadequate and let the wind through. They were undernourished. None of them had much training of work in snow. Huntford describes the expedition as an amalgam of ignorance, inexperience and unpreparedness. Shackleton appears to have been aware of these shortcomings. He had also rapidly formed the opinion that 'Irishmen make better leaders than followers' and thus was not particularly surprised, though pleased, when Scott chose him, together with his friend Wilson, to accompany him on the dash south across the snow that could possibly lead to an attack on the pole.

In fact, conditions were wholly against any such venture. The three men averaged only 4 miles a day at first, the dogs eventually had to be destroyed and Shackleton became ill, partly from scurvy caused by the failure at that time to understand that the cause of this disease was dietary. He may also have had a more serious problem, perhaps a heart condition. By his own account he burst a blood vessel. The documentary evidence as to what actually happened to Shackleton's health is vague, particularly in Shackleton's own written records, but there must certainly have been some serious argument between the three men, particularly between Scott and Shackleton. The two had already disagreed about diet and Scott's casual attitude to scurvy. Each called the other a 'bloody fool', with Scott provoking the incident.

The three men made an odd trio. Wilson was religious and read from the Psalms on Sunday. Scott, who had abandoned orthodox beliefs, countered with *The Origin of Species*, which he got Shackleton and Wilson to read aloud in turn. More fundamentally, Huntford believes that Scott harboured a profound dislike of Shackleton. So when Shackleton's physical weakness gradually became apparent, he could not count on much sympathy from his leader, who put the dash to the south before everything else. Scott even decided to continue the journey after Wilson diagnosed scurvy in his two companions and scurvy, it was known, was a killer. Eventually, very reluctantly, under pressure from both his companions, Scott agreed to turn back. He discarded the skis, shot the dogs and pulled the sledges (on which the skis were strapped). Huntford calls this an 'heroic' farce that has been romanticised as part of the glorious phase of British polar exploration. In fact, the three, often up to their knees in snow, had come to doubt if they could even survive what they knew to be a fairly worthless journey. Shackleton was becoming short of breath and began coughing blood. He was ordered not to pull the sledges and was too big to be carried by the others. He managed to stagger along on a pair of skis. He did not know how to ski, but at least he no longer sank in the snow. Nevertheless he progressively fell behind the other two.

Huntford says that at this point Scott's antagonism to Shackleton became openly apparent, with phrases like 'lame duck' being freely used. As they neared the ship, Shackleton became

They had reached a position, their furthest south, at latitude 82°15'S. by 31 December.

(Left) Shackleton, Scott and Wilson, with sledges and sledge flags in the background, as they set off on their epic foray south.

seriously ill and in later life said that he had heard Scott and Wilson discussing whether he would last the night. Somehow he made a supreme effort and began to recover. He was put on the sledge, on which a sail had been rigged, making the last few miles by ski again.

On their return to base, Scott requested the doctor to make a formal examination of Shackleton, expressing the view that an executive officer should 'enjoy such health that [he] can at any moment be called upon to undergo hardships and exposure'. The doctor wrote in reply that by this standard he could not say that Shackleton would be fit to remain in the polar regions. Privately he wrote that Shackleton had been attacked by 'a sort of asthma'. Scott then told Shackleton that he was to be sent home. The latter's disappointment was intense and he told others that he doubted if his health was the real reason for the decision. According to one member of the party, Scott said,

The doctor wrote that Shackleton, besides scurvy, had 'a sort of asthma' and there were signs, later, that this was a recurrent problem.

'If he does not go back sick, he will go back in disgrace.' Huntford believes that Scott was referring to the fact that Shackleton had somehow avoided having a full medical examination before joining the expedition. He adds: 'Few leaders find it easy to tolerate stronger men under their command. Shackleton had charisma and the power of self-presentation. Scott had neither. He was conventional and ordinary. Shackleton was a spiritual anarchist. He had shown up Scott's failings. . . . Sickness came as a providential pretext. A sick Shackleton would be an admirable excuse for the shortcomings of the journey . . . and divert attention from the monumental bungling which Scott had to conceal.' It did not pass unnoticed that Shackleton and most of the other men being sent home were from the merchant marine, thus leaving behind a more 'pure' naval contingent, which, Scott believed, could make a second attack on the pole.

Shackleton was shattered emotionally by his enforced departure. He was now twenty-nine years old and it must have seemed that his career as an explorer was at an end. He cabled Emily 'BROKEN DOWN IN CHEST RETURNING SOUTHERN SLEDGE JOURNEY SUFFERING SCURVY AND OVERSTRAIN DON'T WORRY NEARLY WELL COMING HOME.' With his customary willpower he stopped off in New Zealand to recover his health and by the time he returned to London he was once more exercising his 'spiritual anarchy' on those in charge of the expedition. Another member writes that Shackleton had sworn 'he meant to return and prove to Scott that he – Shackleton – was a better man than Scott.'

Rather surprisingly Shackleton first took a job as a journalist in Fleet Street, following up a successful stint as editor of the ship *Discovery*'s newspaper. He did not enjoy the job and his old mentor Dr Mill soon helped him to obtain the secretaryship of the Royal Scottish Geographical Society in Edinburgh at a salary of £200 a year. Since her father's death Emily had inherited an independent income of £700 a year and by living, in part, off this they could afford to marry. Shackleton persuaded Emily to give up a honeymoon so that he could get to work on his new job – he felt he had to make it a stepping stone in his self-appointed task of defeating Scott. One weapon to hand was his skill as a public speaker, and he gave lectures on the *Discovery* expedition. Probably as a result of this oratorical ability he was asked to stand for Parliament as a Unionist (Tory). 'I am an Irishman', Shackleton declared 'and I consider myself a true patriot . . . when I say that Ireland should not have Home Rule.' The latter was one of the major political issues of the day. Shackleton had now adopted the stance of an Irishman in most of his dealings, and, like many Irishmen, he attracted friends and enemies in equal numbers.

He resigned from the Royal Scottish Geographical Society and, while waiting for the election to be held, attempted to start a career in business. In this he was following the example of his younger brother Frank who was moving in a wealthy and influential set which, amongst other things, may have been homosexual, and this enabled him to be appointed Dublin Herald at the little Heraldic Court at Dublin Castle, thus enlarging his social milieu still further.

Shackleton was particularly anxious to eliminate from the record any suggestion that he had had to be carried on the sledge, and in November 1904 Scott wrote a letter to the *Daily Mail*, possibly at Shackleton's request, refuting their inference that he had to be carried on the sledge for 150 miles.

Ernest Shackleton now suffered a severe setback in morale when Scott, returned to England, published *The Voyage of the 'Discovery'*, which reopened all the old wounds about Shackleton's breakdown in health. Some of the things Scott wrote on this subject were untrue and Shackleton was incensed and humiliated. As a Freemason he felt that Scott, another, had broken his oath not to wrong a brother Mason. He believed that he could only get satisfaction by himself mounting another expedition to the south and outdoing Scott. Meanwhile, he fought and lost the 1906 election. He engaged himself in further business deals with his brother Frank, now involved in apparently somewhat shady transactions, and then took a job with a leading Scottish industrialist William Beardmore, with whose wife Shackleton was on very friendly terms. Meanwhile he was spending little time with the family (Emily had a son in 1905 when she was 37) although he wrote frequently to his wife of promised El Dorados and the fortunes that were only months away from making. He made trips to London on business and was involved in strange prospective ventures such as chartering ships in Russia. He also expanded his friendship with Elspeth Beardmore and borrowed £1,000 from a wealthy spinster, Elizabeth Dawson-Lambton. This sum he gave to his brother to invest, planning to use it to form the nucleus of a fund to mount his expedition.

Huntford describes the Russian venture as highly speculative and says that at this period Shackleton was in financial straits.

Early in 1906 Shackleton drew up a printed prospectus for the expedition to the Ross Sea and the South Pole, which he sent to seventy businessmen to whom he appealed for financial support. But he was a comparative unknown, and there was no positive response. In February of the following year he announced his plan at a Royal Geographical Society meeting and it was publicised in the press. A novel feature of this revised plan was that he would place little reliance on dogs, replacing them almost entirely with ponies and a motor car, which he optimistically believed would permit a travelling speed of 20–25 miles a day. The plan included nothing in the way of budget forecasts and Shackleton relied on speculative guarantees of money, which he promised he would refund on his return from the sale of a book and from lectures. There would also be exclusive deals with newspapers.

In 1907 Shackleton persuaded one of his brother's City friends to invest in the expedition. Beardmore provided a bank guarantee and supplied the motor car. Huntford suggests that one reason why Beardmore supported the journey to the south was the widely accepted rumour that his wife and Shackleton were in the middle of an affair. With financial backing assured, Shackleton broke news of his plan to Emily, who had just given birth to their second child, a daughter, born just after Christmas 1906.

Meanwhile there were difficult negotiations, conducted by exchange of letters with Scott, who was at sea with the Navy. Both Scott and the Royal Geographical Society regarded Shackleton as an outsider and Scott believed that he had some rights to the next attack on the South Pole. Shackleton, anxious not to alienate his own financial supporters, came to a compromise with Scott, promising that he would not 'trespass' on Scott's preferred route. He had allowed himself only seven months to prepare for his own departure, being anxious to set off well ahead of Scott, and he was still worried about his health. He set up an office in London and threw himself into preparations, at first trying to revive the

(Above) **Emily Shackleton in 1909, five years after marriage, about the time her husband returned in triumph from his own 'Further South' expedition.**

Discovery expedition with himself replacing Scott. For one reason or another, most members of that crew declined to join him, the notable exceptions being Frank Wild and Ernest Joyce. Nansen, with whom he discussed his plans, was dismayed at the way Shackleton acted as an inspired amateur in choice of crew as in almost everything else.

He ignored all the advice given him about dogs (Shackleton was indifferent to animals, according to Huntford) and persisted in putting his faith in ponies and the motor car. Worse still, his City supporter pulled out. Instead of £30,000 he now only had £7,000 and £1,000 from Elizabeth Dawson-Lambton. The ship he had bought, *Nimrod*, was to cost £11,000 but it was small and over forty years old, a battered tramp. His brother Frank was a liability in the matter of finance and was now on the verge of bankruptcy. Less than a month before *Nimrod* was due to sail, the Irish crown jewels were reported stolen and Frank Shackleton was a prime suspect. A major scandal erupted and Shackleton himself was tainted with it. At the last minute he persuaded the Earl of Iveagh, of the Guinness family, to guarantee £2,000 if others brought the total sum for the

15

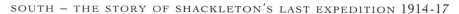

Emily and the children had not been at Cowes but they were staying at Torquay where *Nimrod* anchored in the bay and, together with brother Frank, they came on board.

expedition up to £8,000. Somehow Shackleton managed to persuade supporters to do so but he knew he had to sail towards the south before his creditors caught up with him. Huntford believes that his Masonic connections helped, as they did with his getting recognition from King Edward VII. At Cowes, visiting *Nimrod* with a large royal party, the King told the assembled crew, 'When Captain Scott left in *Discovery* I conferred the Royal Victorian Order on him. I now do the same to you. . . . ' Early in August 1907, *Nimrod* sailed south.

Shackleton did not sail with her. At the last minute he had to return to rescue Frank from a problem with some dishonoured bills. He did so by borrowing another £1,000 from Beardmore, which he was unable to repay before he left (by commercial routes) to join *Nimrod* in Australia. Emily and the family had to exist on her own allowance plus some money from expedition funds – such as these were. The expedition was laden with debts and there was no money to pay the men. Then, with his usual charm, Shackleton proved able to persuade the Australian government to make a grant of £5,000 and the New Zealand government to grant a further £1,000.

With a motley crew, in an overloaded and uncomfortable ship, the voyage out Huntford describes as a 'nightmare'. The captain, England, had never commanded a ship before, and nor had Shackleton. The two soon fell out about how to breach the Great Ice Barrier. Reluctantly, Shackleton agreed to make for McMurdo Sound, the very point he had promised Scott not to touch. 'I have been through a sort of Hell', he told Emily as he described how he had to make the deicision either to turn back or break his word to Scott. 'Each mile I went to the West was a horror to me.' When he heard about Shackleton's decision, Wilson said that he regarded it as inexcusable, and the two men had no further communication with each other.

Once Shackleton's team landed on the ice, the ponies proved useless and the motor car more so. Stores were landed with difficulty and when *Nimrod* finally made off back to New Zealand, it took on board a key member of the party, Mackintosh, who unfortunately had lost an eye during the unloading. Shackleton's later attitude to Mackintosh may well have had something to do with this accident. Shackleton also sent back a secret letter demanding Captain England's resignation on grounds of health. This unfortunate action became public and there was much press comment, some adverse to Shackleton, which was to be detrimental to him in future years.

In their hut on the ice, Shackleton prepared his team for the great push south. They all lived together without distinction – there was no separation of wardroom and messdeck as there had been with Scott. The Boss (this nickname was coined by Wild at the start) had qualities of leadership that were evident to all, as were also his weaknesses, such as an ability to lose his temper rather too quickly. Marshall, the doctor, also found that he had a 'pulm[onary] systolic [heart] murmur' but was not sure whether or not this should disqualify him from the journey south. For his part, Shackleton appeared able to conceal his fears, including fears about his own health.

This is not the place to describe the epic march south of the four men – the Boss himself, Marshall, Wild and Adams. They did not have enough food, although what they did have permitted them to avoid scurvy. The ponies were shot one by one; there were no dogs or skis, and they had to manhandle the sledges. Somehow they reached a point about 100 miles from the pole before turning back, beating Scott's Furthest South by 360 miles. The journey back was terrible: at one point they went for forty hours without solid food. Shackleton became ill again, perhaps with asthma or his 'heart murmur', and Marshall took over temporarily as leader. They had to race to catch the *Nimrod* before it returned to New Zealand, and Shackleton and Wild walked virtually without food or sleep for thirty-six hours to catch her.

According to the *Daily Mail*, King Edward VII 'declared it the greatest geographical event of his reign'.

When he arrived home on 14 June 1909, Shackleton was welcomed as a national hero who had nearly reached the pole. What the public at large did not recognise was that his courage had been shown by his decision to turn back and survive, rather than going on to the pole to perish. Shackleton himself was ready enough to take advantage of his triumph, however it was perceived, even going so far as to cable the Royal Geographical's Secretary to arrange the 'Albert Hall and King's presence' for a big reception meeting.

Already he had plans to return on another expedition, even though Scott had already announced his own intention of attacking the pole again. Indeed there were rumours that the dead-reckoning position claimed by Shackleton (a position, that is, not corroborated by sun-shots) was not his true position and that he had not therefore been within 100 miles of the pole. Despite this, when news of Shackleton's debts leaked out in the press, the Prime Minister, Asquith, personally saw the explorer and arranged for a government grant of £20,000. In the Birthday Honours list Shackleton was knighted.

Money remained a problem. Shackleton wrote a book, *The Heart of the Antarctic*, and travelled all over Europe and the United States lecturing. *Nimrod* was sold. While he was away lecturing

Although the King did not attend (the Prince of Wales came instead), Shackleton gave him a private lecture at Balmoral, by royal command.

Shackleton sent some of his ex-crew to Hungary on a speculative scheme to work a goldmine there. Plans to float a company with Frank had to be abandoned and the reprobate brother was soon bankrupt.

When Scott set off on his second polar expedition in the summer of 1910, backed by a government grant of £20,000, Shackleton was left behind to mope in a rented furnished house the family had taken in Norfolk. By October it was also known that Amundsen was heading south to challenge Scott. Isolated and dismayed, Shackleton left on yet another lecture tour in Europe, where his remuneration was normally only £30 a night.

In May 1911 the family moved to Putney Heath, then quite a fashionable address although these were, in Emily's words, 'the least happy years of his life. They certainly were of mine.' A third child (later Lord Shackleton) was born soon after. The would-be explorer continued restless and moody. One weekend he had another attack of chest pains that might have been heart trouble, but he would not let a doctor examine him. To add to Shackleton's chagrin, on 14 December 1911

(Above left) It is unclear whether this photograph of Adams, Wild and Marshall was taken by Shackleton, or whether he himself is one of the shrouded figures and one of the others was the photographer. *(Right)* Shackleton in 1908.

Amundsen reached the South Pole (the news took several months to reach civilisation). Shackleton cabled him on his 'magnificent achievement', and later sat on a platform at a public meeting in London which the 'geographical establishment' boycotted. The obvious conclusion could be drawn that Shackleton was not totally dismayed to see Scott the loser in the race to the pole.

Shackleton, his financial schemes having come to nothing, was now leading an unsettled life. He wrote to a friend, 'My wife and three children are well. I see little of them, though.' He had taken up with an American lady, Rosalind Chetwynd, who was kept in a Park Lane flat by a rich admirer. Later he visited the United States to attempt to revive interest in a cigarette company, Tabard, which he owned. In January 1913 his brother Frank was charged with fraud at Bow Street magistrates' court, and was later sentenced to 15 months' imprisonment, a major blow that Shackleton took hard.

Simultaneously, the country was wallowing in the news that Scott and his companions had perished at the Pole. Huntford calls this 'glorifying what was not strictly bravery but mindless bravado'. Shackleton, with his record of never having lost a man, as well as his instinct for survival, found the nationalistic heroics hard to take. The publication of another book, *Scott's Last Expedition*, followed, again putting Shackleton's achievements in the shade and showing Scott to be a hero.

Shackleton's mood changed dramatically when, early in December 1913, the Chancellor of the Exchequer, Lloyd George, promised him £10,000 towards financing 'The Imperial Transarctic Expedition' if he could find a matching sum elsewhere. Shackleton claimed that he had a promise of funds from a 'Mr Alfred Harvey', about whose existence no documentary evidence has been found. It is at this point that Shackleton's *South* takes up the story.

PETER KING

(Above) A photographer caught Shackleton in pensive mood on New Year's Eve 1913, standing unknown by the kerb in Oxford Street, perhaps wondering where the finance for the expedition would come from.

PREFACE

AFTER the conquest of the South Pole by Amundsen, who, by a narrow margin of days, was in advance of the British expedition under Scott, only one great main object of Antarctic journeyings remained – the crossing of the South Polar continent from sea to sea.

After hearing of Amundsen's success, I began to make preparations to start a last great journey, so that the first crossing of the last continent should be achieved by a British Expedition.

We failed in this object, but the story of our attempt is the subject of the following pages, and I think, although failure in the actual accomplishment must be recorded, that there are chapters in this book of high adventure, unique experiences, and, above all records of unflinching determination, supreme loyalty and generous self-sacrifice on the part of my men, which will appeal urgently to every one who is interested in the tale of the White Warfare of the South.

The struggles, disappointments and endurance of this small party of Britishers, hidden for nearly two years in the fastnesses of the Polar ice, make a story which is unique in the history of Antarctic exploration.

Owing to the loss of the *Endurance* and the disaster to the *Aurora*, documents relating mainly to the organisation and preparation of the Expedition have been lost, but I will insert here a part of the programme which I prepared in order to arouse the interest of the public in the Expedition.

"The Trans-continental Party

"The first crossing of the Antarctic continent, from sea to sea, via the Pole, apart from its historic value, will be a journey of great scientific importance.

"The distance will be roughly 1,800 miles, and the first half of this, from the Weddell Sea to the Pole, will be over unknown ground. Every step will be an advance in geographical science. It will be learned whether the great Victoria chain of mountains, which has been traced from the Ross Sea to the Pole, extends across the continent and thus links up (except for the ocean break) with the Andes of South America, and whether the great plateau around the Pole dips gradually towards the Weddell Sea.

"Continuous magnetic observations will be taken on the journey. Meteorological conditions will be noted carefully, and ice-formations and the nature of the mountains will be studied.

"Scientific Work by Other Parties

"While the Trans-continental party is carrying out, for the British flag, the greatest Polar journey ever attempted, the other parties will be engaged in important scientific work.

There is no reason for Shackleton to suggest that significant documents were lost. Records and pictorial records certainly disappeared when the *Endurance* sank or those salvaged were abandoned. The *Aurora* (which was purchased in Australia) was not destroyed and after the expedition Shackleton sold her for £10,000, so it is not clear why papers should have been lost. A more likely loss of documents would have been when the expedition office in New Burlington Street closed while Shackleton was in the Antarctic and the manager disappeared.

The Weddell Sea was named after Captain James Weddell who cruised south in 1821-4. The Ross Sea was named after Captain James Ross RN, one of the pioneers of scientific exploration in the Antarctic, who reached the ice pack in 1841.

Graham Land was named after a First Lord of the Admiralty. Enderby Land was in honour of the firm who sent their sealing ships to the Antarctic in the 1830's and encouraged their captains to 'pursue discovery'.

There had been a number of earlier expeditions, notably the Scottish Antarctic Expedition led by Dr William Bruce in 1902 and the German expedition under Dr Wilhelm Filchner in 1911. Shackleton profited from information obtained by both, and planned to follow in Filchner's tracks, landing at Vahsel Bay, found by Filchner. In 1908 Bruce had published a plan to cross Antarctica, which Shackleton at first adopted, although he was later persuaded to change his mind and take two ships.

Douglas Mawson (later Sir Douglas Mawson) had been a physicist on Shackleton's unsuccessful expedition to the South Pole in *Nimrod* in 1907. He went on to become one of the greatest of Australian explorers, leading the Australian Antarctic expedition of 1911. Mawson distrusted Shackleton whom he claimed 'double-crossed one' over money donated towards a joint expedition.

"Two sledging parties will operate from the base on the Weddell Sea. One will travel westwards towards Graham Land, collecting geological specimens, and proving whether there are mountains in that region linked up with those found on the other side of the Pole.

"Another party will travel eastward toward Enderby Land, and a third, remaining at the base, will study the fauna of the land and sea, and the meteorological conditions.

"From the Ross Sea base, on the other side of the Pole, another party will push southward, and probably will await the arrival of the Trans-continental party at the top of the Beardmore Glacier, near Mount Buckley, a region of great importance to the geologist.

"Both the ships of the Expedition will be fully equipped for scientific work. The Weddell Sea ship will try to trace the unknown coast-line of Graham Land.

"The several shore parties and the two ships will thus carry out geographical and scientific work on a scale and over an area never before attempted by one Polar expedition.

"This will be the first use of the Weddell Sea as a base for exploration, and all the parties will open up vast stretches of unknown land. It is appropriate that this work should be carried out under the British flag, since the whole of the area southward to the Pole is British territory.

"How the Continent will be Crossed

"The Weddell Sea ship, with all the members of the Expedition operating from that base, will leave Buenos Ayres in October, 1914, and try to land in November in latitude 78 degrees south.

"Should this be done, the Trans-continental party will start immediately on their 1,800 mile journey, in the hope of accomplishing the march across the Pole and reaching the Ross Sea base in five months. Should the landing be made too late in the season, the party will go into winter quarters, and as early as possible in 1915 set out on the journey.

"The Trans-continental party will be led by Sir Ernest Shackleton, and will consist of six men. The equipment will embody everything that the experience of the leader and his expert advisers can suggest. When this party has reached the area of the Pole, after covering 800 miles of unknown ground, it will strike due north towards the head of the Beardmore Glacier, and there it is hoped to meet the outcoming party from the Ross Sea. Both will join up and make for the Ross Sea base.

"In all, fourteen men will be landed by the *Endurance* on the Weddell Sea. Six will set out on the Trans-continental journey, three will go westward, three eastward, and two will remain at the base.

"The *Aurora* will land six men at the Ross Sea base. They will lay down depots on the route of the Trans-continental party and make a march south to assist that party.

"Should the Trans-continental party succeed in crossing during the first season, its return to civilisation may be expected about April, 1915. The other sections in April, 1916.

"The Ships of the Expedition

"The two ships have been selected.

"The *Endurance*, which will take the Trans-continental party to the Weddell Sea, and will afterwards explore along an unknown coast-line, is a new vessel, specially constructed for Polar work under the supervision of a committee of Polar explorers. To enable her to stay longer at sea, she will carry oil fuel as well as coal. She is of about 350 tons, and this fine vessel, equipped, has cost the Expedition £14,000.

"The *Aurora*, which will take out the Ross Sea party, has been bought from Dr. Mawson. She is similar in all respects to the Terra Nova, of Captain Scott's last Expedition. She is now at Hobart, Tasmania, where the Ross Sea party will join her in October next."

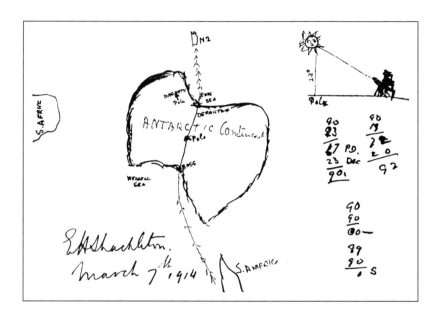

PREFACE

I started the preparations in the middle of 1913, but no public announcement was made until January 13th, 1914, and the first result of this was a flood of applications from all classes of the community to join the adventure. I received nearly 5,000 applications, and from these I picked fifty-six men.

In March, to my great anxiety, I was disappointed in the financial help which had been promised me, and was faced with the fact that I had contracted for a ship and stores, and had engaged the staff, and was not in possession of funds to meet these liabilities.

I immediately began to appeal for help, and met with generous response from all sides. It is impossible to mention every one who supported my application, but I must particularly refer to a munificent gift of £24,000 from the late Sir James Caird, and to one of £10,000 from the British Government. I wish also especially to thank Mr. Dudley Docker, Miss Elizabeth Dawson Lambton, Dame Janet Stancomb Wills, and the Royal Geographical Society, for their generosity.

The only return and privilege an explorer has in the way of acknowledgment for the help given to him is to record on the discovered lands the names of those to whom the Expedition owes its being. I have the honour to place on the new land the names of the above and of other generous contributors to the Expedition.

So the equipment and organisation of the Expedition went on, until towards the end of July everything was ready. And then the war clouds suddenly darkened over Europe.

It had been arranged for the *Endurance* to proceed to Cowes to be inspected by His Majesty, but I received a message to say that the King would be unable to go to Cowes.

We sailed from London on Friday, August 1st, 1914, and anchored off Southend for the whole of Saturday. Growing hourly more

In fact the ship was constructed for a Norwegian shipowner who planned to run 'polar safaris' but the scheme collapsed in 1913. Huntford says she was 'something of a white elephant. With ten cabins, a darkroom for amateur photography, and no cargo space, she was useless for sealing. Nor was she luxurious enough for a yacht ... Shackleton ... appeared like a fairy godmother.' He acquired the ship for £11,600, with several months' credit, as he did not have the money.

(Above) Shackleton sketched this map of Antarctica on the back of a menu card at the annual dinner of the London Devonian Association to show how the two ships would aid his proposed crossing.

Sir James Caird, Bart, was a Dundee jute magnate and a great philanthropist, who asked Shackleton to visit him in June 1914 when, although a certain amount of money had been raised, Shackleton had committed himself to the expedition without adequate funds. Caird was impressed and sent his cheque 'without conditons in the hope that others may make their gifts for this imperial journey also free of all conditions.' However he declined Shackleton's request for more money once war had broken out. Shackleton named an area of coast after him, as well as a boat.

Mr Dudley Docker (later Sir Dudley) a Midlands financier who in 1902 merged several companies and made his reputation as an industrialist. He was on the board of BSA from 1906-12 and arranged a merger with the Daimler car company. His son and daughter-in-law were well-known in the 1950s. He gave £10,000, and one of the boats was named after him.

Miss Elizabeth Dawson-Lambton is described by Huntford as 'a wealthy maiden lady, connected with the Earls of Durham, who migrated between boarding houses and her maiden sisters' homes in Devon ... Shackleton had first met her in 1901, when he showed her over the ship [Scott's *Discovery*] before sailing. Since then her heart had beaten warmly for him.' At that time she gave £1000, which Shackleton's rascally brother Frank misappropriated. This time she gave less, but Shackleton named a glacier after her.

Dame Janet Stancomb Wills is described by Huntford as the adopted daughter of Sir H.W. Wills (later Lord Winterstoke) a tobacco millionaire who was introduced to Shackleton by a journalist friend and supporter on the *Daily Chronicle*. 'Like many older women, she fell quietly in love with him, and wrote a poem beginning 'Into my life you flashed like a meteor out of the dark'. She gave a large sum, and also supported Shackleton's family in his absence. Later still, she loaned more money for exploration. A promontory was named after her, as well as a boat.

21

The Royal Geographical Society, although sceptical about Shackleton's prospects of success, offered a loan of £10,000, of which the explorer said he needed only half. Later, when it came to financing a relief party, and there was no money, the Society was approached for the other half. Shackleton does not mention Lord Iveagh, one of the Guinness family, who guaranteed a loan of £5000, or an Australian banker living in London, Sir Robert Lucas-Tooth, who guaranteed another £5000. Shackleton expected to repay these loans with income from lectures and books.

anxious as the rumours spread, I took the ship to Margate on Sunday afternoon; and on Monday morning I went ashore, and in the morning paper I read the order for general mobilisation.

I immediately returned to the ship, and, having mustered all hands, I told them that I proposed to send a telegram to the Admiralty offering the ship, stores, and, if they agreed, our own services in the event of war. Our only request was that, if war broke out, the Expedition might be considered as a single unit, for there were enough trained and experienced men among us to man a destroyer. Within an hour I received a laconic wire from the Admiralty saying "Proceed." A little later Mr. Winston Churchill wired thanking us for our offer, and saying that the authorities desired that the Expedition should go on.

(Right) Although Emily visited *Endurance*, she and Shackleton had quarrelled once more and he returned home to see her to try to make his peace. He wrote to her on the subject admitting blame 'for all the rows' and adding, 'I expect I have a peculiar nature that the years have hardened'.

Following these definite instructions, the *Endurance* sailed to Plymouth, and on the Tuesday the King sent for me and handed me the Union Jack to carry on the Expedition. On that night, at midnight, war was declared.

On the following Saturday, August 8th, the *Endurance* sailed from Plymouth, obeying the direct orders of the Admiralty.

I make particular reference to this phase of the Expedition, as there was a certain amount of criticism of the Expedition having left the country. Concerning this criticism I wish to say that our preparations had been going on for over a year, that large sums of money had been spent, that we offered to give up the Expedition without even consulting the donors of this money, and that few people imagined at this time that the war would last for years and involve nearly the whole world.

The Expedition was going to a most dangerous and strenuous work, which has nearly always caused a certain percentage of loss of life. Finally, when the Expedition did return, practically all the members who had passed unscathed through the dangers of the Antarctic took their places in the wider field of battle, and the percentage of casualties among them was high.

The voyage to Buenos Ayres was uneventful, and on October 26th we sailed from there for South Georgia, the most southerly outpost of the British Empire. Here, for a month, we were engaged in final preparations.

Apart from private individuals and societies, I wish also most gratefully to acknowledge the assistance rendered by the Dominion Government of New Zealand, the Commonwealth Government of Australia, the Uruguayan Government, and the Chilian Government, which was directly responsible for the rescue of my comrades.

ERNEST SHACKLETON

(Above) Being towed into the harbour. The *Endurance*'s voyage was not exactly uneventful. She arrived in Buenos Aires an unhappy ship with a crew which was insubordinate and drunk. A few of the worst offenders were sacked. Three days after departure, a 19-year-old Welsh sailor was found stowing away in a locker. He was kept on anyway as on leaving Buenos Aires the crew was two men short.

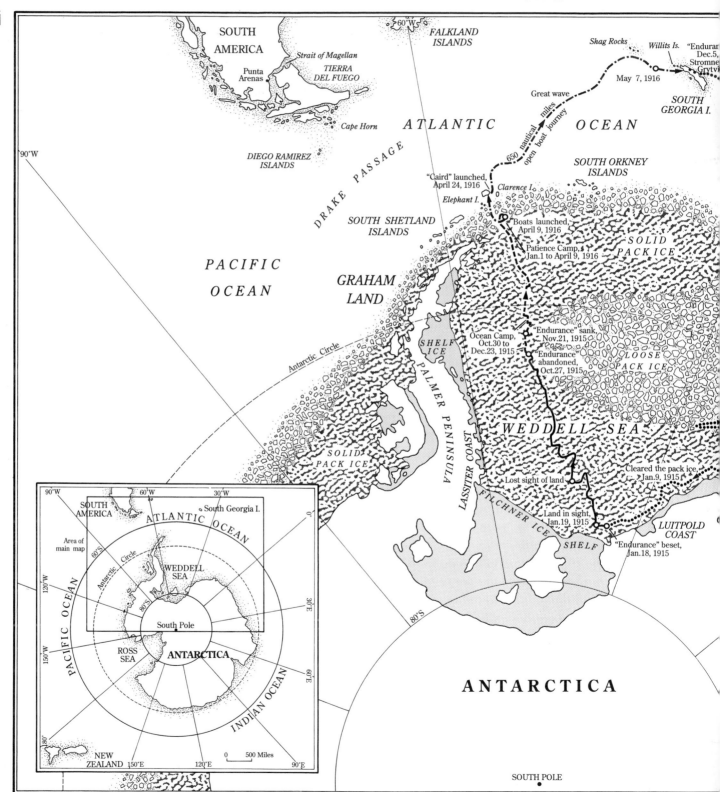

SOUTH
AMERICA

Strait of Magellan

Punta
Arenas

*TIERRA
DEL FUEGO*

Cape Horn

*DIEGO RAMIREZ
ISLANDS*

FALKLAND
ISLANDS

Shag Rocks   *Willits Is.*   "Endura
Dec.5,
Stromne
Grytvi

May 7, 1916

Great wave

SOUTH
GEORGIA I.

ATLANTIC   OCEAN

650 nautical miles
open boat journey

PACIFIC

OCEAN

DRAKE PASSAGE

SOUTH SHETLAND
ISLANDS

GRAHAM
LAND

SOUTH ORKNEY
ISLANDS

"Caird" launched,
April 24, 1916

Clarence I.

Elephant I.

Boats launched,
April 9, 1916

Patience Camp,
Jan.1 to April 9, 1916

SOLID
PACK ICE

Antarctic Circle

*SHELF
ICE*

Ocean Camp,
Oct.30 to
Dec.23, 1915

"Endurance" sank,
Nov.21, 1915

"Endurance"
abandoned,
Oct.27, 1915

LOOSE
PACK
ICE

SOLID
PACK ICE

PALMER PENINSULA

WEDDELL   SEA

Cleared the pack ice,
Jan.9, 1915

Lost sight of land

LASSITER COAST

FILCHNER ICE

Land in sight,
Jan.19, 1915

LUITPOLD
COAST

SHELF

"Endurance" beset,
Jan.18, 1915

90°W

ANTARCTICA

Inset map:

90°W   60°W   30°W

SOUTH
AMERICA   South Georgia I.

Area of
main map

ATLANTIC OCEAN   0°

Antarctic Circle

60°S

WEDDELL
SEA

80°S

30°E

PACIFIC OCEAN

120°W

150°W

South Pole

ANTARCTICA

ROSS
SEA

60°E

INDIAN OCEAN

80°

NEW
ZEALAND   150°E   120°E   90°E

0   500 Miles

SOUTH POLE

30°W

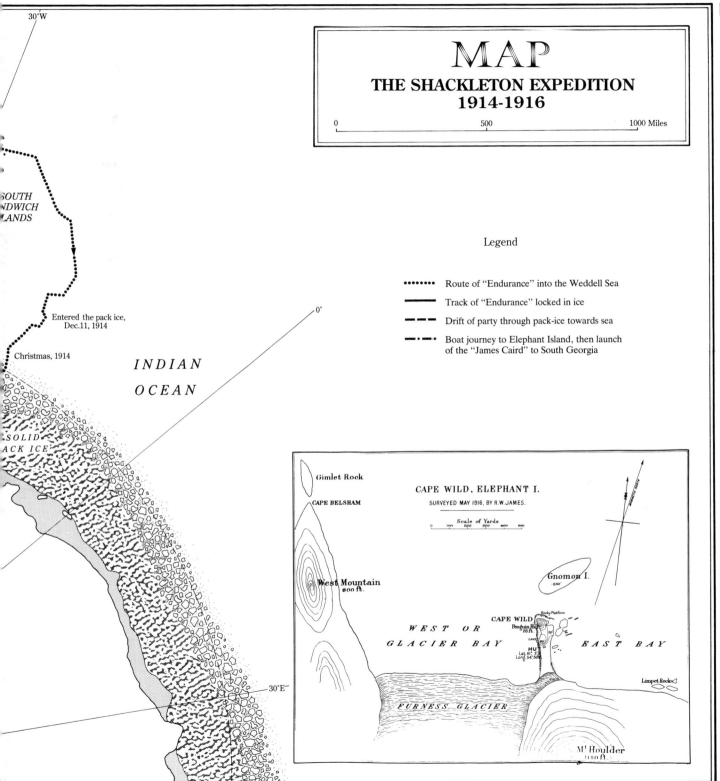

MAP
THE SHACKLETON EXPEDITION
1914-1916

0   500   1000 Miles

SOUTH
SANDWICH
ISLANDS

Entered the pack ice,
Dec.11, 1914

Christmas, 1914

Legend

••••••• Route of "Endurance" into the Weddell Sea

——— Track of "Endurance" locked in ice

– – – Drift of party through pack-ice towards sea

–·–·– Boat journey to Elephant Island, then launch
of the "James Caird" to South Georgia

INDIAN

OCEAN

0°

SOLID
PACK ICE

30°E

Gimlet Rock

CAPE BELSHAM

CAPE WILD, ELEPHANT I.

SURVEYED MAY 1916, BY R.W. JAMES.

Scale of Yards
0   100   200   300   400   500

West Mountain
800 ft.

Gnomon I.
·230·

CAPE WILD
Rocky Platform
Penguin Hill
85 ft.

WEST OR
GLACIER BAY

HUT
Lat. 61° 5'
Long. 54° 50'

EAST BAY

Limpet Rocks

FURNESS GLACIER

Mt Houlder
1140 ft.

Standing on the fo'c'stle head, one of the crew views the first large areas of ice encountered by *Endeavour* – a fragmentary berg in the final stages of decay, soon to disintegrate under wave action and rising temperature.

CHAPTER I

INTO THE WEDDELL SEA

✦

I HAD decided to leave South Georgia about December 5th, 1914, and in the intervals of final preparation I scanned again the plans for the voyage to winter quarters. What welcome was the Weddell sea preparing for us?

Following the advice of the whaling captains at South Georgia, who generously placed their knowledge at my disposal, I had decided to steer to the South Sandwich Group, round Ultima Thule, and work as far to the eastward as the fifteenth meridian west longitude before pushing south. The whalers warned me of the difficulty of getting through the ice in the neighbourhood of the South Sandwich Group, and they thought that the Expedition would have to push through

Shackleton had originally planned to call at Port Stanley in the Falkland Islands rather than South Georgia, but changed his mind when he heard that a German naval squadron was in those waters.

(Left) **A group picture of the shore party at the Weddell Sea base.**

In his fuller account Shackleton added, 'We had hoped that some steamer from the north would bring news of the war and perhaps letters from home before our departure', but although a ship did arrive it brought neither news nor mail and the crew were all 'stoutly pro-German'.

heavy pack in order to reach the Weddell Sea. Probably the best time to get into the Weddell Sea would be about the end of February. Owing to the warnings of the whalers I decided to take the deckload of coal, for if we had to fight our way through to Coats' Land we should need all the fuel we could carry.

At length the day of departure arrived. I gave the order to heave anchor at 8.45 a.m. on December 5th, and the clanking of the windlass broke for us the last link with civilisation. The morning was dull and overcast, but hearts aboard the *Endurance* were light. The long days of preparation were over and the adventure lay ahead.

(Right) The whaling station at Grytviken, a British possession like the rest of South Georgia, but 'one might imagine oneself in Norway' in Reginald James's words, as most of the inhabitants of the island were Norwegian whalers.

With the pack-ice stretching to the horizon, Shackleton knew that it was possible that it might continue for a thousand miles to their landfall at Vahsel Bay.

The wind freshened during the day and all square sail was set, with the foresail reefed in order to give the lookout a clear view ahead, for we did not wish to risk contact with a "growler," one of those treacherous fragments of ice that float with surface awash. During December 6th we made good progress on a south-easterly course, but December 7th brought the first check. At six o'clock on that morning the sea, which had been green in colour on the previous day, changed suddenly to a deep indigo.

Sanders Island and Candlemas were sighted early in the afternoon, and large numbers of bergs, mostly tabular in form, lay to the west of the islands. The presence of so many bergs was ominous, and immediately after passing between the islands we encountered stream-ice. All sail was taken in and we proceeded slowly under steam. At 8 p.m. the *Endurance* was confronted by a belt of heavy pack-ice, half a mile broad and extending north and south. There was clear water

beyond, but the pack in our neighbourhood was impenetrable. This was disconcerting. The noon latitude had been 57° 26′ S., and I had not expected to find pack-ice nearly so far north.

During that night the situation became dangerous. We pushed into the pack in the hope of reaching open water beyond, and found ourselves in a pool which was growing smaller and smaller. Worsley and I were on deck all night, dodging the pack, but some anxious hours passed before we rounded it and were able to set sail once more.

This initial tussle with the pack had been exciting. Pieces of ice and bergs of all sizes were heaving and jostling against each other in the heavy south-westerly swell. In spite of all our care the *Endurance* struck large lumps stern on, but the engines were stopped in time and no harm was done.

During December 9th we again encountered the pack, and after rounding it we steered S. 40° E., and at noon on the 10th we reached lat. 58° 28′ S., long. 20° 28′ W. On the following day we met with loose pack which did not present great difficulties. Worsley, Wild and I, with three officers, kept three watches while we were working through the pack, so that we had two officers on deck all the time. The carpenter had rigged a six-foot wooden semaphore on the bridge to enable the navigating officer to give the seamen or scientists at the wheel the direction and the exact amount of helm required. This device saved time as well as the effort of shouting.

During December 12th and 13th we made fair progress, but on the 14th conditions became more difficult, for the pack was denser than it had been on the previous days. The most careful navigation could not prevent an occasional bump against ice too thick to be broken or pushed aside, but although the propeller received several blows no damage was done. During the afternoon of the 14th a south-westerly gale sprang up, and at 8 p.m. we hove to, stem against a floe, it being impossible to proceed without serious risk of damaging the rudder or propeller.

Shackleton's fears were founded on his knowledge that the *Endurance* was not ideally built for operation in the ice and, as he wrote to Emily, 'I would exchange her for the old *Nimrod* any day'.

(Above) At times the ice field would open up and lay bare the sea. The low air temperature striking the water would produce immense dark clouds of frost smoke. Soon the water would freeze over and become covered with frost-flowers.

The *Endurance* remained against the floe for the next twenty-four hours, when the gale moderated. The pack extended to the horizon in all directions and was broken by innumerable narrow lanes. We made five miles to the south before midnight, and we continued to advance until 4 a.m. on December 17th, when the ice once more became difficult. Very large floes of six-months-old ice lay close together, and some of these floes presented a square mile of unbroken surface.

The morning of December 18th found the *Endurance* proceeding amongst large floes with thin ice between them, and shortly before noon further progress was barred by heavy pack, and we put an ice-anchor on the floe and banked the fires.

I had been prepared for evil conditions in the Weddell Sea, but had hoped that in December and January the pack would be loose, even if no open water was to be found. What we were encountering was fairly dense pack of a very obstinate character.

Pack-ice may be described as a gigantic and interminable jigsaw-puzzle devised by nature. The parts of the puzzle in loose pack have floated slightly apart and become disarranged; at numerous

places they have pressed together again; as the pack gets closer the congested areas grow larger and the parts are jammed harder until it becomes "close pack"; then the whole jigsaw-puzzle becomes so jammed that with care it can be crossed in every direction on foot. Where the parts do not fit closely there is, of course, open water, which freezes over in a few hours after giving off volumes of "frost-smoke." In obedience to renewed pressure this young ice "rafts," thus forming double thicknesses of toffee-like consistency.

All through the winter the drifting pack changes – grows by freezing, thickens by rafting, and corrugates by pressure. If, finally, in its drift it impinges on a coast, such as the western shore of the Weddell Sea, terrific pressure is set up and an inferno of ice-blocks, ridges and hedgerows results, extending possibly for 150 or 200 miles off shore.

I have given this explanation so that the nature of the ice through which we had to push our way for hundreds of miles may be understood.

The conditions did not improve during December 19th, and after proceeding for two hours the *Endurance* was stopped again by heavy floes, and, owing to a heavy gale, we remained moored to a

(Above) The foreground is covered with 'frost-flowers', their pattern a particular favourite of Hurley's. They were formed by a lead opening in the ice and then rapidly freezing over.

Shackleton gives the noon position on 19 December as lat. 62°42′S; long. 17°54′W, showing that they had drifted during the past 24 hours some six miles in a north-easterly direction.

floe during the following day. The members of the staff and crew took advantage of the pause to enjoy a vigorous game of football on the level surface of the floe alongside the ship.

Monday, December 21st, was beautifully fine, and we made an early start through the pack. Petrels of several species, penguins and seals were plentiful, and we saw four small blue whales. At noon we entered a long lead to the southward and passed nine splendid bergs. One huge specimen was shaped like the Rock of Gibraltar but with steeper cliffs, and another had a natural dock which would have contained the *Aquitania*. Hurley brought out his kinematograph-camera to make a

(Above left) Hurley captions this picture 'Self securing film from aloft'. (Above right) Taken on 20 December, with some of the crew at soccer.

record of these bergs. We found long leads during the afternoon, but at midnight the ship was stopped by small, heavy ice-floes, tightly packed against an unbroken plain of ice. The outlook from the mast-head was not encouraging; the big floe was at least fifteen miles long and ten miles wide. I had never seen such an area of unbroken ice in the Ross Sea.

We waited with banked fires for an opportunity to proceed, and during the evening of December 22nd some lanes opened, and we were able again to move towards the south. So we struggled on until Christmas Day, when we were held up by more bad weather. However, we had a really splendid dinner, and in the evening everybody joined in a "sing-song."

The weather was still bad on December 26th and 27th, but on the evening of December 29th the high winds which had prevailed for four and a half days gave way to a gentle southerly breeze, and when the New Year dawned we had pushed and fought the little ship 480 miles through loose and close pack-ice. Our advance through the pack had been in a S. 10° E. direction, and I estimated that the total steaming distance had exceeded 700 miles.

The first hundred miles had been through loose pack, but the greatest hindrances had been the south-westerly gales. The last 250 miles had been through close pack alternating with fine long leads and stretches of open water.

CHAPTER II

NEW LAND

The condition of the pack improved in the evening of New Year's Day, and we progressed rapidly until a moderate gale came up from the east, with continuous snow. Early in the morning of January 2nd we got into thick old pack-ice. The position then was lat. 69° 49′ S., long. 15° 42′ W., and the run for the last twenty-four hours had been 124 miles S. 3° W., which was cheering.

This good run had made me hopeful of sighting the land on the following day, but we were delayed by heavy pack and also by the gale. I was becoming anxious to reach land on account of the dogs, with which I had been greatly pleased when we had started, but, owing to lack of exercise, they were now becoming run down.

The dogs had not been exercised properly for four weeks.

(Left) The deck of the *Endurance* after one of the frequent snowfalls.

When the ship was moored to a floe, 'some enthusiastic foot-ball-players had a game on the ice until, about midnight, Worsley dropped through a hole in rotten ice while retrieving the ball. He had to be retrieved', Shackleton remarks.

Difficulties continued to beset us, and on the 4th we had been steaming and dodging about over an area of twenty square miles for fifty hours, trying to find an opening to the south, south-east, or south-west, but all the leads ran north, north-east, or north-west. It was as if the spirits of the Antarctic were pointing us to the backward track – the track we were determined not to follow.

Our desire was to make easting as well as southing, so that, if possible, we might reach the land east of Ross's farthest South, and well east of Coats' Land.

Solid pack, however, barred the way to the south, but on the 6th, with the ship moored to a floe, I took the opportunity to exercise the dogs. Their excitement when they got on to the floe was intense; several of them managed to get into the water, and their muzzles did not prevent them from having some hot fights. On the following day, when we were able to make some progress,

(Right) Exercising the dogs. This gave the men an opportunity to learn some of the basics which, had they landed at Vahsel Bay as planned, they would have to have learned the hard way. Their professional dog handler had been dropped from the crew.

killer-whales began to be active around us, and I had to exercise caution in allowing any one to leave the ship. These beasts have a habit of locating a resting seal by looking over the edge of a floe, and then striking through the ice from below in search of a meal; they would not distinguish between seal and man.

On the 8th and 9th fortune was with us, and the run southward in blue water, with a path clear ahead and the miles falling away behind us, was a joyful experience after the long struggle through the ice-lanes; but, like other good things, our spell of free movement had to end, and the *Endurance* encountered the ice again at 1 a.m. on the 10th.

In addition to killer whales, they had seen hundreds of crab-eaters and, earlier, petrels, adelies, emperor penguins and sea-leopards.

At noon our position was lat. 72° 02′ S., long. 16° 07′ W., and we were now near the land discovered by Dr. W. S. Bruce, leader of the *Scotia* Expedition, in 1904, and named by him Coats'

Land. Dr. Bruce encountered an ice-barrier in lat. 72° 18′ S., long. 10° W., and from his description of rising slopes of snow and ice, with shoaling water off the barrier-wall, the presence of land was clearly indicated. It was up those slopes, at a point as far south as possible, that I planned to begin the march across the Antarctic continent. All hands now were watching for the coast described by Dr. Bruce, and at 5 p.m. the lookout reported an appearance of land to the south-southeast. It seemed to be an island or a peninsula with a sound on its south side. At the time we were passing through heavy loose pack, and shortly before midnight we broke into a lead of open sea along a barrier edge. The barrier was 70 feet high with cliffs of about 40 feet, and the *Scotia* must have passed this point when pushing to Bruce's farthest south on March 6th, 1904.

'From today onwards to Luitpold Land we are . . . discovering absolutely new land', wrote Worsley.

(Left) This may be the barrier described by Shackleton as 70 feet high with cliffs of about 40 feet, previously seen by Bruce.

Thick and overcast weather impeded our progress on the following days, but on the 12th we were beyond the point reached by the *Scotia*, and the land underlying the ice-sheet, which we were skirting, was new. At 4 p.m. on the 13th, when we were still following the barrier to the south-west, we reached a corner and found it receding abruptly to the south-east. Our way was blocked by very heavy pack, and as we were unable to find an opening we moored the ship to a floe and banked fires.

Several young emperor penguins had been captured and brought aboard on the previous day, and two of them were still alive when the *Endurance* was brought alongside the floe. They promptly hopped on to the ice, turned round, bowed gracefully three times, and retired to the far side of the floe. There is something curiously human about the manners and movements of these birds. I was

The new land they were now reaching Shackleton named the Caird Coast in honour of his patron Sir James Caird.

(Above) **The great glacier berg 180 feet high which menaced the ship. Shackleton named Glacier Bay after it, and had 'reason later to remember it with regret'.**

This run of 124 miles Huntford describes as 'practically the best run of the whole voyage'.

again concerned about the dogs. Some of them appeared to be ailing, and one dog had to be shot on the 12th.

We did not move the ship on the 14th, but on the following day conditions had improved, and in the evening the *Endurance* was moving southward with sails set and we continued to skirt the barrier in clear water. I was watching for possible landing-places, though, as a matter of fact, unless compelled by necessity, I had no intention of landing north of Vahsel Bay, in Luitpold Land. Every mile gained towards the south meant a mile less sledging when the time came for the overland journey.

Shortly before midnight on the 15th we came abreast of the northern edge of a great glacier, projecting beyond the barrier into the sea. It was about 400 ft. high, and at its edge was a large mass of thick bay-ice. The bay formed by the northern edge of this glacier would have made an excellent landing-place, for it was protected from the south-easterly wind and was open only to a northerly wind. I named the place Glacier Bay, and had reason later to remember it with regret.

The *Endurance* steamed along the front of this glacier for about seventeen miles, and at 4 a.m. on the 16th we reached the edge of another hugh glacial overflow from the ice-sheet. We steamed

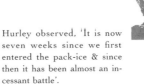

along the front of this tremendous glacier for forty miles and then were held up by solid pack-ice, which appeared to be held by stranded bergs. No further advance was possible for that day, but the noon observation showed that we had gained 124 miles to the south-west during the preceding twenty-four hours. We pushed the ship against a small berg, and a blizzard from the east-north-east prevented us from leaving the shelter of the berg on the following day (Sunday, January 17th).

The land, when the air was clear, seemed to rise to 3,000 feet above the head of the glacier. Caird Coast, as I named it, connects Coats' Land, discovered by Bruce in 1904, with Luitpold Land, discovered by Filchner in 1912. We were now close to the junction with Luitpold Land.

The ship lay under the lee of the stranded berg until 7 a.m. on January 18th, by which time the gale had moderated so much that we could sail to the south-west through a lane which had opened

Hurley observed, 'It is now seven weeks since we first entered the pack-ice & since then it has been almost an incessant battle'.

(Left) Hurley took this picture of the crew once the ship was 'firmly held' in ice.

along the glacier front, and on the morning of the 19th our position was lat. 76° 34' S., long. 31° 30' W. The weather was good, but as the ice had closed around the ship during the night, no advance could be made. A survey of the position on the 20th showed that the *Endurance* was firmly beset. As far as the eye could reach from the masthead the ice was packed heavily and firmly all round the ship in every direction.

Many uneventful days followed. Moderate breezes from the east and south-west had no apparent effect upon the ice, and the ship remained firmly held. On the 27th, the tenth day of inactivity, I decided to let the fires out. We had been burning half a ton of coal a day to keep steam in the boilers, and as the bunkers now contained only sixty-seven tons, representing thirty-three days' steaming, we could not afford this expenditure of coal.

Orde-Lees noted on 24 January, 'It certainly seems not improbable that we may remain . . . incarcerated [and] drift North'.

While *Endurance* was static in the ice, on the other side of the continent, the Ross Sea party were struggling through the snow and ice in a vain attempt to establish stores for Shackleton's party, an epic described in the concluding chapters of this book.

During these days of waiting we gradually collected a stock of seal meat, which the dogs needed, and which also made a very welcome change from our rations.

Not until February 9th did I order steam to be raised in the hope of being able to proceed, but our effort failed. We could break the young ice, but the pack defied us and the ship became jammed against soft floe. As there seemed small chance of making a move, I had the motor crawler and warper put on the floe for a trial run. The motor worked most successfully, running at about six miles an hour over slabs and ridges of ice hidden by a foot or two of soft snow. The surface was worse than we should have expected to face on land or barrier-ice.

No important change in our situation took place during the second part of February. Early in the morning of the 14th I ordered a good head of steam on the engines and sent all hands on to the floe with ice-chisels, prickers, saws and picks. All that day and most of the next we worked strenuously to get the ship into the lead ahead of us. After terrific labour we got the ship a third of the way to the lead, but about 400 yards of heavy ice still separated the *Endurance* from the water, and reluctantly I was compelled to admit that further effort was useless. Every opening we made froze up again quickly owing to the unseasonably low temperature.

(Below) Endurance under full sail in the position where she was finally frozen in.

The crew, after waiting for the
pack to break up, now realised
that *Endurance* was fast in a
sea of ice.

On 20 February, *Endurance* swept past the longitude of Vahsel Bay where they had hoped to make land and begin the trek across to where the Ross Sea party was preparing the ground for them. They were about 60 miles from the Bay.

The abandonment of the attack was a great disappointment to all hands. The men had worked so splendidly that they had deserved success, but the task was beyond our powers. I had not yet abandoned hope of getting clear, but by this time I was beginning to count on the possibility of having to spend a winter in the inhospitable arms of the pack. The sun, which had been above the horizon for two months, set at midnight on the 17th, and, although it would not disappear until April, its slanting rays warned us of the approach of winter. We continued to accumulate a supply of seal meat and blubber, and the excursions across the floes to shoot and bring in the seals provided welcome exercise for all hands.

On the 22nd the *Endurance* reached the farthest south point of her drift, touching the 77th parallel of latitude in long. 35° W. The summer had gone; indeed, it had scarcely been with us at all.

(Above) Strenuous efforts were made on 14-15 February to raft the brash ice astern and break free.

The temperatures were very low both day and night, and as the pack was freezing solidly around the ship, I could no longer doubt that the *Endurance* was confined for the winter.

"We must," I wrote, "wait for the spring, which may bring us better fortune. If I had guessed a month ago that the ice would grip us here, I would have established our base at one of the landing-places at the great glacier. But there seemed no reason to anticipate then that the fates would prove unkind. . . . My chief anxiety is the drift. Where will the vagrant winds and currents carry the ship during the long winter months that are ahead of us? We will go west, no doubt, but how far? And will it be possible to break out of the pack early in the spring and reach Vahsel Bay or some other suitable landing-place? These are momentous questions for us."

The hold of the ship was warmer than their cabins, so Shackleton ordered the construction of cubicles there.

On February 24th we ceased to observe ship routine, and the *Endurance* became a winter station. Orders were given for the after-hold to be cleared and the stores checked so that we might know exactly how we stood for a siege by an Antarctic winter. The dogs went off the ship on the following day, their kennels being placed on the floe along the length of a wire rope to which the

leashes were fastened. They were obviously delighted to get off the ship, and we had already begun the training of teams. Hockey and football on the floe were our chief recreations, and all hands joined in many a strenuous game. We kept our wireless apparatus rigged, but without result. Evidently the distances were too great for our small plant.

(Above) **The dog igloos on the ice, with snow packed round their kennels.**

CHAPTER III

WINTER MONTHS

M ARCH opened with a severe north-easterly gale which lasted until the 3rd. All hands were employed in clearing out the 'tween-decks, which was to be converted into a living-room and dining-room for officers and scientists. Here the carpenter erected the stove that had been intended for the shore hut, and the quarters were made very snug. The dogs seemed indifferent to the blizzard, and were content to lie most of the time curled into tight balls under the snow.

(Opposite) Hurley on the pack ice with his movie camera. Some of this film survives showing the crew trying to raft the ice. This still photograph is almost certainly a montage.

By March 1915 Shackleton had seen the end of all his plans for reaching the south that year and on the sixteenth of the month, Orde-Lees recorded that this 'virtually marks Sir Ernest's acceptance of the inevitable' as they continued to drift north. Despite this major reverse, Shackleton showed great leadership in keeping up the morale of the team. Worsley wrote, 'Shackleton's spirits were wonderfully irrepressible considering the heartbreaking reverses he has had to put up with and the frustration of all his hopes for this year at least. One would think he had never a care on his mind & he is the life & soul of half the skylarking and fooling in the ship.'

(Left) The stove (originally intended for the shore hut) was kept going for the night watch but often attracted other members of the crew.

The bergs within circle of vision had all become familiar shapes and the crew gave them names. Apparently they were all drifting with the pack.

When the gale cleared we found that the pack had been driven in from the north-east and was more firmly consolidated than before. A new berg, probably fifteen miles in length, appeared on the northern horizon, and the sighting of it was of more than passing interest, since in that comparatively shallow sea it was possible for a big berg to become stranded. Then the island of ice would be a centre of tremendous pressure and disturbance amid the drifting pack. We had seen something already of the smashing effect of a contest between berg and floe, and did not wish to see the helpless *Endurance* involved in such a battle of giants.

The quarters in the 'tween-decks were completed by the 10th, and the men took possession of the cubicles which had been built. The largest cubicle contained Macklin, McIlroy, Hurley and Hussey; Clark and Wordie lived opposite in a room called "Auld Reekie." Next came the abode of "The Nuts," or engineers, followed by "The Sailors' Rest," which was inhabited by Cheetham and McNeish.

(Below) Hurley captured the spirit of life in 'The Ritz' during the midwinter of 1915 with (clockwise from top left) the bi-weekly ablutions, a gramophone evening, general activities and a billiards evening.

The new quarters became known as "The Ritz," and meals were served there instead of in the wardroom. Wild, Marston, Crean and Worsley established themselves in cubicles in the wardroom, and by the middle of the month all hands had settled down to the winter routine. I lived alone aft.

The noon position on the 14th was lat. 76° 54′ S., long. 36° 10′ W. The land was visible faintly to the south-east, distant about thirty-six miles. The drift of the ship was still towards the north-west. I had the boilers blown down on the 15th, and the consumption of 2 cwt. of coal per day, to keep the boilers from freezing, ceased. Anyhow there would not be much coal left for steaming purposes in the spring, but I hoped to eke out the supply with blubber.

The training of the dogs in sledge teams continued. The orders used by the drivers were "Mush" (go on), "Gee" (right), "Haw" (left), and "Whoa" (stop). These are the words which Canadian drivers adopted long ago, borrowing them originally from England. The teams rapidly became efficient, but we were losing dogs owing to sickness.

As the days passed the sun sank lower in the sky, the temperature became lower, and the *Endurance* felt the grip of the icy hand of winter; but the month of April was not uneventful. During the night of the 3rd we heard the ice grinding to the eastward, and in the morning we saw that young ice was rafted 8 to 10 feet high in places. This was the first murmur of the danger which was so greatly to threaten us in later months. The ice was heard grinding and creaking during the 4th and the ship vibrated slightly. I gave orders that accumulations of snow, ice and rubbish alongside

(Above) Clark and Wordie in their cabin which they named 'Auld Reekie'. Shackleton lived apart from the others 'alone aft' though he joined in the general activities in 'The Ritz', taking part in guessing games and winning the palm in a 'worst singer' competition.

the *Endurance* should be shovelled away, so that in case of pressure there would be no weight against the topsides to check the ship rising above the ice.

Again, on the 9th, there were signs of pressure, and, although the movement was not serious, I realised that it might be the beginning of trouble for the Expedition. We brought certain stores aboard, and provided space on deck for the dogs in case they had to be removed at short notice from the floe.

The dogs had been divided into six teams of nine dogs each. Wild, Crean, Macklin, McIlroy, Marston and Hurley each had charge of a team, and were fully responsible for their own dogs. We were still losing dogs, and it was unfortunate that we had not the proper remedies for the disease from which they were suffering. By the end of April our mature dogs had decreased to fifty. Our store of seal meat now amounted to 5,000 lb., and I calculated that we had enough meat and blubber to feed the dogs for ninety days without trenching upon the sledging rations.

Training of dogs was difficult because the experienced Canadian doghandler originally selected for the team had been left behind in Latin America. Much of the Hurley film used afterwards for fund-raising purposes featured the dogs because of their popular appeal.

On the 14th a new berg, which was destined to give us cause for anxiety, appeared. It was a big berg, and during the day it increased its apparent altitude and slightly changed its bearing. Evidently it was aground and was holding its position against the drifting pack. During the next twenty-four hours the *Endurance* moved steadily towards the berg. We could see from the mast-head that the pack was piling and rafting against the mass of ice, and it was easy to imagine the fate of the ship if she entered the area of disturbance. She would be crushed like an egg-shell amid the shattering masses.

(Above left) A photograph which Hurley captioned 'Wild and chums' and (above right) Dr Macklin is grooming Mack and Split-up.

The drift of the pack was not constant, and during the succeeding days the berg, which was about three-quarters of a mile long on the side presented to us and probably considerably more than 200 feet high, alternately advanced and receded as the *Endurance* moved with the floe. On Sunday, April 18th, it was only seven miles distant from the ship, but a strong drift to the westward during the night of the 18th relieved our anxiety by carrying the *Endurance* to the lee of the berg, and before the end of the month it was no longer in sight.

We said good-bye to the sun on May 1st and entered the period of twilight, which would be followed by the darkness of midwinter. I wrote: "One feels our helplessness as the long winter night closes upon us. By this time, if fortune had smiled upon the Expedition, we would have been

(Opposite) The dogs were taken out each day for exercise, and some members of the crew attached themselves to specific animals.

(Above) Hussey and Hurley on night watch while away the time playing chess.

Alfred Cheetham was Third Officer and Kerr the Second Engineer.

comfortably and securely established in a shore base, with depôts laid to the south, and plans made for the long march in the spring and summer. Where will we make a landing now? . . . Time alone will tell. I do not think any member of the Expedition is disheartened by our disappointment. All hands are cheery and busy, and will do their best when the time for acting comes. In the meantime we must wait."

The ship's position on Sunday, May 2nd, was lat. 75° 23' S., long. 42° 14' W., and on that day we captured a seal, which was the first we had caught since March 19th. On the following day three emperor penguins appeared and were captured, and on the same afternoon we sighted five more emperors and secured one of them, Kerr and Cheetham fighting a valiant action against two large birds. Kerr rushed at one of them and seized it, but was promptly knocked down by the angry penguin, which jumped on his chest before retiring. Then Cheetham came to Kerr's assistance, and between them they seized another penguin, and bound his bill and led him, muttering muffled protests, to the ship, the bird looking like an inebriated old man between two policemen. This penguin weighed 85 1b.

On May 4th we secured two more emperors, and while Wordie was leading one of them to the ship Wild came along with his dog-team. The dogs, immediately uncontrollable, made a frantic rush for the bird, and were almost upon him when their harness caught on an ice-pylon, which they had tried to pass on both sides at once. The result was a seething tangle of dogs, traces, men and overturned sledge, while the penguin, three yards away, indifferently surveyed the disturbance. During the succeeding days we secured several birds, and they made an important addition to our supply of fresh food.

The month of May passed with few incidents of importance, and the drift of the *Endurance* continued with only occasional reports of pressure during June. The light by now was very bad, except when the friendly moon was above the horizon.

In those days the care of our dog-teams was our heaviest responsibility, and a faint twilight round about noon of each day assisted us in the important work of exercising them. Whatever fate might be in store for us the conditioning and training of the dogs seemed essential, and whenever the weather permitted the teams were taken out by their drivers. Rivalries naturally arose, and on the 15th a great race, the "Antarctic Derby," was run. Considerable betting took place, but the most thrilling wagers were those which concerned stores of chocolate and cigarettes.

A course of about 700 yards had been laid out, and five teams went to the starting point in the dim noon twilight, with a zero temperature and an aurora flickering faintly to the southward. Wild's time for the course was 2 minutes 16 seconds, and in a subsequent race against Hurley's team Wild's dogs completed the course in 2 minutes 9 seconds, although their load was 910 lb., or 130 lb. per dog.

The approach of the returning sun was indicated by beautiful sunrise glows on the horizon in the early days of July. By the 10th numerous cracks and leads extended in all directions to within 300 yards of the ship, but although we heard occasional sounds of moderate pressure, the *Endurance* was not involved.

On the evening of the 13th the most severe blizzard we had experienced in the Weddell Sea swept down upon us, and early in the following morning the kennels to the southern side of the ship

(Above left) Hudson, the Navigating Officer, with penguins for the pot. *(Centre)* Tom Crean (standing) and Alfred Cheetham, both Antarctic veterans, Second and Third Officers respectively, and (*right*) Green the cook carving seal for the larder. Seal blubber, at first disliked, soon became a delicacy. Green was a trained baker and pastry cook but there was little scope for his talents now.

Wild won the 'Derby' at an average speed for the course of 10½ miles per hour. This was in marked contrast to the ship itself, whose average northward drift was about a mile a day, although she moved about four miles a day in various directions and had occasional bursts of speed under the influence of a fresh breeze. They had now reached latitude 74° 45′ South. There were no map references of any real value to them and the nearest known land was 600 miles to the northwest, at Alexander Island.

(Above) A dinner was held on 24 May to celebrate Empire Day and there was another party on Midwinter's Day on 22 June.

Endurance had had a very narrow escape – the major pressure wave had stopped just short and she had risen to the pressures that did reach her, so avoiding being crushed.

were buried under 5 feet of drift. The ship was invisible at a distance of 50 yards, and I gave orders that nobody should go beyond the kennels, for it was impossible to preserve a sense of direction in the raging wind and suffocating drift. The temperature during the blizzard raged from −21° to −33.5° Fahr., and by evening the gale had attained a force of sixty or seventy miles an hour, and the ship was trembling under the attack. We, however, were snug enough in our quarters aboard until the morning of the 14th, when all hands turned out to shovel the snow from deck and kennels. The temperature was then about −30° Fahr., and it was necessary to be on guard against frost-bite.

The weather did not clear until the 16th, and then we saw that the appearance of the surrounding pack had been altered completely by the blizzard. The "island" floe containing the *Endurance* still stood fast, but cracks and masses of ice thrown up by pressure could be seen in all directions.

The ice-pressure, which was indicated by distant rumblings and by the appearance of formidable ridges, was now causing us more and more anxiety. The areas of disturbance were

(Above) At one of their celebrations Shackleton addressed the party in the Ritz with a humorous mock-bombastic speech praising his own accomplishments and deploring the entertainment he was about to see. Orde-Lees, disguised as the Reverend Bubblinglove, replied; Rickinson and McIlroy dressed up as women and performed appropriately; Marston, dressed as a yokel, sang *Widdicombe Fair*, and James, got up as a German professor, gave a dissertation on the Calori. Diet was a subject of perpetual conversation, and no doubt some wag had asked, 'Who *was* Calori?' This singing and joking went on until midnight when a collation of fried bread and onions was served.

gradually approaching the ship. Early on the afternoon of the 22nd a 2-foot crack, running south-west and north-east for a distance of about two miles, approached to within 35 yards of the port quarter.

I had all the sledges brought aboard and set a special watch in case it became necessary hurriedly to get the dogs off the floe. This crack was the result of heavy pressure 300 yards away on the port bow, where huge blocks of ice were piled up in wild and threatening confusion. The pressure at that point was enormous; blocks weighing many tons were raised 15 feet above the level of the floe. I arranged to divide the night watches with Worsley and Wild, and none of us had much rest. The ship was shaken by heavy bumps, and we were on the alert to see that no dogs had fallen into the cracks.

In the morning we saw that our island had been reduced considerably during the night. Our long months of rest and safety seemed to have ended, and a period of stress to have begun.

During the following day I had a store of sledging provisions, oil, matches, and other essentials, placed on the upper deck handy to the starboard quarter boat, so that we should be ready for a sudden emergency. A great deal of ice-pressure was heard and observed in all directions

(Above) Hurley feeding his team in midwinter by the artificial lights he rigged up round the igloos. During the months mid-May to mid-July there was no sunlight throughout the 24 hours.

(Opposite) Hurley's famous picture of *Endurance* covered with heavy rime on a brilliantly clear moonlit night in June 1915. Worsley wrote in his candid way, 'Ship looks like a Christmas cake'.

Shackleton knew that the design of the *Endurance* might well prevent it from rising above the ice and so remaining free to be moved off if a lead opened ahead. Worsley wrote at this time, 'The noise was very loud like an enormous train with squeaky axles being shunted with much bumping and clattering. Mingled with this were the sounds of steamers' whistles starting to blow, cocks crowing, & underfoot moans & groans of damned souls in torment ... It is impressive to stand on the blocks of heavy rafting ice & feel the irresistible forces of Nature working under your very feet as the Weddell Sea North current exerts its slow but mighty force.'

during the 25th, much of it close to the port quarter of the ship. The floe which held the *Endurance* was swung to and fro by the pressure during the day, but came back to the old bearing before midnight.

At this time I wrote: "The ice for miles around is much looser. There are numerous cracks and short leads to the north-east and south-east. Ridges are being forced up in all directions. . . . It would be a relief to be able to make some effort on our own behalf; but we can do nothing until the ice releases our ship. If the floes continue to loosen, we may break out within the next few weeks

(Right) A line of ice mounds were thrown up and joined by cable to act as guidance during blizzards. Hurley, an experienced electrician, also fixed lights on poles to either side of the ship as well as all over the ship itself, so that it could be seen at a distance. Shackleton encouraged walking on the ice wherever possible.

(Opposite) Frank Worsley and Reginald James taking observations with the sextant. Worsley's navigational skills were of a very high order and it is not too much to claim that, on several later occasions, he may have saved his companions from disaster by the accuracy and judgement he showed in his calculations.

and resume the fight. In the meantime the pressure continues, and it is hard to foresee the outcome. All hands are cheered by the indication that the end of the winter darkness is near."

The break-up of our floe came suddenly on Sunday, August 1st, just one year after the *Endurance* left the South-West India Docks on the voyage to the Far South. The position was lat. 72° 26′ S., long. 48° 10′ W. The morning brought a moderate south-westerly gale with heavy snow, and presently, after some warning movements of the ice, the floe began to break up all round us under pressure, and the ship listed over 10 degrees to starboard.

I had the dogs and sledges brought aboard at once and the gangway hoisted. The dogs seemed to realise their danger and behaved most peacefully. The pressure was rapidly cracking the floe, rafting it close to the ship and forcing masses of ice beneath the keel. The *Endurance* listed heavily to port against the gale, and, at the same time, was forced ahead, astern and sideways several times by the grinding floes. She received one or two hard nips, but resisted them without as much as a creak.

(Above) The condition of the ice ahead of the ship in August 1915. A few days later a 90mph blizzard heaved the ice into a chaos of hummocks. In the low temperature the congested hummocks froze together and the ship became immovably gripped.

At one stage it looked as if the ship was to be made the plaything of successive floes, and I was relieved when she came to a standstill with a large piece of our old "dock" under the starboard bilge. I had the boats cleared away ready for lowering, got up some additional stores, and set a double watch. Around us lay the ruins of "Dog Town"; it was a sad sight, but my chief concern just then was about the safety of the rudder, which was being attacked viciously by the ice. I could see that some damage had been done, but it was at the time impossible to make a close examination.

After the ship had come to a standstill in her new position very heavy pressure was set up, but the *Endurance* had been built to withstand the attacks of the ice, and she lifted bravely as the floes drove beneath her. The effects of the pressure around us were awe-inspiring. Mighty blocks of ice, gripped between meeting floes, rose slowly until they jumped like cherry-stones squeezed between thumb and finger. The pressure of millions of tons of moving ice was crushing and smashing inexorably. If the ship was once gripped firmly her fate would be sealed.

By the afternoon of the 2nd the gale had moderated and the pressure had almost ceased. The gale had given us some northing, but it had also severely damaged the rudder of the *Endurance*.

Heavy masses of ice were still jammed against the stern, and it was consequently impossible to ascertain the extent of the damage.

The weather on August 3rd was overcast and misty, and on the following day all hands and the carpenter were busy making and placing kennels on the upper deck, and by nightfall the dogs were comfortably housed and ready for any weather. The sun showed through the clouds above the northern horizon for nearly an hour.

The remaining days of August were comparatively uneventful. The ice around the ship again froze firmly and little movement occurred in our neighbourhood. The training of the dogs proceeded actively, and we continued to drift steadily to the north-west. Minus temperatures

For the crew at large Shackleton persisted in keeping up the myth that they could still sail to safety, writing '*Endurance* had been built to withstand the attacks of the ice' when he knew that she had not. The ice break-up on 1 August caused such consternation that McNeish wrote in his diary, 'I have placed my loved ones fotos inside my Bible . . . & put them in my bag ready to abandon ship.'

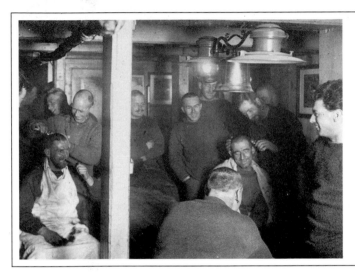

prevailed still, but the daylight was increasing. A sounding on the 17th gave 1,676 fathoms, ten miles west of the charted position of Morell Land. No land could be seen from the mast-head, and I decided that Morell Land must be added to the long list of Antarctic islands and continental coasts which on close investigation have resolved themselves into icebergs.

On August 24th we were two miles north of the latitude of Morell's farthest south, and over 10° of longitude, or more than 200 miles, west of his position. There was some movement of the ice near the ship during the last days of the month, and all hands were called out on the night of the 26th, sounds of pressure having been followed by the cracking of the ice alongside the ship; but the trouble did not develop immediately.

I calculated that we were 250 miles from the nearest known land to the westward, and more than 500 miles from the nearest outpost of civilisation, Wilhelmina Bay. I hoped fervently that we should not have to undertake a march across the moving ice-fields. We knew the *Endurance* to be stout and true, but these were anxious days because no ship ever built by man could live, if taken fairly in the grip of the floes and prevented from rising to the surface of the grinding ice.

(*Above*) Shackleton's team-spirit included participating in a general hair-cutting, first allowing Rickinson to cut his hair which the latter did with a great zest 'till not a vestige of hair is left and his victim looks like one of the Roman Emperors' (Worsley's words). Shackleton then set about his hairdresser and one by one all followed suit until they were reduced to looking 'like convicts', whereupon Hurley took their photographs.

CHAPTER IV

LOSS OF THE ENDURANCE

✦

T HE ice did not seriously trouble us again until the end of September, though during the whole month the floes were seldom entirely without movement. The routine of work and play on the *Endurance* steadily proceeded. Our plans and preparations for any contingency which might arise during the approaching summer had been made, but there was always plenty to do in and about our prisoned ship. Runs with the dogs and vigorous games of hockey and football on the rough, snow-covered floe kept all hands in good condition.

By the middle of September we were running short of fresh meat for the dogs. Nearly five months had passed since we had killed a seal, and penguins had seldom been seen. But on the 23rd

On 4 September McNeish noted that they had 'a real bonfire of 500 gallons of petril [sic] as the motors has turned out useless in those climates'.

(*Left*) Dr Macklin (who, when he joined *Endurance*, had just returned from doctoring in the Malay States) and Commander Greenstreet, an experienced seaman, cooperating in the rather mundane task of boiling blubber for the dogs.

(*Opposite*) To keep up morale in the winter months, Hurley gave regular lantern lectures on the ship. During this time there was no contact with the outside world though in a vain attempt to find out was was happening the crew listened for wireless signals. It had been arranged that the station on the Falkland Islands would send signals every month but it was a thousand miles away and with such primitive apparatus the distance was too great for anything to be received.

On 2 Sept, the situation was so bad that Worsley wrote that they might 'have to get out and walk' as it was 'only 250 miles to the nearest known land to westward'. A few days later he wrote almost hysterically, 'No animal life! – no land! no nothing!!!!' When the break-up came, Worsley wrote (in his book *Endurance*) that Shackleton said to him, 'The ship can't live in this, Skipper . . . You had better make up your mind that it is only a matter of time . . . What the ice gets, the ice keeps.'

we got an emperor penguin, and on the following day, we secured a crab-eater seal. The return of seal-life was most opportune, as we wished to feed the dogs on meat, and seals also meant a supply of blubber to supplement our small remaining stock of coal.

During the last days of September the roar of the pressure grew louder, and I could see that the area of disturbance was rapidly approaching the ship. Stupendous forces were at work, and the fields of firm ice around the *Endurance* were steadily diminishing.

September 30th was a bad day, for at 3 p.m. cracks, which had opened during the night alongside the ship, began to work in a lateral direction. The ship sustained terrific pressure. The decks shuddered and jumped, beams arched, and stanchions buckled and shook. I ordered all hands to stand by in readiness for any emergency. But the ship resisted valiantly, and just when it seemed that the limit of her strength was being reached, one huge floe which was pressing down upon us cracked across and so gave relief.

(Right) Hurley took this shot of the floe cracking up on 29 September 1915 and the other one hour later. 'The pressure was grinding around us' wrote Shackleton, and the day was spent getting the sledges ready to carry the boats. In the afternoon 'Sallie's three youngest pups, Sue's Sirius, and Mrs Chippy, the carpenter's cat, had to be shot. We could not undertake the maintenance of weaklings under the new conditions.'

"The behaviour of our ship in the ice," Worsley wrote, "has been magnificent. Since we have been beset her staunchness and endurance have been almost past belief again and again. It will be sad if such a brave little craft should be finally crushed in the remorseless, slowly strangling grip of the Weddell pack, after ten months of the bravest and most gallant fight ever put up by a ship."

Indeed, the *Endurance* deserved all that could be said in praise of her. Shipwrights had never done sounder or better work. But how long could she continue the fight under such conditions? The vital question for us was whether the ice would open sufficiently to release us before the drift carried us into the dangerous area which we were approaching? With anxious hearts we faced the month of October.

Some of the crew privately expressed less sanguine views. McNeish wrote that the ship was caught in a giant pair of shears which 'buckled the tween deck beems (sic) like a piece of cane we really thought she was going to pieces when the pressure stopped.'

(Left) Huge blocks of ice were thrown up around the *Endurance*. Shackleton asked 'How long could she continue the fight under such conditions? We were drifting into the congested area of the western Weddell Sea, the worst portion of the worst sea in the world.'

On the first day of that month two bull crab-eaters climbed onto the floe close to the ship and were shot by Wild. They were both big animals in prime condition, and all anxiety as to the supply of fresh meat for the dogs was removed. Seal-liver also made a welcome change in our own diet.

Two or three days later we had no doubt that the movement of the ice was increasing. Frost-smoke from opening cracks was showing in all directions during October 6th. In one place it looked like a great prairie fire, at another it resembled a train running before the wind, the smoke rising from the engine straight upward; elsewhere the smoke columns gave the effect of warships steaming in line ahead.

Conditions did not change materially during the next two or three days, but on the 10th a thaw made things uncomfortable for us, and the dogs, who hated wet, looked most unhappy. The thaw indicated that winter was over, and we began preparations to re-occupy the cabins on the main deck. I also made several preparations for working the ship as soon as she was clear.

For several days the temperature remained relatively high, and all hands – amid much noise and laughter – moved on the 12th to their summer quarters in the upper cabins. On the 13th the ship broke free of the floe on which she rested to starboard sufficiently to come upright. The rudder freed itself and, the water being very clear, we could see that it had only suffered a light twist to port at the water-line. It moved quite freely. The propeller, however, was found to be athwartship, and I did not think it advisable to try to deal with it at that stage.

The south-westerly breeze freshened to a gale on the 14th, and the temperature fell from +31° Fahr. to −1° Fahr. The wind died down during the day and the pack opened for five or six miles to the north. Our efforts, however, to force the ship out of the lead failed, and heavy pressure

Shackleton did not show an anxious heart himself and, despite what he must have known, ostentatiously allowed McNeish to build a wheelhouse so that the men at the helm would have protection when they finally broke into the open sea, which by now he must have known was highly improbable. Although the ship broke free on 13 October, it was closed in again a few days later.

(Above) Removing cases of Bovril sledging rations from the ship at night. Hurley was still able, despite the danger, to go about the ship and photograph the deck at close of winter. He took the picture *(opposite)* on the 19 October as the *Endurance* was forced out of the floe. Hurley descended on to the ice during this listing process and took photographs. The ship did not right itself until nightfall.

developed late on Sunday, the 17th. The two floes between which the ship was lying began to close, and the *Endurance* was subjected to a series of tremendously heavy strains. In the engine-room, the weakest point, loud groans, crashes and hammering sounds were heard. For nearly an hour the ship valiantly stood the strain, and then to my great relief, she began to rise with heavy jerks and jars. The ice was getting below us and the immediate danger was past. Our position was lat. 69° 19' S., long. 50° 40' W.

The next attack of the ice came during the afternoon of October 19th. The two floes began to move laterally and exerted great pressure on the ship. Suddenly the floe on the port side cracked and huge pieces of ice shot up from under the port bilge. Within a few seconds the ship heeled over until she had a list of 30 degrees to port, being held under the starboard bilge by the opposing floe. Everything movable on deck and below fell to the lee side, and for a few minutes it looked as if the ship would be thrown upon her beam ends. The midship dog-kennels broke away and crashed down on to the lee kennels, and the howls and barks of the frightened dogs helped to create a perfect pandemonium. Order, however, was soon restored.

(Above) This was another view of the scene on 19 October with *Endurance* clamped in the pressure crack. Shackleton coolly noted that late that afternoon they found a 25-foot whale 'cruising up and down in our pool. It pushed its head up once in characteristic killer fashion', but was judged to be a different specimen.

On 22 October Fisher reports one bright spot: seals began to appear more frequently and a party shot three, which provided fresh livers and hearts for the men, food for the dogs and fuel for the fires.

If the ship had heeled any farther it would have been necessary to release the lee boats and pull them clear, and Worsley was watching to give the alarm. Dinner in the wardroom that evening was a curious affair, for most of the diners had to sit on the deck, their feet against battens and their plates on their knees. At 8 p.m. the floes opened, and within a few minutes the *Endurance* was again nearly upright.

Although the ship was still securely imprisoned in the pool, it was obvious that our chance might come at any moment, and watches were set so as to be ready for working ship. At 11 a.m. on October 20th we gave the engines a gentle trial astern. Everything worked well after eight months of frozen inactivity, except that the bilge-pump and the discharge proved to be frozen up; with some little difficulty they were cleared.

The next two days brought low temperatures with them, and the open leads again froze over. The pack was working, and the roar of pressure ever and anon was heard. We waited for the next move of the gigantic forces arrayed against us, and on Sunday, October 24th, the beginning of the end for the *Endurance* came. The position was lat. 69° 11′ S., long. 51° 5′ W.

We now had twenty-two and a half hours of daylight, and throughout the day we watched the threatening advance of the floes. At 6.45 p.m. the ship sustained heavy pressure in a dangerous position. The onslaught was almost irresistible. The ship groaned and quivered as her starboard quarter was forced against the floe twisting the stern-post and starting the heads and ends of planking. The ice had lateral as well as forward movement, and the ship was twisted and actually bent by the stresses. She began to leak dangerously at once.

The attack of the ice is illustrated roughly in the appended diagram. The shaded portions represent the pool, covered with new ice which afforded no support to the ship, and the arrows indicate the direction of the pressure exercised by the thick floes and pressure-ridges.

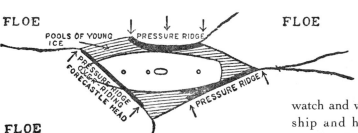

I had the pumps rigged, got up stream, and started the bilge pumps by 8 p.m. By that time the pressure had relaxed. The ship was making water rapidly aft, and all hands worked, watch and watch, during the night, pumping ship and helping the carpenter. By the morning the leak was being kept in check.

On Monday, October 25th, the leak was kept under fairly easily, but the outlook was bad. Heavy pressure-ridges were forming in all directions, and I realised that our respite from pressure

The carpenter and his assistants made a dam astern of the engines with strips of blankets and nailed strips over the seams wherever possible.

Worsley wrote 'This is not a pleasant job . . . the beams and timbers groan and crack all around us like pistol shots. The darkness is almost complete and we mess about in the wet with half-frozen hands.'

(*Left*) Officers and men were still messing separately and leading their separate lives, although Shackleton himself was always able to break the barriers of caste. Macklin described how the Boss 'had a nice way of, every now and then, when he came across you by yourself, getting into conversation and talking to you in an intimate sort of way'. Shackleton insisted, too, on keeping up the Saturday evening ritual of toasting 'Wives and girlfriends'.

could not be prolonged. The pressure-ridges, massive and menacing, testified to the overwhelming nature of the forces at work. Huge blocks of ice, weighing many tons, were lifted into the air and tossed aside as other masses rose beneath them.

I scarcely dared to hope any longer that the *Endurance* would live, and during that anxious day I reviewed all my plans for the sledging journey which we should have to make if we had to take to the ice. As far as forethought could make us we were ready for any contingency. Stores, dogs, sledges and equipment were ready to be moved from the ship at a moment's notice.

The following day was bright and clear, and the sunshine was inspiring. But the roar of pressure continued, new ridges were rising, and as the day wore on I could see the lines of major disturbance were drawing nearer to the ship. The day passed slowly. At 7 p.m. very heavy pressure developed, with twisting strains which racked the ship fore and aft. The butts of planking were opened 4 or 5 inches on the starboard side, and at the same time we could see the ship bending like a bow under titanic pressure. Almost like a living creature she resisted the forces which would crush her; but it was a one-sided battle. Millions of tons of ice pressed inexorably upon the gallant little ship which had dared the challenge of the Antarctic. She was now leaking badly, and at 9 p.m. I gave the order to lower boats, gear, provisions and sledges to the floe, and move them to the flat ice a little way from the ship.

Then came a fateful day – Wednesday, October 27th. The position was lat. 69° 5′ S., long. 51° 30′ W. The temperature was −8.5° Fahr., a gentle southerly breeze was blowing and the sun shone in a clear sky.

"After long months of ceaseless anxiety and strain," I wrote, "after times when hope beat high and times when the outlook was black indeed, the end of the *Endurance* has come. But though we have been compelled to abandon the ship, which is crushed beyond all hope of ever being righted, we are alive and well, and we have stores and equipment for the task that lies before us. The task is to reach land with all the members of the Expedition. It is hard to write what I feel. To a sailor his ship is more than a floating home, and in the *Endurance* I had centred ambitions, hopes and desires. And now she is slowly giving up her sentient life at the very outset of her career. . . . The distance from the point where she became beset to the place where she now rests mortally hurt in the grip of the floes is 573 miles, but the total drift through all observed positions has been 1,186 miles, and we probably covered more than 1,500 miles.

"We are now 346 miles from Paulet Island, the nearest point where there is any possibility of finding food and shelter. A small hut built there by the Swedish Expedition in 1902 is filled with stores left by the Argentine relief ship. . . . The distance to the nearest barrier west of us is about 180 miles, but a party going there would still be about 360 miles from Paulet Island, and there would be no means of sustaining life on the barrier. We could not take food enough from here for the whole journey; the weight would be too great. . . . The attack of the ice reached its climax at 4 p.m. The ship was hove stern up by the pressure, and the driving floe, moving laterally across the stern, split the rudder and tore out the rudder-post and stern-post. Then, while we watched, the ice loosened and the *Endurance* sank a little. The decks were breaking upwards and the water was pouring in below. Again the pressure began, and at 5 p.m. I ordered all hands on to the ice.

"At last the twisting, grinding floes were working their will on the ship. It was a sickening sensation to feel the decks breaking up under one's feet, the great beams bending and then snapping with a noise like heavy gun-fire. The water was overmastering the pumps, and to avoid an explosion when it reached the boilers I ordered the fires to be drawn and the steam let down. The plans for abandoning the ship in case of emergency had been well made, and men and dogs made their way to an unbroken portion of the floes without a hitch.

(Opposite) This picture was taken about a week before *Endurance* finally succumbed to the pressure of the ice. The figure on the right looking over the port rail is said to be Shackleton but the print is not clear enough to be sure about this. Another figure can be seen underneath the boat astern.

Shackleton wrote, 'We were helpless intruders in a strange world, our lives dependent upon the play of grim elementary forces that made a mock of our puny efforts.'

Shackleton continued in this vein in his diary, writing, 'her wounds gaping, she is slowly giving up her sentient life at the very outset of her career'.

'Although this must have been a moment of bitter disappointment for Shackleton', who now had no hope of crossing the continent, Macklin describes how 'he shewed it neither in word or manner . . . Without emotion, melodrama or excitement [he] said "Ship and stores have gone – so now we'll go home." ' Privately Shackleton wrote in his diary, 'I pray God I can manage to get the whole party to civilization.'

In their last hours on the ship, Hurley wrote of how the pressure wave ground towards them, pushing ice slabs through the ice floe. 'Now it is within a few yards of the vessel. We are the embodiment of helpless futility and can only look impotently on. I am quickly down on the moving ice with the camera, expecting every minute to see the sides.'

"Just before leaving I looked down the engine-room skylight as I stood on the quivering deck, and saw the engines dropping sideways as the stays and bed-plates gave way. I cannot describe the impression of relentless destruction which was forced upon me as I looked down and around. The floes, with the force of millions of tons of moving ice behind them, were simply annihilating the ship."

Esssential supplies had been placed on the floe about 100 yards from the ship, but after we had begun to pitch our camp there the ice started to split and smash beneath our feet. Then I had the camp moved to a bigger floe, and boats, stores and camp equipment had to be conveyed across a working pressure-ridge. A pioneer party, with picks and shovels, had to build a snow-causeway before we could get all our possessions across. By 8 p.m. the camp had been pitched again.

We had two pole tents, and three hoop tents which are easily shifted and set up. I took charge of the small pole tent, No. 1, with Hudson, Hurley and James as companions; Wild had the small hoop tent, No. 2, with Wordie, McNeish and McIlroy. The eight forward hands had the large hoop tent, No. 3; Crean had charge of No. 4 hoop tent, with Hussey, Marston and Cheetham; and

(Below) One of the last pictures of *Endurance* still recognisable above the ice.

(Far left) Commander Greenstreet breathing icicles on his beard. He recalled how, on the last night, as they went off to camp on the floe, 'you could hear the ship being crushed up, the ice being ground into her, and you almost felt your own ribs were being crushed . . . It seemed the end of everything.' *(Left)* Dr Macklin, the chief surgeon, wrote that while the men worked at the pumps, 'every muscle ached and revolted at the unspeakable toil'.

Worsley had the other pole tent, No. 5, with Greenstreet, Lees, Clark, Kerr, Rickenson, Macklin, and Blackborrow, the last-named being the youngest of the forward hands.

After the tents had been pitched I mustered all hands and explained the position as briefly and clearly as I could. I told them the distance to the Barrier and the distance to Paulet Island, and stated that I proposed to try to march with equipment across the ice in the direction of Paulet Island. I thanked the men for the steadiness they had shown under trying circumstances, and told them I did not doubt that we should all eventually reach safety provided that they continued to work their utmost and to trust me. Then we had supper, and all hands except the watch turned in.

But, for myself, I could not sleep, and the thoughts which came to me as I walked up and down in the darkness were not particularly cheerful. At midnight I was pacing the ice, listening to the grinding floe and the groans and crashes that told of the death-agony of the *Endurance*, when I noticed suddenly a crack running across our floe right through the camp. The alarm-whistle brought all hands tumbling out, and we moved everything from what was now the smaller portion of the floe to the larger portion. Nothing more could be done then, and the men turned in again; but there was little sleep.

Morning came in chill and cheerless, and all hands were stiff and weary after their first disturbed night on the floe. Just at daybreak I went over to the *Endurance* with Wild and Hurley to retrieve some tins of petrol, which could be used to boil up milk for the rest of the men. The ship represented a painful spectacle of chaos and wreck, but with some difficulty we secured two tins of petrol, and postponed the further examination of the ship until after breakfast, when I went over to the *Endurance* again and examined the wreck more fully.

Only six of the cabins had not been pierced by floes and blocks of ice. All the starboard cabins had been crushed, and the whole of the aft part of the ship had been crushed concertina fashion.

One reason why there was very little sleep was that there were only eighteen reindeer-fur sleeping bags for twenty-eight men; the ten unfortunates who had to have woollen blanket bags were chosen by lot. Shackleton had not planned for the whole expedition to abandon ship, so had made no provision for protection for the party that was intended to remain on board ship.

The forecastle and "The Ritz" were submerged, and the wardroom was three-quarters full of ice. The motor-engine forward had been driven through the galley. In short, scenes of devastation met me on every side. The ship was being crushed remorselessly.

Under a dull, overcast sky I returned to the camp, and, having examined the situation, I thought it wise to move to a larger and apparently stronger floe about 200 yards away. This camp became known as Dump Camp, owing to the amount of stuff that was thrown away there. I decided to issue a complete new set of Burberrys and under-clothing to each man, and also a supply of socks. The camp was quickly transferred to the new floe, and there I began to direct the preparations for the long journey across the floes to Paulet Island or Snow Hill.

Greenstreet, in a conversation with Fisher, said Shackleton's 'first thought was for the men under him. He didn't care if he went without a shirt on his back so long as the men he was leading had sufficient clothing.'

(Above left) Hurley taking his ciné picture, 'unique though sad', of the *Endurance*'s mast structure crashing down, which may still be seen on the film Hurley made and got home to safety. *(Above right)* Dump Camp where so much salvaged from the ship was thrown away.

From the diaries of the party, it is clear that their badinage about tea did not arise, as Shackleton suggests, from 'untroubled' minds, but was an attempt to keep their spirits up. Fisher suggests that this passage may be due to the ghost writer Edward Saunders' interpretation of the incident. Shackleton did not see his draft until 1918.

Meanwhile Hurley had rigged his kinematograph camera, and was getting pictures of the *Endurance* in her death-throes. While he was thus engaged, the foretop and top-gallant mast came down with a run and hung in wreckage on the fore-mast, with the foreyard vertical. The mainmast followed immediately, snapping off about 10 feet above the main deck. The crow's-nest fell within 10 feet of where Hurley was turning the handle of his camera, but he did not stop the machine and so secured a unique, though sad, picture.

The issue of clothing was quickly accomplished, but sleeping-bags were also required. We had eighteen fur bags, and so it was necessary to issue ten of the larger woollen bags in order to provide for the twenty-eight men of the party. As the fur bags were warmer, it seemed fair to distribute them by lot, but some of us older hands did not join in the lottery. Each man who received a woollen bag was also allowed a reindeer-skin to lie upon.

Having apportioned the clothing we turned one of the boats on its side, and supported it with two broken oars to make a lee for the galley. The cook got the blubber-stove going, and presently I heard one man say, "Cook, I like my tea strong." Another joined in, "Cook, I like mine weak." It was good to know that their minds were untroubled, but I thought the time opportune to mention that the tea would be the same for all hands, and that we should be fortunate if two months later we had any tea at all.

During the afternoon the work continued, and the arrangement of the tents and their internal management completed. Each tent had a mess-orderly, the duty being undertaken in alphabetical order.

A quiet night followed, for, although the pressure was grinding around us, our floe was heavy enough to withstand the blows it received. "We are," I wrote on October 29th, "twenty-eight men with forty-nine dogs. All hands this morning were busy preparing gear, fitting boats on sledges, and building and strengthening the sledges to carry the boats. The main motor sledge, with a little fitting from the carpenter, carried our largest boat admirably. The ship was still afloat, with the spurs of the pack driven through her and holding her up. The forecastle-head is under water, the decks are burst up by the pressure, the wreckage lies around in dismal confusion, but over all the blue ensign still flies. . . .

"The number of dog-teams has been increased to seven, Greenstreet taking charge of the additional team. . . . We have ten working sledges to relay with five teams. Wild's and Hurley's teams will haul the cutter with the assistance of four men. The whaler and the other boats will follow, and the men who are hauling them will be able to help with the cutter at the rough places.

(Above) One of the seven dog teams working in very rough conditions. The men were ordered to restrict their personal gear to 2lb apiece, but Hussey was instructed to take his banjo in spite of its weight.

Worsley took charge of the two boats, but he personally believed the minimum required was three. Shackleton decided otherwise, as he was in a hurry to set off across the ice.

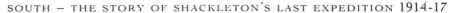

The column was about half a mile in length and Orde-Lees, the only good skier, went back and forth. Shackleton remarked to him, 'Do you know, I had no idea how quickly it was possible for a man on ski to get about.' Orde-Lees was surprised that Shackleton had not thought of this before and trained each man to ski, as Amundsen's speedy journey to the pole had proved the efficacy of skiing long ago.

We cannot hope to make rapid progress, but each mile counts. Crean this afternoon has a bad attack of snow-blindness."

The weather on the morning of October 30th was overcast and misty, with occasional falls of snow. Our sledging and boating rations were still intact, for we were living on extra food brought from the abandoned ship. These provisions would provide full rations for twenty-eight men for fifty-six days, but we could count on enough seal and penguin meat at least to double this time. We could even, if progress proved too difficult and too injurious to the boats – which we had to guard as our ultimate means of salvation – camp on the nearest heavy floe, scour the neighbouring pack for penguins and seals, and await the outward drift of the pack to open and navigable water. But, although this latter plan would have avoided grave dangers, I felt sure that the right thing to do was to attempt a march. It would be, I considered, so much better for the men to feel that they were progressing – even if the progress was slow – towards land and safety, than simply to sit down and wait for the tardy north-westerly drift to take us from the cruel waste of ice.

During that afternoon Wild and I went out in the mist and snow to find a road to the north-east. With difficulty we pioneered a way for at least a mile and a half and then returned by a rather better route to the camp. At 3 p.m. we got under way, leaving Dump Camp a mass of *débris*. The order was that personal gear must not exceed 2 lbs. per man, and this meant that nothing but bare necessaries could be taken on the march. I rather grudged the 2 lbs. allowance, being very anxious to keep weights at a minimum, but some personal belongings could fairly be regarded as indispensable.

(Below) Although Shackleton tore the page from the Bible, which he discarded, MacLeod, a devout Scot, retrieved it because he believed that throwing away a Bible would bring bad luck.

Our journey might be long, and possibly we should have to spend the winter in improvised quarters on an inhospitable coast at the other end. Under such conditions a man needs something to occupy his thoughts, some tangible memento of his home and people beyond the seas. So sovereigns were thrown away and photographs kept.

I tore the fly-leaf out of the Bible which Queen Alexandra had given to the ship, with her own writing on it, and also the wonderful page of Job containing the verse:

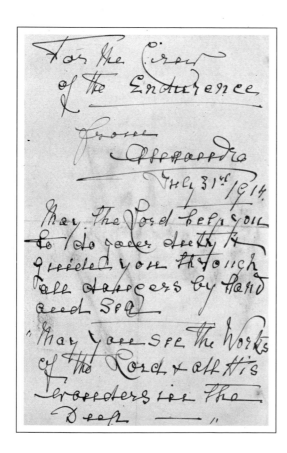

> *"Out of whose womb came the ice?*
> *And the hoary frost of Heaven, who hath gendered it?*
> *The waters are hid as with a stone,*
> *And the face of the deep is frozen."*

The other Bible, which Queen Alexandra had given for the use of the shore party, perished when the ship received her death-blow.

The pioneer sledge party, consisting of Wordie, Hussey, Hudson and myself, carrying picks and shovels, started to break a road through the pressure-ridges for the sledges carrying the boats. The boats, with their gear and the sledges beneath them, each weighed more than a ton. The sledges were the point of weakness. It seemed impossible to prevent them from smashing under their heavy loads when travelling over rough pressure-ice which stretched ahead of us probably for 300 miles.

Very heavy work followed, but both men and dogs worked splendidly. By 5 p.m. we had gained one mile in a north-north-westerly direction, but, although we had only gained a mile in a direct line, the

There were ten sledges in all, plus the sledges which were put under the boats. The whaler was initially mounted on the motor-crawler with sledges under the front part. It was slow work. Pulling the boats all day they only covered a mile in a direct line.

(Left) Shackleton and Wild had together looked out a route that seemed practicable for the sledges.

deviations necessary made the distance travelled at least two miles, and the relays brought the distance marched up to six miles. Some of the dogs had covered at least ten miles. As the condition of the ice ahead was chaotic I gave the order to pitch camp.

During the night snow fell heavily, and, as the temperature had risen to + 25° Fahr., the floor-cloths of the tent were wet through. One of the things we hoped for in those days was a temperature about zero, for then the snow surface would be hard, and our gear would not be troubled by soft snow. Killer-whales were blowing all night, and the ice below us was quite thin enough for them to break through if they wished, but there was no other camping-ground within reach and we had to take the risk.

When morning came it was snowing so heavily that I decided not to strike camp, but the weather cleared later and we struck camp after lunch. I took Rickenson, Kerr, Wordie and Hudson as a break-down gang to pioneer a path among the pressure-ridges. Five dog-teams followed. Wild's and Hurley's were hitched on to the cutter and did splendidly. Indeed, fourteen dogs did as well or even better than eighteen men.

The ice was moving beneath and around us as we worked toward the big floe, and where this floe met the smaller ones there was a mass of pressed-up ice, still in motion, with water between the ridges. But it is wonderful what a dozen men can do with picks and shovels. In ten minutes we could cut a road through a pressure-ridge about 14 feet high, and leave a comparatively smooth path for the sledges and teams.

Wild and Hurley came in for special praise from Shackleton. The 'skipper' was also much admired by the others. A member of the team said, 'very often when we wanted things, instead of going to Shackleton we went to Wild – it was a sort of instinctive thing that you did. Wild was such a tremendously approachable fellow, and always so outstandingly ready to help in every possible way.' Yet Shackleton made it clear that Wild was not in any sense a 'crony' of his.

CHAPTER V

OCEAN CAMP

IN spite of the wet, deep snow, and the halts caused by having to cut a road through the pressure-ridges, we managed to march nearly a mile, but with relays and deviations the actual distance travelled was nearer six miles. As I could see that the men were exhausted I gave orders to pitch the tents under the lee of the two boats, which afforded some protection from the wet snow.

Next day broke cold and still, with the same wet snow, and I decided to find a more solid floe and camp there until conditions were more favourable for a second attempt to escape from our icy prison. To this end we moved our tents and all our gear to a thick, heavy floe about a mile and a half from the wreck, and camped there. This we named "Ocean Camp." It was terribly difficult to shift our two boats, the surface being extraordinarily bad. At times we sank to our hips, and the snow was everywhere 2 feet deep.

This floating lump of ice, about a mile square at first, but later splitting into smaller and smaller

(*Opposite*) Hurley and Shackleton at Ocean Camp. Hurley made the stove out of various components salvaged from the boat. Fisher captions this picture as Patience Camp but Ocean Camp seems more probable.

(*Below*) Towing the *James Caird* away from the *Endurance* was slow work. At times the men sank to their hips in the snow. Shackleton's plan was to march to Paulet Island.

(Right) **The makeshift galley in which the seal and penguin blubber was cooked.**

The stove was in fact devised by Hurley, a trained metalworker who was always making things. It took him two days to construct, as the material was quarter-inch steel and most of the ship's tools had been lost. He also contrived a bilge pump for one of the boats, using the ship's compass, and began making boot crampons 'from sundry bits of iron and screws' for the crossing they hoped to make.

The camp was 1½ miles from the ship, in the centre of a large, thick floe probably about two years old. Wild brought back the wheelhouse which, with the addition of sails and tarpaulins, made a 'very comfortable galley and storehouse' and from the roof flew the King's Union Jack and the burgee of the Royal Clyde Yacht Club.

fragments, was to be our home for nearly two months. With a view to preserving our valuable sledging rations for the inevitable boat journey, I decided that we should live almost entirely on seals and penguins. During these two months we made frequent visits to the vicinity of the ship and retrieved much valuable clothing and food.

As we were to live so largely on seals and penguins which were to provide fuel as well as food, some form of blubber-stove was a necessity. This eventually was most ingeniously contrived from the ship's steel ash-shoot, and it served us successfully during our stay at Ocean Camp.

An attempt was next made to protect the cook against the inclemencies of the weather, and a party under Wild returned from a visit to the ship with the wheel-house practically complete. This, with the addition of some sails and tarpaulins stretched on spars, made a very comfortable storehouse and galley. Food, of course, was so important that I made a strict inventory of all that we possessed.

Early each morning the dog-teams under Wild went to the wreck, and the men made every effort to rescue as much as possible from the ship. This was an extremely difficult task, but we succeeded in adding to our scanty stock between two and three tons of provisions, about half of which was farinaceous food, such as flour and peas, of which we were so short. This sounds a great deal, but at one pound per day it would only last twenty-eight men for three months. Previously to this I had reduced the food allowance to 9½ ounces per man per day.

I had the sledges packed in readiness with the special sledging rations in case of a sudden move, and I tried my hardest to give the utmost possible variety to our meals. We were short of crockery, but small pieces of venesta wood served well as plates for seal steaks; stews and liquids of all sorts were served in the aluminium sledging mugs, of which each man had one. Later on, jelly-tins and biscuit-tin lids were pressed into the service.

Although I had to keep in my mind the necessity for strict economy with our small store of food, I knew how important it was to keep the men cheerful, and that the depression occasioned by our surroundings and precarious position could be somewhat alleviated by increasing the rations, at least until we grew accustomed to our new mode of life. I know from the men's diaries that my efforts in this respect were successful. "It is just," one man wrote, "like school days over again, and very jolly it is too, for the time being!" Later on, as the prospect of wintering in the pack became more apparent, the rations had considerably to be reduced. By that time, however, everybody was more accustomed to the idea and took it quite as a matter of course.

During all this time seal and penguin hunting was our daily occupation, and the supply, if not exhaustible, was always sufficient for our needs. The seals were mostly crab-eaters, and emperor penguins were the general rule. No skuas, Antarctic petrels, nor sea leopards were seen during our two months' stay at Ocean Camp.

In addition to our daily hunt for food, our time was passed in reading the few books we had managed to save from the ship. Our greatest treasure was a portion of the *Encyclopaedia Britannica*, which was continually used to settle our many arguments. The sailors on one occasion were heatedly discussing the subject of "Money and Exchange," and when they discovered that the *Encyclopaedia* did not agree with their views they came to the conclusion that it must be wrong!

The two subjects of most interest to us were our rate of drift and the weather. Worsley's observations showed conclusively that the drift of our floe was almost entirely dependent upon the winds and was not much affected by the currents. Our hope, of course, was to drift northwards to the edge of the pack, and then, when the ice was loose enough, to take to the boats and row to the nearest land. We started off in fine style, drifting north about twenty-two miles in two or three

Although much was rescued from the wreck, Wordie and Clark, two of the scientists, lost all the specimens they had collected. Many diaries and records were lost. Worsley's full dress uniform was dredged up and its owner wrote, 'Sir E. amuses us by donning my cocked hat, boat cloak and sword belt, with a shovel dragging behind for a sword.' Once the carpenters had cut away the tangle of masts and lines on deck, most of the men returned to it, taking considerable risks to salvage possessions stowed below the water line.

(Left) Ocean Camp was a temporary affair because the original decision had been to press on across the snow, but a quorum made up of Shackleton, Wild, Worsley and Hurley decided that conditions were too bad and they would have to wait for the ice to break up. Shackleton conveyed the decision to the rest of the party in terms which implied that all of them had arrived at it by mutual consent.

2 November. Shackleton had insisted that Hurley leave his glass negatives behind on the ship where they had been sealed in boxes and placed in the refrigerator. The carpenters made a hole in the side of the boat and two men went in and fished in the water to find them. Hurley himself, 'bared from head to waist, probed in the mushy ice'.

(Right) Hurley continued to take pictures of the ship while he and other members of the crew were scrambling aboard to retrieve supplies. Vital food stores and other necessities, such as nails pulled out of every available plank, were salvaged.

Practically all the plates were intact and he and Shackleton sat down on the ice and went through the photographs to cut them down to what could be stored in one tin. As a plate was rejected, Hurley smashed it on the ice to prevent any second thoughts. In all, about 150 were kept out of 550. He then had to dump his camera equipment, keeping only a pocket camera and three rolls of film. He also kept the used cinematograph film but not the movie camera. Plates that survived are now in the Royal Geographic Society's photo library.

On 27 October McNeish wrote that the ship 'is going to pieces fast . . . the keel was torn out of her then she filled rapidly.'

(Left) As Endurance sank, trips were still made to her to collect further supplies, even when the deck was 3 to 4 feet under water. Cases below deck were speared with a boat hook, hoisted to the surface and passed to the dog drivers who lashed them on to their sledges.

(Above) Frank Wild examining the wreckage of the *Endurance*. Some prints of this picture are heavily touched-up, and the figure of Wild looks unnatural. Hurley frequently worked on his negatives and this is one of the more obvious examples.

days, but our average rate of progress was slow, and many and varied were the calculations as to when we should reach the pack-edge. On December 12th, 1915, one man wrote, "We are now only 250 miles from Paulet Island, but too much to the east of it. We are approaching the latitudes in which we were at this time last year, on our way down. The ship left South Georgia just a year and a week ago, and reached this latitude four or five miles to the eastward of our present position on January 3rd, 1915."

Thus, after a year's incessant battle with the ice, we had returned to almost identically the same latitude which we had left with such high hopes a year before. But under what conditions now! Our ship crushed and lost, and we drifting on a piece of ice at the mercy of the winds.

As the drift was chiefly affected by the winds, the weather was closely watched by all of us, and Hussey, the meteorologist, was called upon to make forecasts every four hours, and sometimes even more frequently. Our first few days at Ocean Camp were cold and miserable, and at night the temperature dropped to zero, with blinding snow and drift. One-hour watches were instituted, and in such weather were no sinecure.

On November 6th, a dull, overcast day developed into a howling blizzard from the south-west, and only those who were compelled left the shelter of their tent. Deep drifts formed everywhere, but, as we drifted rapidly towards the north, we preferred the screeching blizzard, with its cold, damp wind, to the weather we had previously encountered.

Some beautifully fine days, with glorious sun, followed, and we took this opportunity to dry our sleeping-bags and gear as far as possible, for they had become sodden through our body-heat having thawed the snow which had drifted on to them during the blizzard. Then came several days with comparatively high temperatures, and the result to the surface of our camp was disastrous. "The surface is awful! Not slushy, but elusive. You step out gingerly. All is well for a few paces, then your foot suddenly sinks a couple of feet until it comes to a hard layer."

For some days these high temperatures persisted, and at times, when the sky was clear and the sun shining, we were unbearably hot. I had already made arrangements for a quick move in case of a sudden break-up of the ice, and I took a final survey of the men to note both their mental and physical condition, for our time at Ocean Camp had not been one of unalloyed bliss.

(Above) **At Ocean Camp, Shackleton established a lookout, perhaps as much for the morale of the team as in expectation that there would in fact be anything to see.**

7 November. On this day they drifted over the 69th Parallel. So far they had covered one degree of latitude in seventy days, but now the ice was drifting faster, travelling north at a steady 3 miles a day.

21 November. The ship sinks. Shackleton confided to his diary, 'The stem, the cause of all the trouble, was the last to go under. I cannot write about it.'

The loss of our ship meant more to us than we could ever put into words. After we had settled at Ocean Camp she still remained, nipped by the ice, only her stern showing and her bows overridden and broken by the relentless pack. The tangled mass of ropes, rigging and spars made the scene even more desolate and depressing.

It was almost a relief when the end came. On November 21st, 1915, one of the Expedition wrote in his diary: "This evening, as we were lying in our tents, we heard the Boss call out, 'She's going, boys!' . . . And, sure enough, there was our poor ship a mile and a half away, struggling in her death agony. She went down bows first, her stern raised in the air. She then gave one quick dive and the ice closed over her for ever. . . . Without her our destitution seemed more emphasised, our desolation more complete. The loss of the ship sent a slight wave of depression over the camp . . . . I doubt if there was one amongst us who did not feel some personal emotion when Sir Ernest, standing on the top of the look-out, said somewhat sadly and quietly, 'She's gone, boys.' It must, however, be said that we did not give way to depression for long."

(Below) Ocean Camp with Shackleton at left and Wild next to him.

Indeed, these were rather miserable days, for, with the high temperature, surface-thaw set in, and our bags and clothes were soaked and sodden. To counteract depression I slightly increased

(*Left*) Another view of Ocean Camp, less posed and somewhat less attractive a sight. Their stay there, Shackleton said, had not been one of 'unalloyed bliss'.

Inside the miserable tent in his sleeping bag, Shackleton was wont to quote Browning. Hurley retaliated by reading Keats out loud. Shackleton was reading Kinglake's *Eothen*, another tale of travel, which he described as 'a charming book'. There were clear signs of a fall in morale. As well as increasing the rations on 1 December, Shackleton moved camp by 50 yards to firmer, cleaner snow because their surroundings had become slushy and sordid.

our rations, and this had a splendid effect. Also, owing possibly to the prospects of an early release, our perpetual soakings did not seem greatly to trouble us. The continuance of southerly winds exceeded our best hopes, and by the middle of December I concluded that the ice around us was rotting and breaking up, and that the moment of deliverance was approaching.

After discussing the question with Wild, I, on December 20th, informed all hands that I meant to try and make a march to the west, so that we could reduce the distance between us and Paulet Island. A buzz of pleasurable anticipation went round the camp, and every one was anxious to get on the move. So on the following day Wild, Crean, Hurley and I, with dog-teams, set out westward to survey the route.

After travelling about seven miles we mounted a small berg, and the only place which, as far as we could see, appeared likely to be formidable was a very much cracked-up area between the old floe on which we were and the first of the series of young flat floes about half a mile away.

I decided to keep December 22nd as Christmas Day, and then we consumed most of our small remaining stock of luxuries. For the last time for eight months we really had as much as we could eat. Anchovies in oil, baked beans, and jugged hare made a glorious mixture, such as we had not dreamed of since our school days. Everybody was working at high pressure, packing and repacking sledges and so forth; and as I looked round at the eager faces of the men I could not but hope that this time the fates would be kinder to us than they had been in our last attempt to march across the ice to safety.

15-20 December. Especially after the loss of *Endurance*, Shackleton persisted in the pretence that the party would be home very soon. Orde-Lees records how Shackleton overheard him say, ' "It's all bunk to say we shall be in England by Xmas this year." Himself an inspired optimist, I think he never quite forgave me.' Shackleton does not mention here that for the first two weeks of December he himself was laid up with his mysterious illnesses, which on this occasion he called 'sciatica' and a 'cold'. He allowed the doctors to examine him but not to check his heart. It was after he was up and about again that he found that the ice was breaking up fast and he decided it was now necessary to break camp and move.

CHAPTER VI

THE MARCH BETWEEN

A T 3 a.m. on December 23rd all hands were roused for the purpose of sledging the two boats, the *James Caird* and the *Dudley Docker*, over the dangerously cracked portion to the first of the young floes while the surface still held its night crust. Hot coffee was served, and we started off at half-past four.

Practically all hands had to be harnessed to each boat in succession, and, after much labour and care, we got both boats over the danger-zone. We then returned to Ocean Camp for the tents and the rest of the sledges, and pitched camp by the boats, about one and a quarter miles off. Everybody turned in at 2 p.m., for I intended to sleep by day and march by night, in order to take advantage of the slightly lower temperatures and consequent harder surfaces.

We were off again some six hours later, but were soon brought to a halt by a large open lead, whereupon we camped and turned in without a meal. I was anxious, now that we had started, that

(*Opposite*) Dr Hussey, a young graduate who had been working in the Sudan before he joined the crew, seen here with Samson and an un-named dog.

Hauling the two boats across the ice was terrible drudgery for the men. There was also a sledge, which carried the blubber stove, in the charge of Orde-Lees and Green, the cook. Orde-Lees was now overseeing the distribution of provisions and helped with the cooking. He kept himself somewhat aloof from the others and they regarded him as something of an eccentric. Worsley wrote: 'The "Colonel" really deserves a VC for the gallant way in which he has taken charge of & stuck to the culinary Dept. under the most severe conditions. He wears a furry cap, snow goggles, & a beard, which however is hardly distinguishable from the soot and blubber that covers the rest of his face. He is the living breathing GOL-LIWOG himself.'

(*Left*) While the men exercised themselves as best they could during this period of in-action, Shackleton worked out in meticulous detail what each man was to do if they had to strike camp in a hurry, and a copy of his instructions was pinned to each of the five tents.

(Above) **This picture may have been taken by Hurley when he went with Shackleton, Wild and Crean on 21 December to explore the area to the westward of the camp. This immediately preceded the decision to move off.**

every effort should be made to extricate ourselves, and this temporary check was rather annoying. So, during that afternoon, Wild and I ski-ed out to the crack and found that it had closed up again. We marked out the track with small flags as we returned.

Each day, after all hands had turned in, Wild and I went ahead for two miles or so to reconnoitre the next day's route, marking it with pieces of wood, tins and small flags. It was the duty of the dog-drivers to prepare the track for those who were toiling behind with the heavy boats. These boats were hauled in relays, about sixty yards at a time. Fearing the ice might crack between them and that we should be unable to reach the boat which was in the rear, I did not wish them to be separated by too great a distance. It was gruelling for the men, who worked splendidly. The dogs also were wonderful; without them we could never have transported half the food and gear which we did.

On December 25th, the third day of our march, we wished one another a "Merry Christmas," and as we sat down to our "lunch" of stale, thin bannock and a mug of thin cocoa, we also wondered what they were having at home. But all hands were very cheerful, the prospect of relief from the monotony of life on the floe raising our spirits. High temperatures during Christmas Day made the surface very trying, and at each step we went in over our knees in the soft, wet snow.

The surface was much better on the following day, but the route lay over very hummocky floes, and much work with pick and shovel was required to make it passable for the boat sledges, which were handled in relays by eighteen men under Worsley. On soft surfaces it was killing work.

Had it not been for these cumbrous boats we should have got along at a great rate, but on no account did we dare to abandon them. As it was we had left one boat, the *Stancomb Wills*, behind at Ocean Camp, and the remaining two would barely accommodate the whole party when we could leave the floe.

Still, however, we struggled on with fair success until the early morning of the 28th, when the surface was very soft and our progress, consequently, was slow and tiring. We camped at 5.30 a.m., and I climbed a small tilted berg and saw that the country immediately ahead of us was much broken up. Great open leads intersected the floes at all angles, and the outlook was most unpromising.

On December 29th I wrote: "After a further reconnaissance, the ice ahead proved quite unnegotiable, so at 8.30 p.m. last night, to the intense disappointment of all, instead of forging ahead, we had to retire half a mile so as to get on a stronger floe, and by 10 p.m. we had camped and all hands turned in again. The extra sleep was much needed, however disheartening the check may be."

During the night a crack formed right across the floe, so we hurriedly shifted to a strong old floe about a mile and a half to the east of our position. The ice all around was too broken and soft to sledge over, and yet there was not enough open water to allow us to launch the boats with any degree of safety.

We had been on the march for seven days; rations were short and the men were weak. They were worn out with the hard pulling over soft surfaces, and our stock of sledging food was very small. We had marched seven and a half miles in a direct line, and at this rate it would have taken us over 300 days to reach the land away to the west. As we only had food for forty-two days there was no alternative but to camp once more on the floe and to possess our souls in patience until conditions appeared more favourable for a renewal of the attempt to escape. To this end, we stacked our surplus provisions, the reserve sledging rations being kept lashed on the sledges, and brought what gear we could from our but lately deserted Ocean Camp.

Our new home, which we were to occupy for nearly three and a half months, we called "Patience Camp."

Shackleton does not mention an incident that upset him very much. This happened when, returning to the main party from an advance sortie with Hurley, he found that Harry McNeish had refused to obey an order from Worsley, the deputy leader, to continue work. McNeish thought the concept of marching over the ice was misguided and, as he was suffering from piles, every step was painful. He thought that with his carpentry skills he could have built a sloop in which they could all have sailed to safety. Shackleton rapidly called a meeting of all hands and read out Ship's Articles. He then took McNeish to one side and told him that he, as Master, would have him shot if he continued to disobey orders. McNeish gave in, but Shackleton never forgave him for challenging his leadership and he was one of four sailors from whom the Polar Medal was withheld on their return.

29 December. Shackleton wrote in his private diary, 'I do not like retreating but prudence demands this course.' They were barely 10 miles from Ocean Camp.

CHAPTER VII
PATIENCE CAMP

THE apathy which seemed to fall upon some of the men at our great disappointment was soon dispelled. Parties were sent out daily to look for seals and penguins, for our supply of food was a cause of perpetual anxiety – so small and inadequate was it. I sent Hurley and Macklin to bring back the food we had left at Ocean Camp, and they returned with quite a good load.

We were, of course, very short of the farinaceous element in our diet. The flour would last ten weeks. After that our sledging rations would last us less than three months. Our meals had to consist mainly of seal and penguin, and, although this was such a valuable antidote against scurvy that not a single case of the disease occurred among our party, it was nevertheless a badly-adjusted diet, and we felt weak and enervated in consequence.

The cook deserved much praise for the way he stuck to his job under very severe conditions. At first his galley was only partially protected, and the eddies drove the pungent blubber smoke in all directions. After a few days we were able to build him an igloo of ice-blocks, with a tarpaulin over the top as a roof.

Shackleton probably named this camp because the word Patience reflected his mood. One entry in his diary reads, 'Put footsteps of courage into stirrups of patience'; in another entry he wrote the words 'Waiting, Waiting, Waiting', and on another day 'Patience, Patience, Patience.'

(Left) This is perhaps the igloo of ice-blocks which formed the galley, as the first one, made of tarpaulin, provided only partial protection against the wind.

(Opposite) A selection of the many dog portraits taken by Hurley. Some have been captioned by him in the various albums of prints which survive, but most remain unknown heroes.

The rations were short because Shackleton had kept them short. Macklin wrote in a private code in his diary, not wishing it to be seen, 'The Boss was a bit improvident in not getting in all the food possible whilst the going was good.' When Orde-Lees raised the subject in public, Shackleton snapped at him, 'It will do some of the people good to go hungry; their bloody appetites are too big.' Orde-Lees went off on solo skiing expeditions to hunt for food, but he took such risks that Worsley was put in charge of him and then, when they became separated by 200 yards, both were confined to camp. Shackleton's care for the safety of each individual was obsessive, but admirable.

Some of the men had been pressing Shackleton to fetch the third boat, particularly Worsley.

"Our rations," I wrote at this time, "are just sufficient to keep us alive, but we all feel that we could eat twice as much as we get. . . . Our craving for bread and butter is very real, not because we cannot get it, but because the system feels the need of it."

Owing to this shortage of food, and the fact that we needed all we could get for ourselves, I had to order all the dogs except two teams to be shot. It was the worst job we had had throughout the Expedition, and we felt their loss keenly. I continually rearranged the weekly menu, for the slightest variation was of great value, and the mere fact that the men did not know what was coming gave them a sort of mental speculation.

On January 26th I wrote: "We are now very short of blubber, and, in consequence, one stove has to be shut down. We only get one hot beverage a day, tea at breakfast. For the rest we have iced water. Sometimes we are even short of this, so we take a few chips of ice in a tobacco tin to bed with us. In the morning there is about a spoonful of water in the tin, and one has to lie very still all night so as not to spill it."

To provide some variety in the food, I began to use the sledging ration at half strength twice a week.

The ice between us and the Ocean Camp was very broken, but I decided to send Macklin and Hurley back with their dogs to see if there was any more food which could be added to our scanty stock. I gave them written instructions to take no undue risk or cross any wide-open leads, and, although they both fell more than once through the thin ice up to their waists, they managed to reach the camp. It looked, they said, "like a village that had been razed to the ground and deserted by its inhabitants." They collected what food they could find and brought it back to the camp, and as their report seemed to show that the road was favourable, on February 2nd I sent back eighteen men under Wild to bring all the remainder of the food and the third boat, the *Stancomb Wills*. This excursion was also successful, and one excellent result of the trip was the recovery of two cases of lentils weighing 42 lbs. each.

On the following day Macklin and Crean also started to the camp to make a further selection of the gear, but they found that several leads had opened up during the night, and they had to return

(*Right*) Mundane tasks occupied them because, as James wrote, 'the worst thing is having to kill time. It seems such a waste, yet there is nothing else to do. I don't find any theoretical work which I might do possible in the present environment.'

when within a mile and a half of their destination. We were never again able to reach the abandoned camp, but there was very little left there which would have been useful to us.

By the middle of February the blubber question was a serious one. Our meat supply was very low indeed. Fortunately, however, we caught two seals and four emperor penguins, and next day we captured forty adelies.

On Leap Year Day, February 29th, we held a special celebration, more to cheer the men than for any other reason. We used the last of our cocoa, and for the future water, with an occasional drink of weak milk, was our only beverage. Three lumps of sugar were now issued daily to each man.

Later on both seals and penguins seemed studiously to avoid us, and, on taking stock of our provisions on March 21st, I found that we had only meat enough to last us for ten days, and that the blubber would not even last for that time. So we had to make our midday meal off one biscuit.

Our meals were now practically all seal meat, with the biscuit at midday; and I calculated that at this rate, allowing for a certain number of penguins and seals being caught, we could last for nearly six months. But we were all very weak, and as soon as it seemed likely that we should leave our floe and take to the boats I should have considerably to increase the ration.

One day a large sea-leopard climbed on to the floe and attacked one of the men, and Wild, hearing the shouting, ran out and shot it. When it was cut up we found several undigested fish in its stomach. These we fried in some of its blubber, and so had our only "fresh" fish meal during the whole of our drift on the ice.

On April 2nd the last two teams of dogs had to be shot, and the carcasses were dressed for food. We ate some of the cooked dog-meat, and it was not at all bad – just like beef, but, of course, very tough. On April 5th we killed two seals, and this, with the sea-leopard of a few days before, enabled us slightly to increase our ration; and everybody at once felt much happier – such is the effect of hunger appeased. On cold days a few strips of raw blubber were served out to all hands,

Green, the cook, told Fisher that one day, 'I was crying my eyes out. I was absolutely done ... The Boss turned up, asked me how I was getting on. "Oh, all right," I said. He said, "What are you going to do with all the money when you get home?" I said, "I'm coming on another expedition with you if I can." He turned to the Captain he said, "Would you believe it, he hasn't had enough, he wants to come again."'

Shackleton also spent much of his time moving around the tents and encouraging the inmates. He played innumerable games of bridge and gave instruction to those who needed it. He also recited poetry at great length.

and it was a wonderful fortification against the cold. Our stock of forty days' sledging rations remained practically untouched, but once in the boats they were used at full strength.

When we first settled down at Patience Camp the weather was very mild, and, as a rule, during the first half of January it remained comparatively warm and calm. This meant that our drift northwards, which depended almost entirely on the wind, was checked. On January 18th, however, we had a howling south-westerly gale, which increased next day to a regular blizzard with much drift. This lasted for six days, and then the drift subsided somewhat, although the southerly wind continued, and we were able to get a glimpse of the sun. This showed us to have drifted eighty-four miles north in six days, the longest drift we had made. By this amazing leap we had crossed the Antarctic Circle, and were now 146 miles from the nearest land to the west of us – Snow Hill – and 357 miles from the South Orkneys, the first land directly to the north of us.

The wind was now the vital factor with us and the one topic of any real interest. Varying fortunes followed, but on March 13th a south-easterly gale sprang up and lasted for five days. This sent us twenty miles north, and from this date our good fortune, as far as the wind was concerned, never left us for any length of time.

On the 20th we experienced the worst blizzard we had met up to this time, though still worse were to come after we had landed on Elephant Island. As the blizzard eased up, the temperature dropped and it became bitterly cold; and in our weak condition, with torn, greasy clothes, we felt these sudden variations in temperature much more than we should otherwise have done. For two or three days it was impossible to do anything but get inside one's frozen sleeping-bag and try to get warm. Too cold to read or sew, we had to keep our hands well inside and pass the time in talking to each other.

Two days of brilliant warm sunshine succeeded this period of cold, and on March 29th we experienced what was to us the most amazing weather. It began to rain hard, and we had seen no rain since leaving South Georgia sixteen months before. We regarded it as our first touch with civilisation.

Although the general drift of our ice-floe had indicated that we must eventually drift north, our progress in that direction was by no means uninterrupted. We were at the mercy of the wind, and could no more control our drift than we could control the weather.

By February 22nd we were still eighty miles from Paulet Island, which was now our objective. There was a hut there and some stores which had been taken there by the ship which went to the rescue of Nordenskjöld's Expedition in 1904, and whose fitting out and equipment I had been in charge of. We remarked how strange it would be if these very cases of provisions, which I had ordered and sent out so many years previously, were now to support us during the coming winter.

But this was not to be. By March 17th we were exactly on a level with Paulet Island, but sixty miles to the east. It might have been 600 miles for all the chance we had of reaching it by sledging across the broken ice in the condition in which it was at that time.

Subsequently our thoughts turned first towards the Danger Islands and then towards Joinville Island; but in each case it would have been ridiculous to attempt to reach the land, for the ice was too loose and broken to march over, and yet not open enough for us to be able to launch our boats.

For the next few days we saw ourselves slowly drifting past the land which we could not reach, and towards the end of March we saw Mount Haddington fade away into the distance.

Our hopes were now centred on Elephant Island or Clarence Island, which lay 100 miles almost due north of us. If we failed to reach either of them we could try for South Georgia, but our chances of reaching it were very small.

New Year's Day was celebrated with 'Dinner of pancake made from flour & water fried in seal blubber. Supper stewed seal meat & cocoa, then we turn into our sleeping bags on the snow & dream of the Loved ones at Home & Happy Days to come . . .' So wrote McNeish. Although food made them happier, there was a general feeling of malaise. Hussey had even ceased to play the banjo that Shackleton had insisted on saving from the wreck. This may have been because, as McNeish put it, 'his 6 tunes is heart-breaking'. Orde-Lees was another one whose music was not appreciated; Worsley complained, he 'makes night hideous with a star turn on his nasal trombone'. Orde-Lees was often the centre of a quarrel, perhaps partly because as the only 'regular' officer on board he held himself somewhat aloof.

Towards the end of March when the ice floes began to break up, Shackleton had two men on constant watch because he had now made the decision that they would have to take the boats to reach land, as they were drifting past Paulet Island and would be lost if they drifted further away and out into the Atlantic. On 2 April the last of the dogs had been shot and the sledges abandoned, so an overland march was no longer realistic even if it had been possible. (Thus he adopted McNeish's view, though never forgiving the carpenter for expressing it.)

(Opposite) The dogs named by Hurley as (clockwise from top left) Samson, Lupoid, Owd Bob and Soldier.

93

CHAPTER VIII

EFFORTS TO ESCAPE FROM THE ICE

A T daylight on April 7th the long-desired peak of Clarence Island came into view, but not until Worsley, Wild and Hurley had unanimously confirmed my observation was I satisfied that I was really looking at land. The island was still more than sixty miles away, but to our eyes it had something of the appearance of home. The longing to feel solid earth under our feet filled our hearts.

I wrote on this day: "The swell is more marked today, and I feel sure we are at the verge of the floe-ice. One strong gale followed by a calm would scatter the pack, I think, and then we could push through. I have been thinking much of our prospects. . . . The island is the last outpost of the south and our final chance of a landing-place. Beyond it lies the broad Atlantic. Our little boats may be compelled any day now to sail unsheltered over the open sea, with a thousand leagues of ocean separating them from the land to the north and east. It seems vital that we should land on Clarence Island or its neighbour, Elephant Island."

A little later, after reviewing the whole situation in the light of our circumstances, I made up my mind that we should try to reach Deception Island. Clarence Island and Elephant Island lay comparatively near to us and were separated by some eighty miles of water from Prince George Island, which was about 150 miles away from our camp on the berg. From this island a chain of similar islands extends westward, terminating in Deception Island.

We knew from the Admiralty sailing directions that there were stores for the use of shipwrecked mariners on Deception Island, and it was possible that the summer whalers had not yet deserted its harbour. Also we knew that a small church had been erected there for the benefit of the whalers, and from this building we could get a supply of timber and construct a reasonably seaworthy boat if dire necessity compelled us. In any case, the worst that could befall us when we had reached Deception Island would be a wait until the whalers returned about the middle of November.

The swell increased in the night of April 7th, and the movement of the ice became more pronounced. The situation was rapidly becoming critical, and it was imperative that we should get solid ground under our feet as quickly as possible. There were twenty-eight men on our floating cake of ice, which was steadily dwindling under the influence of wind, weather, charging floes and heavy swell. I confess that the burden of responsibility sat heavily on my shoulders, but, on the other hand, I was stimulated and cheered by the loyal attitude of the men.

At 6.30 p.m. a particularly heavy shock went through our floe. The watchman and other members of the party made an immediate inspection, and found a crack right under the *James Caird*

During their voyage icebergs and clouds had deceived their eyes so often into thinking they saw land ahead that Shackleton needed the confirmation of the others that this time it was no illusion.

(Opposite) Another picture of the 'frost-flowers'. Hurley captioned this one, 'As sea water freezes, salt is exposed in tiny molecules and if the air is calm these become nucleii about which the flowers grow in exquisite crystals.'

and between the two other boats and the main camp. Within five minutes the boats were over the crack and close to the tents. We were now on a triangular raft of ice, the three sides measuring, roughly, 90, 100, and 120 yards. I felt that the time for launching the boats was approaching; indeed, it was obvious that, even if the conditions were unfavourable for a start during the coming day, we could not stay safely on the floe much longer, for the floe might split right under our camp. If anything of the kind occurred we had made preparations for quick action, but our case would have been desperate if the ice had broken into small pieces not large enough to support our party, and not loose enough to permit us the use of the boats.

The following day was Sunday, but it was no day of rest for us. In fact it saw both our forced departure from the floe on which we had lived for nearly six months and also the start of our journeyings in the boats.

"This," I wrote, "has been an eventful day for us. . . . At 7 a.m. the long swell from the northwest was coming in more freely than on the previous day and was driving the floes together in the utmost confusion . . . . Our own floe was suffering in the general disturbance, and after breakfast I ordered the tents to be struck and everything prepared for an immediate start when the boats could be launched."

I had decided to take the *James Caird* myself, with Wild and eleven men. This was the largest of our boats, and she carried the major portion of our stores. Worsley had charge of the *Dudley Docker* with nine men, and Hudson and Crean were the senior men in the *Stancomb Wills*.

Soon after breakfast the ice closed again, and we were standing by, with our preparations as complete as we could make them, when at 11 a.m. our floe suddenly split right across under the boats. We rushed our gear on to the larger of the two pieces, and watched anxiously for the next development. The crack had cut right through the site of my tent. Our home was being shattered under our feet, and we had a sense of loss and incompleteness hard to describe, for during all those months on the floe we had almost ceased to realise that it was but a sheet of ice floating on unfathomed seas.

The call to action came at 1 p.m., after we had all eaten a good meal of seal meat. We could not take all our meat with us, so we regarded each pound eaten as a pound saved! The *Dudley Docker* and the *Stancomb Wills* were quickly launched. Stores were thrown in, and the two boats were pulled clear of the immediate floes towards a pool of open water three miles broad, in which floated a lone and mighty berg.

The *James Caird* was the last boat to leave, heavily loaded with stores and odds and ends of camp equipment. Many things regarded by us as essentials at that time were to be discarded later on. Man can sustain life with very scanty means, and the trappings of civilisation are soon cast aside in the face of stern realities.

The three boats were a mile away from our floe home at 2 p.m., and then we had a narrow escape from a rush of foam-clad water and tossing ice that approached us, like the tidal bore of a river. It was an unusual and startling experience; the effect of tidal action on ice is not often as marked as it was on that day, and if we had failed to pull clear of the advancing ice, accompanied as it was by a large wave, we should certainly have been swamped.

For an hour we pulled hard to windward of the berg which lay in the open water. The swell was crashing on its perpendicular sides and throwing spray to a height of 60 feet. Under other conditions we might have paused to have admired the spectacle; but night was coming on fast, and we needed a camping-place. So we hastened forward in the twilight in search of a flat, old floe, and presently found a fairly large piece rocking in the swell. It was not by any means an ideal camping-place, but darkness had overtaken us. We hauled the boats up, and by 8 p.m the tents were pitched

and the blubber-stove was burning cheerily. Soon all hands were well fed and happy in their tents, and snatches of song came to me as I wrote up my log.

An intangible feeling of uneasiness made me leave my tent about 11 p.m. to glance round the quiet camp, and I had started to walk across the floe to warn the watchman to look carefully for cracks when the floe lifted on the crest of a swell and cracked under my feet as I was passing the men's tent.

The men were in one of the dome-shaped tents, and it began to stretch apart as the ice opened. A muffled sound, suggestive of suffocation, came from the stretching tent. I rushed forward, helped some men to come out from under the canvas, and called out, "Are you all right?" "There are two in the water," someone answered.

The crack had widened to about 4 feet, and as I threw myself down at the edge I saw a whitish object floating in the water. It was a sleeping-bag with a man inside. I was able to grasp it, and, with a heave, lifted man and bag on to the floe. A few seconds later the ice-edges came together

(*Above*) Hurley captioned this, 'At last we reached the northern margin of the Polar Sea. We managed to launch the boats and the course was set for Elephant Island, 150 miles to the north.' It appears to be one of his composite pictures. Wordie mentioned that Hurley showed the crew some colour photos which were 'a make-up, and savoured rather of "ciney" acting'.

The ice had just happened to break where Holness was lying. 'He couldn't help himself – it dropped him into the drink', in the words of Walter How.

When Shackleton hauled Holness out of the water and asked him if he was all right, he replied 'Yes, Boss, only thing I'm thinking about is my baccy I'd left in the bag.' There was no change of dry clothes to give him, so he had to be kept on the run all night long, and every movement he made with his legs and arms produced a crackle of icy clothes. 'He got over it,' commented Walter How.

again with tremendous force. Fortunately, there had been but one man in the water, the rescued bag containing Holness, who was wet but otherwise unscathed.

Almost immediately the crack began again to open. The *James Caird* and my tent were on one side of the opening and the remaining two boats and the rest of the camp were on the other side. With help I struck my tent, and then all hands manned the painter and rushed the *James Caird* across the opening crack. We held on to the rope while, one by one, the men left on our side jumped the channel or scrambled over by means of the boat.

Finally I was left alone. The night had swallowed all the others, and the rapid movement of the ice forced me to let go the painter. For a moment I felt that my piece of rocking floe was the loneliest place in the world. But Wild's quick brain had immediately grasped the situation, and the boat was already being manned and hauled to the ice-edge. Two or three minutes later she reached me, and I was ferried across to the camp.

We were now on a piece of flat ice about 200 feet long and 100 feet wide. There was no more sleep for any of us during that night, but, although our position was almost as critical as possible, we were cheered by the fact that we were on the move at last, and no longer drifting helplessly at the mercy of wind and current.

The first glimmerings of dawn came at 6 a.m., and two hours later the pack opened and we launched our boats. The *James Caird* was in the lead, with the *Stancomb Wills* next and the *Dudley Docker* in the rear. Our way was across the open sea, and soon after noon we swung round the north

Macklin wrote, 'I think his taking of those overloaded boats through the ice, with seventeen hours of darkness in the twenty-four, breaking up and grinding of floes, and the whole set of conditions of the seven days we were in the boats, constituted a truly remarkable piece of leadership.'

(*Right*) A Hurley composite, using his photograph for the background. He captioned it, 'The escape through the surging pack-ice was a superb feat of seamanship but it took a severe toll of all hands. Most were suffering from frostbite and severe privation.'

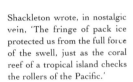

end of the pack and laid a course to the westward. Immediately our boats began to make heavy weather. They shipped sprays which froze as they fell and covered men and gear with ice.

It was soon clear that we could not proceed safely, so I put the *James Caird* round and ran for shelter of the pack again, the other boats following. By 3 p.m. we were back inside the outer line of ice where the sea was not breaking, but all hands were cold and tired. A big floeberg resting peacefully caught my eye, and half an hour later we had hauled up the boats and pitched camp for the night. Every one of us needed rest after the troubles of the previous night and the unaccustomed strain of the last thirty-six hours at the oars.

Our berg appeared well able to withstand the battering of the sea, and looked too deep and massive to be seriously affected by the swell; but it was not as safe as it looked, and when daylight came we saw that the pack had closed round it, and that in the heavy swell we could not possibly launch our boats.

The highest point of the berg was about 15 feet above sea-level, and during the day Worsley, Wild and I were continually climbing to this point and staring out to the horizon in search of a break in the pack. After long hours had dragged past, far away on the lift of the swell, a dark break in the tossing field of ice appeared. I do not think I had ever quite so keenly felt the anxiety which belongs to leadership.

When I looked down at the camp I could see that my companions were waiting with more than ordinary interest to learn what I thought about it all. After one particularly heavy collision somebody shouted sharply, "She has cracked in the middle." This turned out to be a mere surface-break in the snow, but the carpenter mentioned calmly that earlier in the day he had actually gone adrift on a fragment of ice. He had been standing near the edge of our camping-ground when the ice under his feet parted from the parent mass, but a quick jump over the widening gap saved him.

The hours dragged on. One of the anxieties in my mind was the chance that the current would drive us through the eighty-mile gap between Clarence Island and Prince George Island into the open Atlantic; but slowly the open water came nearer, and at noon it had almost reached us. A long lane, narrow but navigable, stretched out to the south-west horizon.

Our chance came a little later, and we rushed our boats over the edge of the reeling berg and swung them clear of the ice-foot as it rose beneath them. We flung stores and gear aboard and within a few minutes were away. With the rolling ice on either side of us the three boats made progress down the lane, and presently we saw a wider stretch of water to the west which seemed to offer us release from the grip of the pack. At the head of an ice-tongue, which nearly closed the gap leading to this wider stretch, was a wave-worn berg shaped like some curious antediluvian monster, an icy Cerberus guarding the way.

At dusk we made fast to a heavy floe, but our hopes of a quiet night were quickly shattered, for we were soon compelled to cast off because pieces of loose ice began to work round the floe. Constant rain and snow squalls blotted out the stars and soaked us through, and at times it was only by shouting to each other that we could keep the boats together. Nobody, owing to the severe cold, had any sleep, and since we could only see a few yards ahead we did not dare to pull fast enough to keep ourselves warm.

All around us we could hear the killer-whales blowing, their short, sharp hisses sounding like sudden escapes of steam. They were a source of great anxiety, for a boat could easily have been capsized by one of them coming up to blow; and we had an uneasy feeling that the white bottoms of the boats would look like ice from below.

Early on the morning of April 12th the weather improved and the wind dropped. At dawn I looked around at the faces of my companions in the *James Caird* and saw pinched and drawn

Shackleton wrote, in nostalgic vein, 'The fringe of pack ice protected us from the full force of the swell, just as the coral reef of a tropical island checks the rollers of the Pacific.'

He does not mention it here, but a great piece of ice had broken off within eight feet of Shackleton's tent.

The killer whales also kept them awake by blowing in the lanes around the floe. At 3 a.m. the stove was lit and each man had a cup of hot milk.

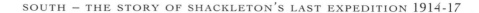

They had now been going for three days and nights, without much sleep – indeed it is probable that Shackleton himself hardly slept at all.

(*Right*) This iceberg appears to have been photographed by Hurley, but curiously it also appears in the book by Ernest Joyce based on his log of the Ross Sea voyage. That log, published in book form in 1929, includes a number of snapshots of that party and its surroundings, including one captioned 'Stevens and his camera', so Stevens may have taken this picture.

Hudson was in nominal charge of the *Stancomb Wills* but he had not fully recovered from his breakdown and Crean, the second mate, was effectively in command. Worsley was in charge of the *Dudley Docker* and his performance in the open boats, which were frightening in heavy seas, won him new respect from the men. He had learnt to handle them in New Zealand, where he grew up.

features. Wild sat at the rudder with the same calm, confident expression which he would have worn under happier conditions. But all the men, though evidently suffering, were doing their best to be cheerful, and the prospect of a hot breakfast was inspiring.

I told all the boats that directly we could find a suitable floe the cooker would be started and that hot milk and Bovril would soon make us all feel better. Away we rowed to the westward through the open pack, and the hunger of the men could be gauged by the floes they considered suitable for our camping-place. At eight o'clock a respectable floe appeared ahead and we pulled up to it. The galley was landed, and presently the welcome steam rose from the cooking food, as the blubber-stove flared and smoked. Never did a cook work under more anxious scrutiny.

Worsley, Crean and I stayed in our respective boats to keep them steady and prevent collisions with the floe, but the other men were able to stretch their limbs and run to and fro in the "kitchen," as somebody called it.

The sun was now rising gloriously, our Burberry suits were drying and the ice was melting off our beards, and the steaming food had given us new vigour. Within an hour we were off again to the west with all sails set. We had been making westward with oars and sails since April 9th and fair easterly winds had prevailed. Hopes ran high as to the noon observation for position. Optimists thought that we had gained sixty miles towards our goal, and the most cautious gave us at least thirty miles. As noon approached I saw Worsley ready to take his observation, and after he had got it we waited eagerly for him to work out the sight. The result was a grievous disappointment. Instead of making a good run to the westward we had made a big drift to the south-east. After a whispered consultation with Worsley and Wild I announced that we had not made as much

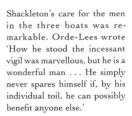

progress as we had hoped for, but I did not think it wise to inform the hands that we were actually thirty miles to the east of the position which we had occupied when leaving the floe on the 9th.

The question of our course now demanded further consideration. Deception Island seemed to be beyond our reach. The wind was foul for Elephant Island, and, as the sea was clear to the south-west, I discussed with Worsley and Wild the advisability of proceeding to Hope Bay on the mainland of the Antarctic Continent, now only eighty miles distant. Elephant Island was the nearest land, but it lay outside the main body of pack, and even if the wind had been fair we should have hesitated at that time to face the high sea which was running in the open.

We laid a course roughly for Hope Bay, and again the boats moved on. I gave Worsley a line for a berg ahead and told him, if possible, to make fast before darkness set in. This was about 3 p.m., and towards dusk the *Dudley Docker* came beating down towards us, and Worsley reported that he had been close to the berg and had found it unapproachable.

The news was bad, but two miles away we could see a larger piece of ice, and to it we managed, after some trouble, to secure the boats. I brought my boat bow on to the floe, while Howe, with the painter in his hand, stood ready to jump. He just managed to get a footing on the edge of the floe and make the painter fast to a hummock, but there was no possibility of getting the galley ashore, so we started the Primus lamps.

The other two boats were fastened alongside the *James Caird*, but in the rough, choppy sea they began to bump so heavily that I had to slack away the painter of the *Stancomb Wills* and put her astern. Much ice was coming round the floe and had to be poled off. Then the *Dudley Docker*, being the heavier boat, began to damage the *James Caird*, and I slacked the *Dudley Docker* away. The *James Caird* remained moored to the ice, with the other two boats in line behind her. The darkness had become complete, and we strained our eyes to see the fragments of ice which threatened us.

As the light improved the wind shifted to the southeast, and drove the boats broadside on towards the jagged floe of ice. There was no time to cast off, so we had to cut the painter of the *James Caird* and pole her off, thus losing much valuable rope.

Then we pushed away from the floe and all night long lay in the open, freezing sea. The boats were attached to one another by their painters, and most of the time the *Dudley Docker* kept the other boats up to the swell, the men who were rowing being in better case than those of us who were inactive.

The temperature was down to 4° below zero, and a film of ice formed on the surface of the sea. When we were not on watch we lay in each other's arms for warmth. Our frozen suits thawed where our bodies met, and, as the slightest movement exposed these comparatively warm spots to the biting air, we clung motionless. Occasionally, from an almost clear sky, snow showers fell silently on the sea, and lay a thin shroud of white over our bodies and our boats.

Shackleton's care for the men in the three boats was remarkable. Orde-Lees wrote 'How he stood the incessant vigil was marvellous, but he is a wonderful man . . . He simply never spares himself if, by his individual toil, he can possibly benefit anyone else.'

As the *Stancomb Wills* could not keep up with the other two boats, Shackleton's boat took her in tow.

(Above) This picture is described by Hurley as 'a remarkable remnant of a berg floating bottom-up after overturning. The black is mud and rock gouged out by the glacier from its point of origin. Eighttenths of the bulk of the berg is below the sea.'

CHAPTER IX

ESCAPE
FROM THE ICE

THE dawn of April 13th came clear and bright, but most of the men were now looking seriously worn and strained. Their lips were cracked, and the beards of even the younger men might have been those of patriarchs, for the frost and salt spray had made them white. Obviously it was imperative for us to land quickly, and I decided to run for Elephant Island. The wind had shifted fair for that rocky isle, then about 100 miles away, and the pack which separated us from Hope Bay had closed up during the night.

At 6 a.m. we made a distribution of stores among the three boats, in view of the possibility that they might be separated. Hot breakfast was out of the question, but I gave orders that all hands might eat as much as they pleased, this concession being partly due to the fact that we should have to jettison some of our stores when we reached the open sea, and partly to the hope that a liberal

In the longer edition of *South* there is no new chapter starting 13 April. That day Hurley lost his mittens, so Shackleton 'at once divested himself of his own, and in spite of the fact that he was standing up in the most exposed position of all, the while he insisted on Hurley's acceptence of the mitts, and on the latter's protesting, Sir Ernest was on the point of throwing them overboard rather than wear them when one of his subordinates had to go without; as a consequence, Sir Ernest had one finger rather severely frost-bitten'.

(Left) Frank Wild in his winter and *(right)* summer gear.

Wordie listed the crew of each boat as follows:

James Caird
Boss
Wild
Vincent
McArty
McNeish
Clark
Hurley
Wordie
Hussey
James
Green

Dudley Docker
Worsley
Greenstreet
Cheetham
McLeod
Macklin
Kerr
Holness
Lees
Marston

Stancomb Wills
Hudson
Crean
Howe
Bakewell
Rickinson
McIlroy
Stevenson
Blackborrow

Orde-Lees relieved his thirst by risking the consequences 'whatever they may be' of drinking sea water. 'Some say that one goes mad. Maybe I am or was, but I did not hesitate to drink with discretion small quantities.'

(Opposite) George Marston *(top left)*, the artist who had also been on *Nimrod*; *(top right)* Dr James McIlroy, the second surgeon; *(bottom left)* Leonard Hussey, a medical student whose selection as a member of the expedition seemed another of Shackleton's aimless decisions, though he kept his colleagues amused; *(bottom right)* James Wordie, geologist, who became perhaps the most distinguished survivor.

meal would compensate to some extent for the lack of warm food and shelter. Unfortunately some of the men could not take advantage of the extra food owing to sea sickness, and it was hard indeed that this devastating sickness should have been added to the sufferings which they already had to bear.

We ran before the wind through the loose pack, a man in the bow of each boat trying to pole off with a broken oar the lumps of ice which could not be avoided. I regarded speed as essential. The *James Caird* was in the lead and bore the brunt of the encounters with the lurking fragments, then came the *Dudley Docker*, and the *Stancomb Wills* followed. I gave orders that the boats should keep thirty to forty yards apart, so that the danger of a collision, if one boat was checked by the ice, should be reduced.

We made our way through the lanes until at noon we suddenly shot out of the pack into the open ocean. Sails were soon up, and, with the sun shining brightly, we enjoyed for a few hours a sense of the freedom and magic of the sea. At last we were free from the ice, in water which our ships could navigate; thoughts of home came to birth once more, and the difficulties ahead of us dwindled in fancy almost to nothing.

During the afternoon the wind freshened and the deeply-laden boats shipped much water, and steered badly in the rising sea. I had laid the course for Elephant Island, and we made such good progress that, had not the danger of the boats being separated been too great, I should have been tempted to carry on through the night. But it was imperative that the party should be kept together, and also I thought it possible that we might overrun our goal in the darkness and be unable to return. So we made a sea-anchor of oars and hove to, and though we did what we could to make things comfortable during the hours of darkness there was really little that could be done. A terrible night followed, and I doubted if all of the men would survive it. The temperature was below zero and the wind penetrated our clothes and chilled us almost unbearably.

One of our troubles was lack of water, for we had emerged so suddenly from the pack into the open sea that we had not had time to take aboard ice for melting in the cookers, and without ice we could not have hot food. The condition of most of the men was pitiable. All of us had swollen mouths and could hardly touch the food. I longed intensely for the dawn, and at last daylight came; and a magnificent sunrise heralded in what we hoped would be our last day in the boats.

By this time we were all dreadfully thirsty, and although we could get momentary relief by chewing pieces of raw seal meat and swallowing the blood, our thirst was soon redoubled owing to the saltiness of the flesh. I gave orders, therefore, that meat should only be served out at stated times during the day, or when thirst seemed to threaten the reason of any particular individual.

In the full daylight Elephant Island showed cold and severe. The island was on the bearings Worsley had laid down, and I congratulated him on the accuracy of his navigation under most difficult circumstances. The *Stancomb Wills* came up and McIlroy reported that Blackborrow's feet were severely frostbitten, but, unfortunate as this was, nothing could be done. Most of the men were frostbitten to some extent, and it was interesting to notice that the "old-timers," Wild, Crean, Hurley and I, were all right. Apparently we were acclimatised to ordinary Antarctic temperature, though we discovered later that we were not immune.

Progress was slow during the day, but gradually Elephant Island came nearer. We would have given all the tea in China for a lump of ice to melt into water, but no ice was within our reach. Always, while I attended to the other boats, signalling and ordering, Wild sat at the tiller of the *James Caird*. He seemed unmoved by fatigue and unshaken by privation.

About 4 p.m. a stiff breeze came up ahead and impeded our progress. When darkness set in our goal was still some miles away. A heavy sea was running, and we soon lost sight of the *Stancomb*

'The rope grew heavy with ice as the unseen seas surged past us and our little craft tossed to the motion of the waters.' Shackleton's powers of description are remarkable.

Wills, astern of the *James Caird* at the length of the painter (the *James Caird* having taken her permanently in tow), but occasionally the white gleam of broken water revealed her presence. When the darkness was complete I sat in the stern with my hand on the painter so that I might know if the other boat broke away, and I kept that position during the night.

It was a stern night. Harder and harder blew the wind, and fiercer and fiercer grew the sea. The temperature had fallen very low, and it seemed that the general discomfort of our situation could scarcely have been increased. But the land looming ahead was a beacon of safety, and I think that, in spite of our pitiable sufferings, we were all buoyed up by the hope that the coming day would see the end of our immediate troubles.

Towards midnight the wind shifted, and this change enabled us to bear up closer to the island. A little later the *Dudley Docker* ran down to the *James Caird*, and Worsley shouted a suggestion that he should go ahead and search for a landing-place. I told him he could try, but that he must not lose sight of the *James Caird*. Just as he left a heavy snow-squall came down, and in the darkness the boats parted.

This separation made me anxious during the remaining hours of the night, for I could not be sure that all was well with the missing boat; but my anxiety was, as a matter of fact, groundless. I will quote extracts of Worsley's own account of what happened to the *Dudley Docker*.

They are not strictly 'extracts' but a précis of the fuller extracts quoted in *South*. They were nonetheless placed in quotation marks in the earlier edition.

"About midnight we lost sight of the *James Caird* with the *Stancomb Wills* in tow, but not long after saw the light of the *James Caird's* compass-lamp, which Sir Ernest was flashing on the sail to guide us. We answered by lighting our candle under the tent and letting the light shine through. With this candle our poor fellows lit their pipes, their only solace, as our raging thirst prevented us from eating anything. By this time we had got into a bad tide-rip, which, combined with the heavy, lumpy sea, made it almost impossible to keep the *Dudley Docker* from swamping. As it was we shipped several bad seas over the stern as well as abeam and over the bows.

"Lees, who owned himself to be a rotten oarsman, made good here by strenuous bailing, in which he was well seconded by Cheetham. Greenstreet, a splendid fellow, relieved me at the tiller and helped generally. He and Macklin were my chief supports as stoke-oars throughout. McLeod and Cheetham were two good sailors and oars. We had now had 108 hours of toil, tumbling, freezing and soaking, with little or no sleep. I think Sir Ernest, Wild, Greenstreet and I could say that we had no sleep at all.

Worsley describes Cheetham as 'a pirate to his fingertips [who] in the height of the gale that night was buying matches from me for bottles of champagne . . . The champagne is to be paid when he opens his "pub" in Hull and I happen to pass that way.'

"The temperature was 20° below freezing-point. Greenstreet's right foot got badly frost-bitten, but Lees restored it by holding it in his sweater against his stomach. We were close to the land as the morning approached, but we could see nothing of it through the snow and spindrift. My eyes began to fail me. I could not see or judge distance properly, and found myself falling asleep momentarily at the tiller. At 3 a.m. Greenstreet relieved me there. I was so cramped from long hours in the constrained position I was forced to assume at the tiller that the other men had to pull me amidships and straighten me out like a jack-knife, first rubbing my thighs, groin and stomach.

"At daylight we found ourselves close alongside the land, but the weather was so thick we could not see where to make for a landing. I had again taken the tiller after an hour's rest and I ran the *Dudley Docker* off before the gale, following the coast around to the north. At first this course was fairly risky, but by 8 a.m. we had obtained a slight lee from the land. Then I was able to keep her very close in, along a glacier front, with the object of picking up lumps of fresh-water ice as we sailed through them. Our thirst was intense. We soon had some ice aboard, and for the next hour and a half we sucked and chewed fragments with greedy relish.

Worsley was navigating as well as he could by his little pocket compass, the boat compass having been smashed.

"All this time we had seen no possible landing-place, but at 9.30 a.m. we spied a narrow, rocky beach at the base of some very high crags and cliffs, and made for it. To our joy we sighted the

James Caird and the *Stancomb Wills* sailing into the same haven just ahead of us. So delighted were we that we gave three cheers."

Our experiences on the *James Caird* had been similar, although we had been unable to keep up to windward as well as the *Dudley Docker* had done. The weather was very thick in the morning, indeed at 7 a.m. we were right under the cliffs before we saw them. We also picked up pieces of ice and sucked them eagerly. At 9 a.m. at the north-west end of the island we saw a narrow beach at the foot of the cliffs; outside lay a fringe of rocks heavily beaten by the surf, but with a narrow channel showing as a break in the foaming water. Unattractive as the spot was for a landing-place I decided that we must risk it. Two days and nights without drink or hot food had played havoc with most of the men, and we could not assume that any safer haven was within reach.

The *Stancomb Wills* was the lighter and handier boat, and I called her alongside with the intention of taking her through the gap first to ascertain the possibilities of a landing. Just as I was climbing into the *Stancomb Wills* I saw the *Dudley Docker*, and the sight took a great load off my mind.

(*Above*) The first landing on Elephant Island after seven days and nights in the open boats. Hurley captioned this 'we landed on solid rock for the first time in sixteen long months.'

The *James Caird* has survived and may still be seen at Dulwich College, Shackleton's school.

(Above) The helpless men were carried ashore on to the island and the boats hauled up. Hurley wrote, 'It was an inhospitable place, devoid of any vegetation, covered with glaciers and swept by ice-laden surges of the south Atlantic Ocean.'

Blackborrow was helped over the side of the boat so as to be first ashore, but he collapsed in the surf. Macklin said that 'Shackleton himself looked gaunt and haggard and could scarcely speak above a whisper.'

Rowing carefully we brought the *Stancomb Wills* towards the opening in the reef, then, with a few strong strokes, we shot through on the top of a swell and ran the boat on to a stony beach. The next swell lifted her a little farther. It was the first landing ever made on Elephant Island, and I thought the honour should belong to Blackborrow, the youngest member of the Expedition, but I had forgotten that his frost-bitten feet would prevent him from appreciating the honour thrust upon him.

We landed the cook with his blubber-stove, a supply of fuel, and some packets of dried milk, and also several of the men. Then the rest of us pulled out again to pilot the other boats through the channel, and within a few minutes the three boats were aground.

When I landed for the second time a curious spectacle met my eyes. Some of the men were reeling about the beach as if they were intoxicated. They were laughing uproariously, picking up stones and letting handfuls of pebbles trickle between their fingers, like misers gloating over hoarded gold. I remember that Wild came ashore as I was looking at the men, and stood beside me as easy and unconcerned as if he had stepped out of his car for a stroll in the Park.

The stores were soon ashore, but our strength was nearly exhausted, and it was heavy work

The first meal on Elephant Island; hot milk and then seal steak and blubber. *(Left to right)* Orde-Lees, Wordie, Clark, Richardson, Greenstreet, How, Shackleton, Bakewell, Kerr and Wild.

carrying our goods over the rough pebbles and rocks to the foot of the cliff. We did not, however, dare to leave anything within reach of the tide. There was no rest for the cook during that day. The blubber-stove flared and spluttered fiercely as he cooked meal after meal. We drank water and ate seal meat until every man had reached his limit.

The tents were pitched with oars for supports, and by 3 p.m. our camp was in order, and most of the men turned in early for a safe and glorious sleep.

Before getting into the tents, Wild, Worsley and Hurley accompanied me on an inspection of our beach, and we found the outlook to be anything but cheering. Obvious signs showed that at spring tides our little beach would be covered by the water right up to the foot of the cliffs. Clearly we should have to find some better resting-place, but I decided not to share this unwelcome news with the men until they had enjoyed the full sweetness of comparatively untroubled rest.

The accompanying plan will show our exact position more clearly than I can describe it. The cliffs at the back of the beach were inaccessible except at two points where there were steep snow-slopes.

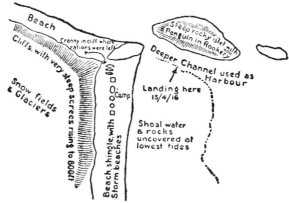

Elephant Island is about 23 miles long, east to west, and about 13 miles at its widest. It is a kind of desert island, made of very little except rock and ice. While the Shackleton party were on it the beach was permanently awash. It was not on the route of any ships on those seas – whalers or sealers – and nobody would look for Shackleton there. Port Stanley in the Falkland Islands was 550 miles away.

Hurley recorded, 'It is regrettable to state that many conducted themselves [on this sea journey] in a manner unworthy of gentlemen & British sailors. Some whom it was anticipated would be the bulwarks of the party "stove in". In the majority of cases those suffering from severe frostbites could be traced to negligence, whilst the numerous cases of temporary aberration are excusable under the plea of intense privation and suffering. Amongst those that stand meritorious, Sir E. had mentioned Wild – a tower of strength ... C. Crean ... who piloted the *Wills*; McNeish (carpenter) Vincent (AB) McCarthy (AB) Marston (*Dudley Docker*) & Self.' (Despite this comment, Shackleton refused McNeish the Polar Medal, although Wordie always took him along to their commemoration dinners as his guest in the later years.)

Worsley said that in a 'confidential talk' soon after landing Shackleton said, 'Thank God I haven't killed one of my men!' Worsley told him, 'We all know that you have worked superhumanly to look after us.' Rather gruffly the reply was 'Superhuman effort ... isn't worth a damn unless it achieves results.'

Apart from the shortage of oars, Shackleton reported that the current here was running as fast as five miles an hour.

We were not worried about food, for, apart from our rations, there were seals on the beach, and there was also a ringed penguin rookery within reach.

These attractions, however, were overridden by the fact that the beach was open to the attack of wind and sea from the north-east and east. Before turning in that night I studied the whole position most carefully, and came to the reluctant conclusion that we must move on.

Early next morning all hands were astir. The sun shone brightly and we spread out our wet gear to dry and made the beach look like a particularly disreputable gipsy camp. I had decided to send Wild along the coast in the *Stancomb Wills* to look for a new camping-ground, on which I hoped the party would be able to live for weeks or even months in safety.

Wild, accompanied by Marston, Crean, Vincent and McCarthy, pushed off in the *Stancomb Wills* at 11 a.m. and proceeded westward along the coast. Then Hurley and I walked along the beach towards the west, searching for a place where we could get the boats ashore and make a permanent camp in the event of Wild's search proving fruitless. But after three hours' vain toil we had to turn back.

The *Stancomb Wills* had not returned by nightfall, but at 8 p.m. we heard a hail in the distance and soon, like a pale ghost out of the darkness, the boat appeared. I was awaiting Wild's report most anxiously, and was greatly relieved when he told me that he had discovered a sandy spot, seven miles to the west, about 200 yards long, running out at right angles to the coast and terminating at the seaward end in a mass of rock.

Wild said that this place was the only possible camping-ground he had seen, and that, although in very heavy gales it might be spray-blown, he did not think that the seas would actually break over it. The boats could be run on a shelving beach, and, in any case, it would be a great improvement on our very narrow beach.

After hearing this good news I was eager to get away before the weather, which had been fine for two days, changed, and I told all hands that we should make an early start on the following morning.

The morning of April 17th came fine and clear; the sea was smooth, but in the offing we could see a line of pack which seemed to be approaching. The appearance of ice emphasised the importance of getting away promptly, for it would have been a serious matter had we been imprisoned on the beach by the pack. The preparations for leaving the beach took longer than I had expected, and, indeed, some of the men were reluctant to leave the barren safety of the beach and to venture once more on the ocean. A mishap befell us when we were launching the boats, for we were using oars as rollers, and three of these were broken, leaving us short for the journey which had still to be undertaken.

But the move was absolutely necessary, and by 11 a.m. we were away, the *James Caird* leading. Almost immediately a southerly gale sprang up, and we were straining at the oars with the gale on our bows. Never had we found a severer task. The wind shifted from south to south-west, and the shortage of oars became a serious matter. After two hours of strenuous labour we were almost exhausted, but then we were fortunate enough to find some shelter behind a point of rock; and there we rested while we ate our cold ration.

After half an hour's pause I gave the order to start again. The *Dudley Docker* was pulling with three oars, and she fell away to leeward in a particularly heavy squall. I anxiously watched her battling up against wind and sea, but could do nothing to help her, as the *James Caird*, being the heavier boat, was hard pressed to make any progress. The only thing to do was to go ahead and hope for the best. All hands were wet to the skin and many of them were feeling the cold severely.

We forged on slowly, and passed inside a great pillar of rock standing out to sea and towering

(Left) It is unclear whether Hurley took this picture as they changed sites on the island, or later as the small party set off to get help. The boat is the *Stancomb Wills*.

to a height of about 2,400 feet. A line of reef stretched between the shore and this pillar, and at first I thought that we should have to face the raging sea outside, but a break in the white surf revealed a gap in the reef and we laboured through. The *Stancomb Wills* followed safely, but I had lost sight of the *Dudley Docker*, and as she had been making so much leeway it was obvious she would have to go outside the pillar. It was a bad time, but I dared not pause to see what had happened to her. At last, about 5 p.m., the *James Caird* and the *Stancomb Wills* reached calmer water, and we saw Wild's beach just ahead of us. I looked back for the *Dudley Docker*, but looked in vain.

Rocks studded the shallow water round the spit, and the sea surged amongst them. I ordered the *Stancomb Wills* to run on to the beach at the place which looked smoothest, and in a few moments the boat was ashore, the men jumping out and holding her against the receding wave. When I saw that she was safe I ran the *James Caird* in. We slipped the painter round a rock, and then began to get out the stores and gear, working like men possessed, for the boats could not be pulled up until they had been emptied.

We were still labouring at the boats when I saw Rickenson turn white and stagger in the surf. His heart had been temporarily unequal to the strain placed upon it, and he needed prompt medical attention. He was one of those eager souls who do more than their share of work, and who will try to do more than they are physically capable of doing. Like many of the members of the Expedition he was suffering from bad salt-water boils.

I was very anxious about the *Dudley Docker*, but within half an hour the missing boat appeared and presently reached the smoother water of the bay. We watched her coming in with that sense of relief which the mariner feels when he crosses the harbour bay.

The tide was going out rapidly, and Worsley lightened the *Dudley Docker* by placing some cases on an outer rock, from which they were afterwards retrieved. Then he beached his boat, and with many hands at work we soon had our three craft above high-water mark.

The name of the Chief Engineer is spelt Rickinson by Fisher and Huntford, no doubt correctly.

In fact some of the men were seriously ill. Blackborrow would have to be operated on for frostbite, and there were four others on the sick-list, including Rickinson with heart trouble and Hudson with his mental problems. In a letter written to his wife in June from Port Stanley, Shackleton said, 'Towards the end, about ten of the party were off their heads'. But Fisher believes this was exaggeration, Shackleton's way of expressing his own fear of emotional expression, the reverse of his own iron control.

(Right) Cape Wild. Hurley described it as being 'like the courtyard of a prison, measuring only 250 yards long by 50 yards wide.' He adds, 'This was to be our home for another five months.'

The spit was named Cape Wild or, by some, Cape Bloody Wild.

The spit was by no means an ideal camping-ground; it was rough, bleak, and inhospitable, but some of the larger rocks sheltered us a little from the wind, and, as we clustered round the blubber-stove, we were quite a cheerful company. After all, another stage of the homeward journey was finished, and for an hour we could afford to forget the problems of the future.

The snow had made it impossible for us to find the tideline, and we were uncertain how far the sea would encroach upon our beach. I pitched my tent on the seaward side of the camp so that I might have early warning of danger, and, sure enough, about 2 a.m. a little wave forced its way under the tent-cloth. After this practical demonstration that we had not gone far enough away from the sea, we took down our tents and re-pitched them close against the high rocks at the seaward end of the spit, where large boulders made an uncomfortable resting-place. Snow was falling heavily, and it was difficult to see where we could find safety. Then all hands helped to pull the boats farther up the beach, and at this task we suffered a serious misfortune.

Two of our bags of clothing had been placed under the bilge of the *James Caird*, and, before we realised the danger, a wave had lifted the boat and carried the two bags into the surf. We had no chance to recover them. But this was not our only misfortune, for in the early morning our big eight-man tent was blown to pieces.

A southerly gale was blowing on the morning of April 18th, and drifting snow covered everything. The outlook indeed was cheerless, but much work had got to be done. Some sea-elephants were lying about the beach, and we killed several of the younger ones for their meat and blubber. The big tent could not be replaced, and in order to provide shelter for the men we turned the *Dudley Docker* upside down and wedged up the weather side with boulders. We also lashed the

They only carried four bags of spare clothing, so half was lost.

painter and stern rope round the heaviest rocks which we could find, so as to guard against the danger of the boat being moved by the wind.

The gale continued all day, while I made a careful examination of the spit to ascertain its possibilities as a camping-ground. Apparently some of the beach lay above high-water mark, and the rocks which stood above the shingle gave a measure of shelter. At the seaward end of the spit were the high rocks which I have mentioned, and there – we had noted with satisfaction on landing – were a few thousand ringed penguins and some gentoos.

But at 8 a.m. on this morning I noticed the ringed penguins mustering in orderly fashion close to the water edge. At first I thought that they were preparing for the daily fishing excursion, but presently realised that they were on the point of migrating. Hurriedly I organised a raid upon them, but we were too late; only a few of the weaker ones fell victims to our needs, the main army took to the sea and we saw them no more.

The gentoo penguins, however, remained with us, and, although they were few in numbers, the weight of the legs and breast is greater than that of the adelie, a point that particularly appealed to us.

The deserted rookery was sure at all times to be above high-water mark, and we mounted the rocky ledge to search for a place on which to pitch our tents. The disadvantages of a camp on the rookery were obvious – the smell, to put it mildly, was strong; but our choice of sites was small, and during that afternoon we dug out a site for two tents in the *débris* of the rookery and levelled it off with snow and rocks.

My tent, No. 1, was pitched close under the cliff, and there I lived during my stay on Elephant

(Above) **The bleak Elephant Island: without vegetation or shelter, but with food and water. Some of the party were now in a bad way – Wordie estimated that about eight 'are broken down and unable to work'.**

Despite the loss of the ringed penguin (often known now as the chinstrap penguin) there was plenty of fresh food on Elephant Island in the early days: seal, sea elephant and the gentoos that sometimes came ashore. The glacier ice provided unlimited drinking water.

In addition to morale problems, there were social difficulties. Orde-Lees wrote, 'Piled close upon one another as we are, we have been given to understand that we are on an equal footing and, of course, the sailors, like most people of their class . . . become objectionably familiar & have revolting habits.' He admitted, 'There is one brilliant exception, Bakewell, a Canadian of some refinement, who is always respectful, as well as being self-respectful.' Hurley agreed. 'Our sailors are a very meagre set, ignorant, illiterate and of complaining disposition . . . Even as regards endurance, the genteel born have proved himself [sic] far more capable of sustaining prolonged exertion.'

It was on 18 April that the *Dudley Docker* was turned upside down because the big tent could not be replaced and some shelter was needed for the men who had been in it.

Island. Crean's tent was close by, and the other three tents, which had fairly clean snow under them, were some yards away. The fifth tent was a ramshackle affair. The material of the torn eight-man tent had been drawn over a rough framework of oars, and thus shelter of a kind was provided for the men who occupied it.

On April 18th we took to our sleeping-bags early, but my companions and I in No. 1 tent were not destined to spend a pleasant night. The heat of our bodies soon melted the snow and refuse beneath us, and the floor of the tent became an evil-smelling yellow mud. Additionally, the snow drifting from the cliff above us weighted the sides of the tent, and during the night a particularly stormy gust brought our little home down on top of us. There, however, we stayed until the morning, for it was hopeless to set about re-pitching the tent amid a raging storm and in the darkness of the night.

On the morning of April 19th the weather was still bad, and some of the men were showing signs of demoralisation and were disinclined to leave their tents when the hour came for turning out. It was apparent that they were thinking more of the discomforts of the moment than of the good fortune which had brought us to sound ground and comparative safety; and only by rather drastic methods were they induced to turn to.

The southerly gale was still so severe that I was blown down as I went along the beach to kill a seal. The cooking pots from No. 2 tent at the same moment took a flying run into the sea, but as nearly all our cooking was done over the blubber-stove these pots were fortunately not essential. The galley was set up by the rocks close to my tent, in a hole we had dug through the *débris* of the penguin rookery. Cases of stores gave some shelter from the wind, and a spread sail kept some of the snow off the cook while he was working. He had not much idle time; the amount of seal and sea-elephant steak and blubber consumed by our hungry party was almost incredible, and he earned everybody's gratitude by his unflagging energy in preparing meals which, to us at least, were savoury and satisfying.

Frankly, we needed all the comfort which hot food could give us. The icy fingers of the gale pushed relentlessly through our worn garments and tattered tents. The snow swathed us and our gear, and set traps for our stumbling feet. The rising sea beat against the rocks and shingle, and tossed fragments of floe-ice within a few feet of our boats. The consoling feature of the situation was that our camp was safe. We could endure the discomforts, and I felt that all of us would be benefited by this opportunity to rest and recuperate.

CHAPTER X

PREPARATIONS FOR THE BOAT JOURNEY

THE increasing sea made it necessary for us to drag our boats farther up the beach, and when this was done I discussed with Wild and Worsley the chances of reaching South Georgia before the winter locked the sea against us. For every conceivable reason some effort to secure relief had got to be made. The health and mental condition of several men were causing me serious anxiety, and the food supply was also a vital consideration. I did not dare confidently to count upon supplies of meat and blubber, for animals seemed to have deserted the beach, and the winter was near.

The conclusion was forced upon me that a boat journey in search of relief was necessary and must not be delayed. The nearest port where assistance could certainly be secured was Port Stanley, in the Falkland Islands, 540 miles away; but we could scarcely hope to beat up against the prevailing north-westerly wind in a frail and weakened boat with a small sail area.

It was not difficult to decide that South Georgia, which was over 800 miles away but lay in the area of west winds, must be our objective. I could count upon finding whalers at any of the whaling-stations on the east coast, and, provided that the sea was clear of ice and that the boat survived the great seas, a boat party might make the voyage and be back with relief within a month.

The hazards of a boat journey across 800 miles of stormy sub-Antarctic ocean were obvious, but I calculated that at the worst this venture would add nothing to the risks of the men left on the island. The boat would not require to take more than one month's provisions for six men, for if we did not make South Georgia in that time we were sure to go under. A consideration which also influenced me was that there was no chance at all of any search being made for us on Elephant Island.

The perils of the proposed journey were extreme, and the risk was justified solely by our urgent need of assistance. The ocean south of Cape Horn in the middle of May is known to be the most tempestuous area of water in the world, and the gales are almost unceasing. We had to face these conditions in a small and weather-beaten boat, already strained by the work of the previous months. Worsley and Wild realised that the attempt must be made, and asked to be allowed to accompany me on the voyage.

I had at once to tell Wild that he must stay behind, for I relied upon him to hold the party together while I was away, and, should our attempt to bring help end in failure, to make the best of his way to Deception Island in the spring. I determined to take Worsley with me as I had a very high opinion of his accuracy and quickness as a navigator – an opinion that was only enhanced during our journey.

The chance that a rescue team, if and when it was sent out, would look for them on Elephant Island was remote. 'The world was as completely cut off from us as though we had come from another planet. I have experienced a good many strange things in my time, but this situation of detachment from the living world was one of the most memorable.' These are Worsley's words.

Another factor influencing the decision to go immediately for help was that the two doctors told Shackleton that they would almost certainly have to operate on Blackborrow's frost-bitten feet, and Shackleton was not sure that they would be able to save his life.

Two days after arriving on the island, Shackleton asked for volunteers. Many of the men did not want to go back on the sea, including Orde-Lees, who thought the plan to try to reach Georgia 'the forlornest forlorn hope conceivable'. The two doctors, though they volunteered, had to stay behind to amputate Blackborrow's toes, which were gangrenous. Shackleton took McNeish, despite his 'mutiny' five months before, partly because he thought he would be a disruptive influence at the base. Vincent, who had been disrated from bosun for bullying, was taken for similar reasons; both were good seamen. Both McCarthy and Crean were Irish and Huntford suggests that this is why Shackleton selected them, ensuring that half the crew was Irish. Worsley was in charge of the boat, and Shackleton called him 'Skipper' throughout the boat journey. (In *South* and in Huntford McCarthy is referred to as such, but Fisher calls him McCarty.)

Four other men were required, and, although I thought of leaving Crean as a right-hand man for Wild, he begged so hard to come that, after consulting Wild, I promised to take him. Then I called the men together, explained my plan, and asked for volunteers. Many came forward at once, and I finally selected McNeish, McCarthy and Vincent, in addition to Worsley and Crean. McIlroy and Macklin were both anxious to go but realised that their duty lay on the island with the sick men. The crew seemed a strong one, and as I looked at the men I felt confidence increasing.

After the decision was made, I walked through the blizzard with Worsley and Wild to examine the *James Caird*. The 20-foot boat had never looked big, but when I viewed her in the light of our new undertaking she seemed in some mysterious way to have shrunk. She was an ordinary ship's whaler, fairly strong, but showing signs of the strain she had endured. Standing beside her, and looking at the fringe of the tumultuous sea, there was no doubt that our voyage would be a big adventure.

I called McCarthy, the carpenter, and asked him if he could do anything to make the ship more seaworthy. He asked at once if he was to go with me, and seemed quite pleased when I answered "Yes." He was over fifty years of age and not altogether fit, but he was very quick and had a good knowledge of sailing-boats. He told me that he could contrive some sort of covering for the *James Caird* if he was allowed to use the lids of the cases and the four sledge-runners, which we had lashed inside the boat for use in the event of a landing on Graham Land at Wilhelmina Bay. He proposed to complete the covering with some of our canvas, and immediately began to make his plans.

Noon had passed, the gale was more severe than ever, and the tents were being so buffeted and battered by the wind that it did not appear possible for them to hold out for many more days. So we made our way to the snow-slope at the shoreward end of the spit, with the intention of digging a

(Right) Preparing the *James Caird* for the relief voyage. The case for going, said Shackleton, 'had to be argued in some detail, since all hands knew that the perils of the proposed journey were extreme'.

hole in the snow large enough to shelter the whole party. But after examining the spot we saw that any hole which we could dig would in all probability be quickly filled by the drift.

On the following morning (April 20th) the gale was stronger than ever and no work could be done. A seal came up on the beach during that day, and so urgent was our need of food and blubber that I called all hands, and organised a line of beaters instead of simply walking up to the seal and hitting it on the nose. We were prepared to fall *en masse* upon this seal if it tried to escape. The kill was made with a pick-handle, and in a few minutes we had five days' food and six days' fuel stowed away in a place of safety above high-water mark.

During this day the cook, who had worked very well, suddenly collapsed, and to replace him I selected one of the men who had expressed a desire to lie down and die. The task of keeping the galley fire alight was both strenuous and difficult, and it took his thoughts away from the chances of immediate dissolution. In fact, I found him a little later gravely concerned over the drying of a naturally not over-clean pair of socks, which were hung up close to our evening milk.

There was a lull in the bad weather on April 21st, and the carpenter was able to collect material for the decking of the *James Caird*. He fitted the mast of the *Stancomb Wills* fore and aft inside the *James Caird* as a hog-back, and thus strengthened the keel with the object of preventing our boat from buckling in heavy seas. He had not enough wood to provide a deck, but by using the sledge runners and box lids he made a framework extending from the forecastle aft to a well. It was a patched-up affair, but it provided a base for a canvas covering.

We had a bolt of canvas frozen stiff, and this material had to be thawed out foot by foot over the blubber-stove so that it might be sewn into the form of a cover. When it had been nailed and screwed into position it certainly gave an appearance of safety to the boat, though I had an uneasy feeling that it bore a strong likeness to stage scenery. But, as events proved, the covering served its purpose well, and without it we certainly could not have lived through the voyage.

Another fierce gale blew on April 22nd, and our preparations for the voyage were again interfered with. Blackborrow's feet were giving him much pain, and McIlroy and Macklin thought that an operation would soon be necessary. At that time they thought that they had no chloroform, but they found some in the medicine chest after we had left.

We had begun to set aside stores for the boat journey, and to choose the essential equipment from the scanty stock at our disposal. Two ten-gallon casks had to be filled with water melted down from ice collected at the foot of the glacier; a slow business, as the blubber-stove had to be kept going all night and the watchman emptied the water into the casks from the pot in which the ice was melted. An attempt to dig a hole in the snow to provide a site for camp failed, the snow drifting down unceasingly from the inland ice.

The weather was fine on April 23rd, and we hurried forward our preparations. About noon, however, a storm came on, with driving snow and heavy squalls. Occasionally the air cleared for a few minutes, and we could see a line of pack-ice, five miles out, driving across from west to east. This sight increased my desire to get away quickly, for winter was advancing, and the pack might soon close completely round the island and prevent our departure for days or even weeks. I did not think that ice would remain continuously around Elephant Island during the winter, because the strong winds and fast currents would keep it in motion.

Worsley, Wild and I climbed to the summit of the seaward rocks, and examined the ice from a better vantage-point than the beach offered. The belt of pack outside appeared to be broken enough for our purposes, and I decided that, unless conditions forbade it, we would make a start on the following morning. The decision having been made, I spent the rest of the day looking over the boat, gear and stores, and discussing plans with Worsley and Wild.

McCarthy, a seaman, is sometimes referred to as the carpenter, but most of the difficult carpentry work was done by McNeish, an ingenious shipwright who had already raised the freeboard of *James Caird* by 10 inches using wood salvaged from *Endurance*. There was no wood on the island.

The others helped Crean sew up the canvas and blankets. McNeish wrote, 'They had rather a job as it was frozen stiff. They had to pull the needle through with a pair of pinchers.'

Shackleton was worried that it might be thought he was deserting his men left behind, but they all knew that he was incapable of being inactive. In Macklin's words, 'Shackleton sitting still and doing nothing wasn't Shackleton at all.'

(Above) **Preparing to launch the *James Caird*. The crew of six was to be Worsley as master, Crean, McNeish, McCarthy, Vincent and Shackleton himself.**

Our last night on Elephant Island was cold and uncomfortable, and we turned out at dawn. After breakfast we launched the *Stancomb Wills* and loaded her with stores, gear and ballast, which were to be transferred to the *James Caird* when the heavier boat had been launched. The ballast weighed about 1,000 lb., and, in addition, we had gathered a number of round boulders, and a good deal of ice to supplement our two casks of water.

The stores taken in the *James Caird*, which would last six men for one month, were as follows:-

30	boxes of matches.	*Food.*		*Instruments.*
6½	gallons paraffin.	3 cases sledging rations	= 300 rations.	Sextant.
1	tin methylated spirit.	2 cases nut food	= 200 rations.	Binoculars.
10	boxes of flamers.	2 cases biscuits	= 600 biscuits.	Prismatic Compass.
1	box of blue lights.	1 case lump sugar.		Sea-anchor.
2	Primus stoves with spare parts and prickers.	30 packets of Trumilk.		Charts.
1	Nansen aluminium cooker.	1 tin of Bovril cubes.		Aneroid.
6	sleeping-bags.	1 tin of Cerebos salt.		
A	few spare socks.	36 gallons of water.		
A	few candles and some blubber oil in an oil-bag.	112 lb. of ice.		

(Left) The *Stancomb Wills* was launched first, loaded with supplies to be transferred to the *Caird* which was dragged out – the men up to their waists in the water – half an hour later.

The *Stancomb Wills* had to make four trips out to where the *James Caird* was anchored.

(Left) When the *Caird* was afloat in the surf she nearly capsized amongst the rocks before the crew could get her clear, and two men were thrown into the water. It was discovered that the bottom plug had been left out, and Worsley quickly found the cork and replaced it.

On one of its trips out to the *Caird*, the *Wills* became half-filled with water and had to be turned over and emptied before the return journey.

(Right) The *Caird* anchored about 100 yards offshore, loaded with 19 bags of ballast which, with the supplies, had been ferried from the beach. At 12.30 in the afternoon, 'with a final wave of the hand, and three squawky cheers from us and the penguins, Sir Ernest and his crew set off on their perilous journey'. So wrote Orde-Lees in his diary.

This photograph does not seem to have survived.

The party on shore was optimistic. Orde-Lees wrote, 'The *Caird* is an excellent sailor, & guided by providence, shd make South Georgia in 14 days . . . How we shall count the days.'

The swell was slight when we launched the *Stancomb Wills*, but half an hour later, when we were pulling down the *James Caird*, the swell suddenly increased, and made things difficult. Many of us got wet to the waist while dragging the boat out – a serious matter in that climate. When the *James Caird* was launched she nearly capsized, and Vincent and the carpenter, who were on deck, were thrown into the water – a piece of really bad luck as they would have small chance of drying their clothes after we started. Hurley, who had the eye of the professional photographer for "incidents," secured a picture of the upset, and I firmly believe he would have liked the two men to remain in the water until he could "snap" them at close quarters! But, regardless of his feelings, we hauled them out immediately.

The *James Caird* was soon clear of the breakers, and the *Stancomb Wills* came alongside, transferred her load, and went back to the shore for more. On this second journey the water-casks were towed behind the *Stancomb Wills*, and the swell, which was rapidly increasing, drove the boat on to the rocks, where one of the casks was slightly stove in. This accident proved later on to be serious, since some sea water had entered the casks and made the contents brackish.

By midday the *James Caird* was ready for the voyage. Vincent and the carpenter had secured some dry clothes by exchange with members of the shore-party, and the boat's crew was standing by, waiting for the order to cast off. I went ashore in the *Stancomb Wills* and had a last word with Wild. Secure in the knowledge that he would act wisely I told him that I trusted the party to him, and then I said "good-bye" to the men. Within a few minutes I was again aboard the *James Caird*, and the crew of the *Stancomb Wills* shook hands with us and offered us the last good wishes.

Then, setting our jib, we cut the painter and moved away to the north-east. The men who were staying behind made a pathetic little group on the beach, but they waved to us and gave three hearty cheers. There was hope in their hearts, and they trusted us to bring the help which they so sorely needed.

CHAPTER XI

THE BEGINNING OF THE BOAT JOURNEY

I HAD all sails set, and the *James Caird* quickly dipped the beach and its line of dark figures. The westerly wind took us rapidly to the line of pack, and as we entered it I stood up with my arm around the mast directing the steering. The pack thickened and we were forced to turn almost due east, running before the wind towards a gap which I had seen in the morning from the high ground. At 4 p.m. we found the channel, and, dropping sail, we rowed through without touching the ice, and by 5.30 p.m. we were clear of the pack with open water before us. Soon the swell became very heavy, and when it was time for our first evening meal we had great difficulty in keeping the Primus lamp alight and preventing the hoosh from splashing out of the pot.

Three men were needed to attend to the cooking, and all their operations had to be conducted in the confined space under the decking, where the men lay or knelt and adjusted themselves as best they could to the angles of our cases and ballast. It was uncomfortable, but we found consolation in the reflection that without the decking we could not have used the cooker at all.

The tale of the next sixteen days is one of supreme strife amid heaving waters, for the sub-Antarctic Ocean fully lived up to its evil winter reputation. I decided to run north for at least two days while the wind held, and thus get into warmer weather before turning to the east and laying a course for South Georgia.

We took two-hourly spells at the tiller. The men who were not on watch crawled into the sodden sleeping-bags and tried to forget their troubles for a period. But there was no comfort in the boat, indeed the first night aboard the boat was one of acute discomfort for us all, and we were heartily glad when dawn came and we could begin to prepare a hot breakfast.

Cramped in our narrow quarters and continually wet from the spray, we suffered severely from cold throughout the journey. We fought the seas and the winds, and at the same time had a daily struggle to keep ourselves alive. At times we were in dire peril. Generally we were encouraged by the knowledge that we were progressing towards the desired land, but there were days and nights when we lay hove to, drifting across the storm-whitened seas, and watching the uprearing masses of water, flung to and fro by Nature in the pride of her strength.

Nearly always there were gales. So small was our boat and so great were the seas that often our sail flapped idly in the calm between the crests of two waves. Then we would climb the next slope, and catch the fully fury of the gale where the wool-like whiteness of the breaking water surged around us. But we had our moments of laughter – rare, it is true, but hearty enough.

On the third day out the wind came up strong and worked into a gale from the north-west. We stood away to the east, but the increasing seas discovered the weaknesses of our decking. The

Eighteen months after the start of his expedition, Shackleton now faced his most difficult task. Furthermore, although the five men with him in the boat had worked as fishermen or sailors, Shackleton himself had no such background. He was amazingly fit but he now had to cross 800 miles of one of the stormiest seas in the world. He told Worsley, 'Do you know I know nothing about boat sailing', and when Worsley laughed said crossly, 'I'm telling you that I don't.'

Once he reached the coast of South Georgia he then had to get across land to a whaling station, and from there to one of the South American ports to find a relief ship. A small error of navigation would allow them to miss South Georgia – a small speck in a large ocean.

Shackleton records that this description of the epic boat journey is based on 'scanty notes made day by day' dealing with the bare facts of distances, positions and weather, but their memories retained incidents 'never to be forgotten'.

(*Opposite, clockwise from top left*) **Shackleton, Crean, Wild and Hurley.**

continuous blows shifted the box lids and sledge-runners so that the canvas sagged down and accumulated water. Then icy trickles, distinct from the driving sprays, poured fore and aft into the boat. We did what we could to secure the decking, but our means were very limited, and the water continued to enter the boat at a dozen points.

Much bailing was necessary, but nothing could prevent our gear from becoming sodden. The searching runnels from the canvas were really more unpleasant than the sudden definite douches of the sprays. There were no dry places in the boat, and at last we simply covered our heads with our Burberrys and endured the all-pervading water. The bailing was work for the watch.

None of us, however, had any real rest. The perpetual motion of the boat made repose impossible; we were cold, sore and anxious. In the semi-darkness of the day we moved on hands and knees under the decking. By 6 p.m. the darkness was complete, and not until 7 a.m. could we see one another under the thwarts. We had a few scraps of candle, but we preserved them carefully so that we might have light at meal-times. There was one fairly dry spot in the boat, under the solid original decking at the bows, and there we managed to protect some of our biscuit from the salt water. But I do not think any of us got the taste of salt out of our mouths during the voyage.

The clothing was inadequate. Oilskins had disappeared when *Endurance* was abandoned, and their reindeer footwear was intended for land not sea.

The difficulty of movement in the boat would have had its humorous side if it had not caused so many aches and pains. In order to move along the boat we had to crawl under the thwarts, and our knees suffered considerably. When a watch turned out I had to direct each man by name when and where to move, for if all hands had crawled about at the same time the result would have been dire confusion and many bruises.

Then there was the trim of the boat to be considered. The order of the watch was four hours on and four hours off, three men to the watch. One man had the tiller ropes, the second man attended to the sail, and the third bailed for all he was worth. Sometimes, when the water in the boat had been reduced to reasonable proportions, we could use our pump, which Hurley had made from the Flinders' bar case of our ship's standard compass. Though its capacity was small this pump was quite effective.

Shackleton kept 'scanty notes made day by day'. He was not inclined to write humorously, but Worsley's memoirs resulted in such comic comments as, 'My unworthy hands held the aluminium cooker that was to receive the sacred HOOSH, and Crean the High Priest of Cookery and Tender of the Sacred Flame gave instructions.'

While the new watch was shivering in the wind and spray, the men who had been relieved groped hurriedly among the soaking sleeping-bags, and tried to steal some of the warmth created by the last occupants; but it was not always possible to find even this comfort when we went off watch. The boulders which we had taken aboard for ballast had to be shifted continually in order to trim the boat and give access to the pump, which became choked with hairs from the moulting sleeping-bags and finniskoe.

The moving of the boulders was weary and painful work. As ballast they were useful, but as weights to be moved about in cramped quarters they were simply appalling. They spared no portion of our poor bodies. Another of our troubles was the chafing of our legs by our wet clothes, and our pain was increased by the bite of the salt water. At the time we thought that we never slept, but in fact we dozed off uncomfortably, to be roused quickly by some new ache or by another call to effort. My own share of the general discomfort was increased by a finely-developed bout of sciatica, which had begun on the floe several months earlier.

Shackleton insisted on regular meals. Bovril hoosh for eight o'clock breakfast with two biscuits, nutfood and sugar. Lunch was raw sledging ration washed down with a panikin of hot milk. Tea was the same. At night they had another hot drink. If Shackleton saw that one of the men was showing signs of strain, he would order hot milk. Worsley noticed 'a touch of the woman' about the leader's solicitude.

Our meals were regular in spite of the gales. Attention to this was essential, since the conditions of the voyage made ever-increasing calls upon our vitality. The meals, which consisted chiefly of Bovril sledging-ration, were the bright beacons in these cold and stormy days. Finding ourselves in need of an oil lamp to eke out our supply of candles, we emptied one of our two tins of Virol in the manner which most appealed to us, and fitted it with a wick made by shredding a bit of canvas. This lamp was of great assistance to us at night. Since we had 6½ gallons of petroleum we were fairly well off for fuel.

Before Shackleton set off for South Georgia, the Royal Geographical Society in London held meetings to discuss a rescue. A lengthy account of the society's negative attitude to Shackleton is given by Fisher: the President, Douglas Freshfield, said, 'We should firmly decline further contributions. The speculative syndicate who are running Shackleton's project must find the funds.' Alas, the syndicate no longer existed. An appeal to Asquith, the Prime Minister, led to the Admiralty taking on the task at public expense.

(Below left) Reginald James, the physicist and *(below right)* Captain Thomas Orde-Lees, the only regular officer of the expedition and therefore rather distrusted by some of the others. He was a man of many parts who left a fascinatingly frank diary, still available at the Scott Polar Research Institute.

A severe south-westerly gale on the fourth day out forced us to heave to. The delay was vexatious, since up to that time we had been making sixty to seventy miles a day, good going with our limited sail area. We hove to under double-reefed mainsail and our little jigger, and waited for the gale to blow itself out. The weather, however, did not improve, and on the fifth day we were obliged to take in the double-reefed mainsail and hoist our small jib instead.

We put out a sea-anchor to keep the boat's head up to the sea. This anchor consisted of a triangular canvas bag fastened to the end of the painter and allowed to stream out from the bows. The boat was high enough to catch the wind, and, as she drifted to leeward, the drag of the anchor kept her head to windward. Thus our boat took most of the seas more or less end on, but even then we shipped a great deal of water, which necessitated unceasing bailing and pumping. A thousand times it seemed as if the *James Caird* must be engulfed; but the boat lived.

The gale had its birthplace above the Antarctic Continent, and its freezing breath lowered the temperature far towards zero. The spray froze upon the boat and gave bows, sides and decking a heavy coat of mail. This ice reduced the buoyancy of the boat, and to that extent was an added peril; but from one point of view it possessed a notable advantage. The water ceased to drop and trickle from the canvas, and the spray came in solely at the well in the after part of the boat. We could not allow the load of ice to increase beyond a certain point, and in turn we crawled about the decking forward, chipping and picking at it with what tools we had.

When daylight came on the sixth day we saw and felt that the *James Caird* had lost her resiliency. She was not rising to the oncoming seas. The weight of the ice was having its effect, and she was becoming more like a log than a boat. The situation called for immediate action. First of all

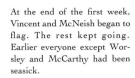

we broke away the spare oars, which were encased in ice and frozen to the sides of the boat, and threw them overboard. We kept two oars for use when we got inshore. Then two of the fur sleeping-bags went over the side, weighing probably 40 lb. each. We still had four bags, three in use and one in reserve should a member of the party permanently break down. The reduction of weight relieved the boat to some extent, and vigorous chipping and scraping, by which we got rid of a lot of ice, helped more. The *James Caird* lifted to the endless waves as though she lived again.

At the end of the first week, Vincent and McNeish began to flag. The rest kept going. Earlier everyone except Worsley and McCarthy had been seasick.

About 11 a.m. the boat suddenly fell off into the trough of the sea. The painter had parted and the sea-anchor had gone. This was serious. The boat went away to leeward, and we had no chance to recover the anchor and our valuable rope, which had been our only means of keeping the boat's head up to the sea without the risk of hoisting sail in a gale. Now we had to set the sail and trust to its holding. While the *James Caird* rolled in the trough, we beat the frozen canvas until the bulk of the ice had cracked off it, and then we hoisted it. The frozen gear worked protestingly, but after a struggle our little craft came up to the wind again, and we breathed more freely.

Skin frost-bites were troubling us, and we had developed large blisters on our fingers and hands, but we held the boat up to the gale during the day, enduring as best we could discomforts amounting to pain. Our thoughts did not embrace much more than the necessities of the hour. Every surge of the sea was an enemy to be watched and circumvented. Night fell early, and in the lagging hours of darkness we were cheered by an improvement in the weather. The wind dropped, the snow-squalls became less frequent, and the sea moderated.

When the morning of the seventh day dawned there was not much wind, and we shook the reef out of the sail and laid our course once more for South Georgia. The sun came out bright and clear, and presently Worsley got a snap for longitude. We hoped that the sky would remain clear until noon so that we could get the latitude, for we had been six days out without an observation, and our dead reckoning naturally was uncertain.

The boat on that morning must have presented a strange appearance. All hands basked in the sunshine. We hung our sleeping-bags to the mast, and our socks and other gear were spread all over the deck. Porpoises came blowing round the boat, and Cape pigeons wheeled and swooped within a few feet of us. These little black-and-white birds have an air of friendliness which is not possessed by the great circling albatross.

We revelled in the warmth of the sun during that day. Life, after all, was not so bad. Our gear was drying, and we could have a hot meal in more or less comfort. The swell was still heavy, but it was not breaking, and the boat rode easily. At noon Worsley balanced himself on the gunwale and clung with one hand to the stay of the main-mast while he got a snap of the sun. The result was more than encouraging. We had done over 380 miles and were getting on for half-way to South Georgia. It looked as if we were going to get through.

Shackleton observed, 'The albatross, of the black or sooty variety, had watched with hard, bright eyes, and seems to have quite impersonal interest in our struggle to keep afloat amid the battering seas. In addition . . . a small bird, unknown to me . . . appeared always to be in a fussy, bustling state . . . It irritated me.' Shackleton actually swore at it, the only occasion on which he was heard to swear on this journey.

CHAPTER XII

THE END OF THE BOAT JOURNEY

DURING the afternoon the wind freshened to a good stiff breeze, and the *James Caird* made satisfactory progress. I had not realised until the sunlight came how small our boat really was. So low in the water were we that each succeeding swell cut off our view of the skyline. At one moment the consciousness of the forces arrayed against us would be almost overwhelming, and then hope and confidence would rise again as our boat rose to a wave and tossed aside the crest in a sparkling shower. My gun and some cartridges were stowed aboard the boat as a precaution against a shortage of food, but we were not disposed to destroy our little neighbours, the Cape pigeons, even for the sake of fresh meat. We might have shot an albatross, but the wandering king of the ocean aroused in us something of the feeling that inspired, too late, the Ancient Mariner.

The eighth, ninth and tenth days of the voyage had few features worthy of special note. The wind blew hard during these days, and the strain of navigating the boat was unceasing, but we kept on advancing towards our goal and felt that we were going to succeed. We still suffered severely from the cold, for our vitality was declining owing to shortage of food, exposure, and the necessity of maintaining our cramped positions day and night. I found that it was now absolutely necessary to prepare hot milk for all hands during the night, in order to sustain life until dawn. This involved an increased drain upon our small supply of matches, and our supply already was very small indeed. One of the memories which comes to me of those days is of Crean singing at the tiller. He always sang while he was steering, but nobody ever discovered what the song was.

On the tenth night Worsley could not straighten his body after his spell at the tiller. He was thoroughly cramped, and we had to drag him beneath the decking and massage him before he could unbend himself and get into a sleeping-bag.

A hard north-westerly gale came up on the eleventh day (May 5th), and in the late afternoon it shifted to the south-west. The sky was overcast and occasional snow-squalls added to the discomfort produced by a tremendous cross-sea – the worst, I thought, which we had encountered. At midnight I was at the tiller, and suddenly noticed a line of clear sky between the south and south-west. I called to the other men that the sky was clearing, and then, a moment later, realised that what I had seen was not a rift in the clouds but the white crest of an enormous wave.

During twenty-six years' experience of the ocean in all its moods I had never seen a wave so gigantic. It was a mighty upheaval of the ocean, a thing quite apart from the big white-capped seas which had abeen our tireless enemies for many days. I shouted, "For God's sake, hold on! It's got us!" Then came a moment of suspense which seemed to last for hours. We felt our boat lifted and flung forward like a cork in breaking surf. We were in a seething chaos of tortured water; but

Shackleton minimises the terrors of the journey. The sea was grey as well as mountainous, and the weather was icy. The men were beginning to suffer from exposure, particularly McNeish. Their lips were cracked and their mouths swollen.

Worsley said that by a Sherlock Holmes system of deduction, they found that the song was 'The Wearin' O' the Green'. Huntford points out that almost at the same time, the Easter Monday Rising in Dublin was resounding to the same song.

(Opposite) An artist's impression, probably by George Marston, who remained behind on Elephant Island. He had been the official artist on Shackleton's earlier expedition, and wrote well about his experiences. He was also an accomplished comedian at crew entertainments. This reconstruction of the sighting of South Georgia is captioned, in the original edition of *South*, *'In sight of our Goal.'*

Shackleton now insisted that they should hove to, but without a sea anchor the boat bobbed about and shipped water. The glass on the compass broke and had to be repaired with a piece of plaster from the first-aid box. It was the thirteenth day of their voyage.

Vincent, a young man, was one of the strongest on the boat, but now he became a passenger. Worsley and Shackleton wondered if they could reach land with a reduced crew and they discussed what to do if they missed a landfall on South Georgia. In any case they would have no water 'so we dropped the discussion as it was so futile'.

somehow the boat lived through it, half-full of water, sagging to the dead weight and shuddering under the blow. We bailed with the energy of men fighting for life, flinging the water over the sides with every receptacle which came into our hands; and after ten minutes of uncertainty we felt the boat renew her life beneath us. She floated again, and ceased to lurch drunkenly as though dazed by the attack of the sea. Earnestly we hoped that never again should we encounter such a wave.

The conditions of the boat, uncomfortable before, were made worse by this deluge of water. All our gear was thoroughly wet again, and our cooking-stove was floating about in the bottom of the boat. Not until 3 a.m., when we were all chilled to the limit of endurance, did we manage to get the stove alight and to make ourselves hot drinks. The carpenter was suffering particularly, but he showed grit and spirit. Vincent, however, had collapsed, and for the past week had ceased to be an active member of the crew.

On the following day (May 6th) the weather improved, and we got a glimpse of the sun. Worsley's observation showed that we were not more than 100 miles from the north-west corner of South Georgia. Two more days, with a favourable wind, and we should sight the promised land. I hoped that there would be no delay, as our supply of water was running very low. The hot drink at night was essential, but I decided that the daily allowance of water must be cut down to half a pint per man. Our lumps of ice had gone some days before; we were dependent upon the water which we had brought from Elephant Island, and our thirst was increased by the fact that we were at this time using the brackish water in the breaker which had been slightly stove in when the boat was being loaded. Some sea-water had entered it.

Thirst took possession of us, but I dared not permit the allowance of water to be increased, because an unfavourable wind might have driven us away from the island and have lengthened our voyage by several days. Lack of water is always the most severe privation which men can be condemned to endure, and we found that the salt water in our clothing and the salt spray which lashed our faces made our thirst quickly grow to a burning pain. I had to be very firm in refusing to allow any one to anticipate the morrow's allowance, which sometimes I was begged to do.

I had altered the course to the east so as to make sure of striking the island, which would have been impossible to regain if we had run past the northern end. The course was laid on our scrap of chart for a point some thirty miles down the coast. That day and the following day passed for us in a sort of nightmare. Our mouths were dry and our tongues were swollen. The wind was still strong and the heavy sea forced us to navigate carefully. But any thought of our peril from the waves was buried beneath the consciousness of our raging thirst. The bright moments were those when we each received our one mug of hot milk during the long, bitter watches of the night.

Things were bad for us in those days, but the end was approaching. The morning of May 8th broke thick and stormy, with squalls from the north-west. We searched the waters ahead for a sign of land, and, although we searched in vain, we were cheered by a sense that the goal was near. About 10 a.m. we passed a little bit of kelp, a glad signal of the proximity of land. An hour later we saw two shags sitting on a big mass of kelp, and we knew then that we must be within ten or fifteen miles of the shore. These birds are as sure an indication of the proximity of land as a lighthouse is, for they never venture far to sea.

Although Worsley had hoped to navigate round the north coast, so reaching a whaling station, he afterwards agreed with Shackleton's strategy, since both the desperate state of the men and the shortage of water would have prevented success.

We gazed ahead with increasing eagerness, and at 12.30 p.m., through a rift in the clouds, McCarthy caught a glimpse of the black cliffs of South Georgia, just fourteen days after our departure from Elephant Island. It was a glad moment. Thirst-ridden, chilled, and weak as we were, happiness irradiated us. The job was nearly done.

We stood in towards the shore to look for a landing-place, and presently we could see the green tussock-grass on the ledges above the surf-beaten rocks. Ahead of us, and to the south, blind rollers showed the presence of uncharted reefs along the coast. The rocky coast appeared to descend sheer to the sea. Our need of water and rest was almost desperate, but to have attempted a landing at that time would have been suicidal.

Night was approaching and the weather indications were unfavourable. We could do nothing but haul off until the following morning, so we stood away on the starboard tack until we had made what appeared to be a safe offing. Then we hove to in the high westerly swell. The hours passed slowly as we waited the dawn; our thirst was a torment and we could scarcely touch our food, the cold seemed to strike right through our weakened bodies.

At 5 a.m. the wind shifted to the north-west, and quickly increased to one of the worst hurricanes any of us had ever experienced. A great cross-sea was running and the wind simply shrieked as it converted the whole seascape into a haze of driving spray. Down into the valleys, up to tossing heights, straining until her seams opened, swung our little boat, brave still but labouring heavily. We knew that the wind and set of the sea were driving us ashore, but we could do nothing.

The dawn revealed a storm-torn ocean, and the morning passed without bringing us a sight of the land; but at 1 p.m., through a rift in the flying mists, we got a glimpse of the huge crags of the island and realised that our position had become desperate. We were on a dead lee shore, and we could gauge our approach to the unseen cliffs by the roar of the breakers against the sheer walls of rock. I ordered the double-reefed mainsail to be set in the hope that we might claw off, and this attempt increased the strain upon the boat.

The *James Caird* was bumping heavily, and the water was pouring in everywhere. Our thirst

Although irradiated by their happiness, the sight before them must have been very bleak. Captain Cook had described it as 'savage and horrible' when he first saw it 140 years earlier. This south coast was uninhabited and probably uninhabitable. The whaling stations were on the north coast. It was a triumph for Worsley's navigational skill that they had arrived at all.

It took an hour to change the sail, but then Worsley's seamanship enabled them to edge out, almost inch by inch, to sea. Meanwhile, the men were bailing out as each wave struck the boat and the bow planks opened and let in water. They were fighting for their lives. Worsley wrote later, 'I felt a sharp resentment that we should all be going in such a way and in sight of our goal.'

(Left) Penguins on the shore of South Georgia. It was, however, the young albatrosses that provided essential food on landing.

129

This was a Force 10 storm, worse than anything experienced on the voyage. By noon it reached hurricane force. The boat and its crew seemed doomed.

was forgotten in the realisation of our imminent danger, as we bailed unceasingly and from time to time adjusted our weights; occasional glimpses showed that the shore was nearer.

I knew that Annewkow Island lay to the south of us, but our small and badly marked chart showed uncertain reefs in the passage between the island and the mainland, and I dared not trust it, though, as a last resort, we could try to lie under the lee of the island.

The afternoon wore away as we edged down the coast, and the approach of evening found us still some distance from Annewkow Island; dimly in the twilight we could see a snow-capped mountain looming above us. The chance of surviving the night seemed small, and I think most of us felt that the end was very near. Just after 6 p.m., as the boat was in the yeasty backwash from the seas flung from this iron-bound coast, just when things looked their worst, they changed for the best; so thin is the line which divides success from failure.

This is a good example of how Shackleton incorporated other diaries into his account. The phrase 'snapped like a carrot' is actually Worsley's. He added, 'Providence had certainly held us in the hollow of his hand.'

The wind suddenly shifted, and we were free once more to make an offing. Almost as soon as the gale eased the pin which locked the mast to the thwart fell out. Throughout the hurricane it must have been on the point of doing this, and if it had nothing could have saved us. The mast would have snapped like a carrot. Our backstays had carried away once before, when iced up, and were not too strongly fastened. We were thankful indeed for the mercy which had held the pin in its place during the hurricane.

We stood off shore again, tired almost to the point of apathy. Our water had long been finished. The last was about a pint of hairy liquid, which we strained through a bit of gauze from the medicine chest. The pangs of thirst attacked us with redoubled intensity, and I felt that at almost any risk we must make a landing on the following day. The night wore on. We were very tired and longed for day. When at last dawn came there was hardly any wind, but a high cross-sea was running. We made slow progress towards the shore.

They had not drunk anything for forty-eight hours. The hairy quality was reindeer fur.

About 8 a.m. the wind backed to the north-west and threatened another blow. In the meantime we had sighted a big indentation which I thought must be King Haakon Bay, and I decided that we must land there. We set the bows of the boat towards the bay, and ran before the freshening gale. Soon we had angry reefs on either side. Great glaciers came down to the sea and offered no landing-place. The sea spouted on the reefs and thundered against the shore. About noon we sighted a line of jagged reef, like blackened teeth, which seemed to bar the entrance to the bay. Inside, fairly smooth water stretched eight or nine miles to the head of the bay.

A gap in the reef appeared, and we made for it, but the fates had another rebuff for us. The wind shifted and blew from the east right out of the bay. We could see the way through the reef, but we could not approach it directly. That afternoon we bore up, tacking five times in the strong wind. The last tack enabled us to get through, and at last we were in the wide mouth of the bay.

The *James Caird* tacked back and forth across the fjord entrance for four hours until Worsley saw the little cove and, after another hour, managed to effect entrance.

Dusk was approaching. A small cove, with a boulder-strewn beach guarded by a reef, made a break in the cliffs on the south side of the bay, and we turned in that direction. I stood in the bows, and directed the steering as we ran through the kelp and made the passage of the reef. The entrance was so narrow that we had to take in the oars, and the swell was piling itself right over the reef into the cove. But in a minute or two we were inside, and in the gathering darkness the *James Caird* ran in on a swell and touched the beach.

I sprang ashore with the short painter, and held on when the boat went out with the backward surge. When the boat came in again three men got ashore and held the painter while I climbed some rocks with another line. A slip on the wet rocks 20 feet up nearly closed my part of the story, just when we were achieving safety. A jagged piece of rock held me and also sorely bruised me. I, however, made fast the line, and in a few minutes we were all safe on the beach, with the boat floating in the surging water just off the shore.

It was 10 May 1916, the seventeenth day after they had left Elephant Island.

We heard a gurgling sound which was sweet music in our ears, and, peering round, we found a stream of fresh water almost at our feet. A moment later we were down on our knees drinking the pure, ice-cold water in long draughts which put new life into us. It was a splendid moment.

(Above) Hurley described how these 'small ice fragments have been cast from the sea face of numerous glaciers and present a crystal foreground to the heights of the 8,000 ft summits of the Allardyce Range'. The range is the backbone of South Georgia, running north-west and south-east.

CHAPTER XIII
KING HAAKON BAY

Our next task was to get the stores and ballast out of the boat so that we might secure her for the night, and having taken out the stores and gear and ballast, we tried to pull the empty boat up the beach. By this effort we discovered how weak we were, for our united strength was not enough to get the *James Caird* clear of the water. Time after time we pulled together but without avail, and I saw that we must have food and rest before we beached the boat.

We made fast a line to a heavy boulder, and set a watch to fend the boat off the rocks of the

(Opposite) Hurley was not, of course, one of the boat party, nor did they carry a camera. These pictures of South Georgia were taken later, when Hurley made a special expedition to gather still and ciné material for his publicity film, or possibly on an earlier visits to South Georgia.

Shackleton does not mention here that in mooring the boat he slipped and, as he described it in the full edition, 'nearly closed my part of the story' on the rocks. Fortunately he was only badly bruised.

(Left) Another reconstruction with the foreground probably by Marston and a photograph by Hurley used for background and sky. It is not clear from Hurley's caption if this is based on a photograph he took on Elephant Island.

Another omission in this account is that Shackleton also took the second watch to enable Worsley to recover from the ordeal of his strenuous seamanship in bringing them to safety.

In order to lighten the boat so that the weakened men could lift it, the two carpenters first cut off the superstructure, the deck and foresides.

Huntford says that 'the hospitable promontory which had given them a haven was already called Cape Rosa; and Rosa was what Shackleton's mistress Rosalind Chetwynd called herself'.

It was not really a cave but a recess in the cliff sheltered by icicles in front.

beach. Then I sent Crean round to the left side of the cove, about thirty yards away, where I had noticed a little cave as we were running in. He could not see much in the darkness, but reported that the place certainly promised some shelter. We carried the sleeping-bags round and found a mere hollow in the rock-face, with a shingle floor sloping at a steep angle to the sea. There we prepared a hot meal, and when the food was finished I ordered the men to turn in. I took the first watch beside the *James Caird*, which was still afloat in the tossing water just off the beach.

Fending the boat off the rocks in the darkness was awkward work, and during the next few hours I laboured to keep her clear of the beach. Occasionally I had to rush into the seething water. Then, as a wave receded, I let the boat out on the alpine rope so as to avoid a sudden jerk. The *James Caird* could only be dimly seen in the cove, where the high black cliffs made the darkness almost complete, and the strain upon one's attention was great.

After several hours had passed my desire for sleep became irresistible and I called Crean. While he was taking charge of the boat she got adrift, and we had some anxious moments; but fortunately she went across towards the cave and we secured her unharmed. I arranged for one-hour watches during the remainder of the night, and then took Crean's place among the sleeping men.

The sea went down in the early hours of the morning (May 11th), and, having braced ourselves with another meal, we again started to get the boat ashore. We waited for Byron's "great ninth wave," and when it lifted the *James Caird* in we held her, and, by dint of great exertion, worked her round broadside to the sea. Inch by inch we dragged her up until we reached the fringe of the tussock-grass and knew that the boat was above high-water mark. The completion of this task removed our immediate anxieties, and we were free to examine our surroundings and plan the next move. The day was bright and clear.

King Haakon Bay is an eight-mile sound penetrating the coast of South Georgia in an easterly direction. The northern and southern side of the sound were formed by steep mountain-ranges, their flanks being furrowed by mighty glaciers. It was obvious that our way inland from the cove was barred, and that we must sail to the head of the sound. Several magnificent peaks and crags gazed out across their snowy domains to the sparkling waters of the sound.

Our cove lay a little inside the southern headland of King Haakon Bay. A narrow break in the cliffs, which were about 100 feet high, formed the entrance to the cove. Our cave was a recess in the cliff on the left-hand of the beach. The rocky face of the cliff was undercut at this point, and the shingle thrown up by the waves formed a steep slope, which we reduced to about one in six by scraping the stones away from the inside. Later we strewed the rough floor with the dead, nearly dry leaves of the tussock-grass, and thus formed a slightly soft bed for our sleeping-bags.

Water had trickled down the face of the cliff and formed long icicles, which hung down in front of the cave to the length of about 15 feet. These icicles provided shelter, and when we had spread our sails below them, with the assistance of the oars, we had quarters which, under the circumstances, were reasonably comfortable. The camp at least was dry, and we moved our gear there with confidence. We also built a fireplace and

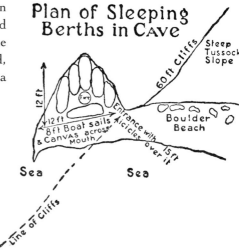

Plan of Sleeping Berths in Cave

The *James Caird* had been damaged during the voyage and again during their first night ashore. They cut off her deck and topsides to make her light enough to handle.

(Left) South Georgia island, surrounded by hundreds of miles of open sea, is home for seabirds, penguins and seals. The Clapmatch or Fur Seal, an original inhabitant according to Hurley, had long been exterminated, but the sea-elephants survived in plentiful numbers in their rookeries where 'they breed, sleep and grunt incessantly'. However in the spot where the party had landed, there was no sign of one.

arranged our sleeping-bags and blankets around it. The cave was about 8 feet deep and 12 feet wide at the entrance.

While the camp was being arranged Crean and I climbed the tussock slope behind the beach, and reached the top of a headland overlooking the sound. There we found the nests of albatrosses, and to our delight the nests contained young birds. The fledglings were fat and lusty, and we had no hesitation in deciding that some of them must die at an early age.

At this stage our most pressing anxiety was about fuel. We had rations for ten more days, and we knew now that we could get birds for food; but if we were to have hot meals fuel must be secured. Our store of petroleum was running low, and it was necessary to keep some of it for the overland journey which lay before us. A sea-elephant or a seal would have provided fuel as well as food, but we could not see a sign of either. During the morning we started a fire in the cave with wood from the top sides of the boat, and, in spite of the dense smoke, we enjoyed the warmth and the splendid stew which Crean, who was cook for the day, provided for us.

Four young albatrosses went into the pot, with a Bovril ration for thickening. The flesh was white and succulent, and the bones, not fully formed, almost melted in our mouths. That was a memorable meal. Afterwards we dried our tobacco in the embers of the fire and smoked contentedly, but an attempt to dry our soaked clothes was not successful. Until we could secure blubber or driftwood we could not afford to have a fire except for cooking.

The final stage of the journey was still before us. I realised that the condition of the party generally, and of McNeish and Vincent in particular, would prevent us putting to sea again except

Worsley wrote, 'The Boss and I discussed making enough money to start another expedition by taking . . . baby albatrosses and selling them to the epicures of Europe and New York at £50 a piece, quite ignoring the fact that there is a regulation forbidding the killing of these chicks.'

Worsley suggested making for Prince Olav Harbour, the closest whaling station, but Shackleton doubted whether it was manned in winter.

Worsley had taken a noon sun sight to prove to himself that they were in fact where he had said they were – King Haakon Bay.

under pressure of absolute necessity. I also doubted if our boat in its weakened condition could weather the island. By sea we were still 150 miles away from Stromness Whaling Station.

The alternative was to attempt the crossing of the island. If we could not get over we must try to get food and fuel enough to keep us through the winter, but such a task was almost hopeless. On Elephant Island were twenty-two men whose plight was worse than ours, and who were waiting the relief which we alone could secure for them. Somehow or other we had got to push on, though several days must elapse before our strength would be sufficiently recovered for us to row or sail the last nine miles up to the head of the bay. In the meantime we could make what preparations were possible.

Shortly before midnight a gale sprang up suddenly from the north-east, with rain and sleet showers, and when daylight came the temperature was the highest we had experienced for several months. The icicles overhanging our cave were melting down in streams, and we had to move smartly when passing in and out unless one wished to be struck by the falling lumps. A fragment weighing 15 or 20 lb. crashed down while we were having breakfast.

Our party spent a quiet day, attending to clothing and gear, checking stores, eating and resting. We had previously discovered that when we were landing from the boat on May 10th we had lost the rudder. The *James Caird* had been bumping heavily astern as we scrambled ashore, and evidently the rudder had then been knocked off. A careful search of the beach and rocks failed to reveal the missing rudder, and this was a serious loss, even if the voyage to the sound could be made in good weather.

In the afternoon Crean and McCarthy brought down six young albatrosses, so we were well supplied with fresh food. The air temperature on that night was probably not lower than 38° or 40° Fahr., and the unaccustomed warmth made us quite uncomfortable in our sleeping quarters. The ice in the cove was rearing and crashing on the beach, but with firm land beneath our feet the noise of it did not trouble us.

The bay was still filled with ice on the morning of Saturday, May 13th, but the tide took it all away in the afternoon. Then a strange thing happened. The rudder, with all the broad Atlantic to sail in, came bobbing back into our cove. Nearer and nearer it came as we waited anxiously on the shore, oars in hand; and at last we were able to seize it. Surely a remarkable salvage!

The day was bright and clear; our clothes were drying and our strength was returning. In the afternoon we began to prepare the *James Caird* for the journey to the head of King Haakon Bay. During the morning of this day (May 13th) Worsley and I tramped across the hills in a north-easterly direction for the purpose of getting a view of the sound, and possibly gathering useful information for the next stage of our journey. It was exhausting work, but after covering about two and a half miles in two hours we were able to look east up the bay. We, however, could not see very much of the country which we should have to cross in order to reach the whaling station on the other side of the island. Some gentoo penguins and a young sea-elephant which we found were killed by Worsley.

When we got back to the cave, tired and hungry, we found a splendid meal of stewed albatross chicken waiting for us. We had carried a quantity of blubber and the sea-elephant's liver in our blouses, and produced our treasures as a surprise for the men. Rough climbing on the way back had nearly persuaded us to throw the stuff away, but we held on and had our reward at the camp.

The long bay had been a magnificent sight, even to eyes which had dwelt long enough on grandeur and were hungry for the familiar things of every-day life. Its green-blue waters were being beaten to fury by the gale. The mountains peered through the mists, and between them huge glaciers poured down from the great ice-slopes which lay behind. We counted twelve glaciers,

According to Worsley, Shackleton, with his usual love of leg-pulling, pretended that Worsley had saved Shackleton's life. 'Our tale of course was not believed.' The story he told was that he had been attacked by a savage sea-elephant, though in fact the two men had succeeded in stunning it with a stone before knifing it.

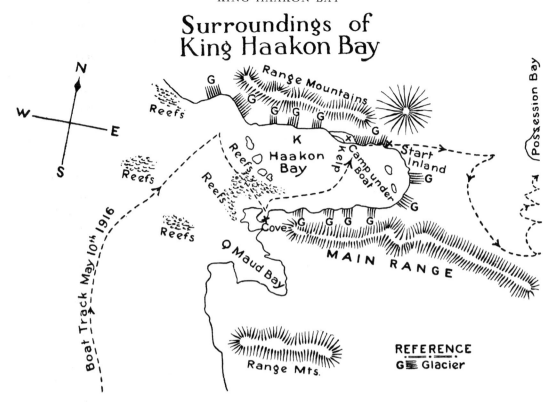

Surroundings of King Haakon Bay

N
W — E
S

Range Mountains

Reefs

G G G G G G G G G

K

Reefs

Haakon Bay

Reefs

Kelp

x Camp under
Boat

x Start
Inland

G

G

Reefs

Cove

G G G G

MAIN RANGE

G

(Possession Bay)

Boat Track May 10ᵗʰ 1916

Q Maud Bay

Range Mts.

REFERENCE
G≡ Glacier

(Left) The coast at King Haa-kon Bay was imperfectly charted, and they had no means of identifying exactly where they were by appear-ance, though Worsley's sight proved their location. This map did not appear in the shorter version of *South.*

and every few minutes we heard the great roar caused by masses of ice calving from the parent streams.

On May 14th we made our preparations for an early start on the following day, should the weather hold fair. All hands were recovering from the chafing caused by our wet clothes during the boat journey. We paid our last visit to the nests of the albatrosses. Each nest consisted of a mound over a foot high of tussock-grass, roots and a little earth. The albatross lays one egg, and very rarely two. We did not enjoy attacking these birds, but our hunger was so great that each time we killed one we felt a little less remorseful.

May 15th was a great day. We made our hoosh at 7.30 a.m., and then loaded up the boat and gave her a flying launch down the steep beach into the surf. A gusty north-westerly wind was blowing, but the *James Caird* headed to the sea as if anxious to face the battle of the waves once more. As we sailed merrily up the bay the sun broke through the mists and made the tossing waters sparkle around us. We were a curious-looking party on that bright morning, but we were feeling happy.

The wind blew fresh and strong, and a small sea broke on the coast as we advanced. We had hoped to find sea-elephants on the upper beaches, and our expectations were realised. As we neared the head of the bay we heard the roar of the bulls, and soon afterwards we saw their great unwieldy forms lying on a shelving beach towards the bay-head.

We rounded a high, glacier-worn bluff on the north side, and soon after noon we ran the boat ashore on a low beach of sand and pebbles, with tussock-grass growing above high-water mark. Hundreds of sea-elephants were lying about, enough to provide food and blubber for years and years. Our landing-place was about a mile and a half west of the north-east corner of the bay. Just

As they set off on 'the 15th, Worsley wrote, 'we felt happy and excited ... the weather was fine, the prospects good ... and ahead of us was action – action always doubly-inspiring after enforced inactivity.'

They had made a run of roughly 30 miles when they came ashore at about midday.

(Above) After leaving the cave, the boat party could see along the shore sea-elephants in such numbers that they would have provided blubber for months ahead.

À la Peggotty. Shackleton called this Peggotty Camp after the Dickens character in *David Copperfield* who lived in a house made out of a boat. Shackleton describes them as 'a curious looking party'. They broke into song and 'but for our Robinson Crusoe appearance we might have been mistaken for a picnic party in a Norwegian fiord'.

east of us was a glacier-snout ending on the beach but giving a passage towards the head of the bay, except at high-water or when a very heavy surf was running.

A cold rain had begun to fall, and as quickly as possible we hauled the *James Caird* up above high-water mark, and turned her over just to the east side of the bluff. The spot was separated from the mountain side by a low bank, rising 20 or 30 feet above sea-level.

We soon converted the boat into a very comfortable cabin *à la* Peggotty, turfing it round with tussocks. One side of the *James Caird* rested on stones so as to afford a low entrance, and when we had finished she looked as if she had grown there. A sea-elephant provided us with fuel and meat, and that evening found a well-fed and fairly contented party in Peggotty Camp.

Our camp, as I have said, lay on the north side of King Haakon Bay near the head. The path towards the whaling stations led round the seaward end of the snouted glacier on the east side of the camp, and up a snow-slope which seemed to lead to a pass in the great Allardyce range, which forms the main backbone of South Georgia. The range dipped opposite the bay into a well-defined pass from east to west.

I planned to climb to the pass, and then be guided by the configuration of the country in the selection of a route eastward to Stromness Bay, where the whaling stations were established in the minor bays, Leith, Husvik and Stromness. On Tuesday, May 16th, the weather was bad, and we stayed under the boat nearly all day. The quarters were cramped but gave full protection from the weather, and we regarded our little cabin with much satisfaction, abundant meals adding to our contentment.

A fresh breeze was blowing on the following morning, with misty squalls, sleet and rain. I took Worsley with me on a pioneer journey to the west for the purpose of examining the country to be crossed at the beginning of the overland journey. We went round the seaward end of the snouted glacier, and tramped about a mile, crossing some big ridges of scree and moraines on our way. We found good going for a sledge as far as the north-east corner of the bay, but a snow squall obscured the view and we did not get much information regarding the conditions farther on. I had satisfied myself, however, that we could reach a good snow-slope leading apparently to the inland ice. Worsley reckoned from the chart that the distance from our camp to Husvik was seventeen geographical miles, but we could not expect to follow a direct line. The carpenter started to make a sledge for the overland journey, but the materials at his disposal were limited in quantity and scarcely suitable in quality.

We overhauled our gear on Thursday, May 18th, and hauled our sledge to the lower edge of the snouted glacier. The sledge proved heavy and cumbrous, and I realised that three men would be unable to manage it amid the snow-plains, glaciers and peaks of the interior. Worsley and Crean

Shackleton knew that, because it was winter, he would have to try a rush across the island travelling day and night, hoping for fine weather and moonlight.

Crean was an experienced snow traveller. He had been one of the last men to see Scott alive four years before.

Because he was still unable to start on the land crossing due to the bad weather, Shackleton was, according to Worsley, 'more discouraged, worried and nearer to depression than I had ever seen him'. He burst out, 'Skipper, I'll never make another expedition!' But as soon as fair weather was in the offing the change in him 'was remarkable. He seemed to tauten and gain strength.'

(*Left*) Hurley took this picture looking west on a calm day. It shows Moraine Fiord, an ice river which has its origins in the high-levels of the interior of South Georgia.

Huntford notes at this point a change in Shackleton's character. On the open-boat journey, he says, Shackleton had crossed an invisible line and left his youth behind and 'passed into the twilight world that divides it from maturity'.

Shackleton scribbled in McNeish's diary, 'I am about to try and reach Husvik . . . for relief for our party. I am leaving you in charge.' Huntford describes this as 'psychologically correct' although the younger McCarthy was the stronger man. Shackleton continued, 'You will remain here until relief arrives.' After itemising the stores he concludes, 'In the event of my non-return you had better after the winter try to sail round to the [north] coast. I trust to have returned in a few days.'

The three men were plodding slowly in an exhausted state over snowfields up to 3,000 feet thick with no knowledge of what lay ahead. McNeish had made them a sledge out of driftwood but Shackleton discarded it at the outset as too heavy for them. Huntford describes their equipment as 'grossly inadequate'. As usual Worsley navigated, using a sketchy German chart of South Georgia (which was like a blueprint) and two compasses. One was a sledging compass which he found 'useless'; he stuck to the other, a small hand compass that had been given to him in Switzerland five years before.

were coming with me, and, after consultation, we decided to leave the sleeping-bags behind and made the journey in very light marching order.

We decided to take three days' provisions for each man in the form of sledging ration and biscuit, the Primus lamp filled with oil, the small cooker, the carpenter's adze (for use as an ice-axe), and the alpine rope, which made a total length of 50 feet when knotted, and would help us to lower ourselves down steep slopes or cross crevassed glaciers.

We had two boxes of matches left, one full and the other partially used. We decided to leave the full box at the camp and to take the second box, which contained forty-eight matches. I was unfortunate as regards foot-gear, as I had given away my heavy boots on the floe, and only had a lighter pair in poor condition. The carpenter helped me by putting several screws into the sole of each boot with the object of providing a grip on the ice. The screws came out of the *James Caird*.

We turned in early that night, but troubled thoughts kept me from sleeping. The task before the overland party would in all probability be heavy, and we were going to leave a weak party behind us in the camp. Vincent was still in the same condition and could not march. McNeish was pretty well broken up. These two men could not manage for themselves, and I had to leave McCarthy to look after them. Should we fail to reach the whaling station McCarthy might have a difficult task.

We had very scanty knowledge of the interior, for no man had ever penetrated from the coast of South Georgia at any point, and I knew that the whalers regarded the country as inaccessible.

At 2 a.m. on the Friday morning we turned out, and an hour later our hoosh was ready. The full moon was shining in a practically cloudless sky, and we made a start as soon as we had eaten our meal. Our first difficulty was to get round the edge of the snouted glacier, which had points like fingers projecting into the sea. The waves were reaching the points of these fingers, and we had to rush from one recess to another when the waters receded. We soon reached the east side of the glacier, and began to ascend a snow-slope, heading due east on the last lap of our long trail.

The snow-surface was disappointing, and as we sank over our ankles at each step our progress was slow. After two hours' steady climbing we were 2,500 feet above sea level, and the bright moonlight showed us that the interior was tremendously broken. High peaks, impassable cliffs, steep snow-slopes, and sharply descending glaciers could be seen in all directions, with stretches of snow-plain overlaying the ice-sheet of the interior. The slope which we were ascending mounted to a ridge, and our course lay direct to the top. The moon, which was a good friend to us, threw a long shadow at one point and told us that the surface was broken in our path. Thus warned we avoided a huge hole capable of swallowing an army. The bay was now about three miles away.

I had hoped to get a view of the country ahead of us from the top of this slope, but as the surface became more level a thick fog drifted down. Under these conditions we roped ourselves together as a precaution against holes, crevasses and precipices, and I broke trail through the soft snow. With almost the full length of rope between myself and the last man we could steer an approximately straight course, for if I veered to the right or left when marching into the blank wall of fog, the last man on the rope could shout a direction. So, like a ship with its "port," "starboard," "steady," we tramped through the fog for the next two hours.

Then, as daylight came, the fog partially lifted, and, from a height of about 3,000 feet, we looked down on what seemed to be a huge frozen lake, with its farther shores still obscured by fog. We halted there to eat a bit of biscuit, and to discuss whether we would go down and cross the flat surface of the lake or keep on the ridge we had already reached. I decided to go down, as the lake lay on our course. After an hour's fairly easy travel through the snow we began to meet crevasses, which showed that we were on a glacier. Later on the fog lifted completely and then we saw that

140

(Above) Another of Hurley's pictures of South Georgia, this one of the Neumayer Glacier.

our lake stretched to the horizon, and suddenly we realised that we were looking down upon the open sea on the east coast of the island.

Evidently we were at the top of Possession Bay, and the island at that point could not be more than five miles across from the head of King Haakon Bay. Our rough chart was inaccurate, and there was nothing for it but to start up the glacier again. That was about seven o'clock, and in two hours we had more than recovered our lost ground.

We regained the ridge and then struck south-east, for the chart showed that two more bays indented the coast before Stromness. It was comforting to know that we should have the eastern water in sight during our journey, although we could see that there was no way around the shoreline owing to steep cliffs and glaciers.

Men lived in houses lit by electric light on the east coast. News of the outside world awaited us there, and, above all, the east coast meant for us the means of rescuing the twenty-two men left on Elephant Island.

This was about 8 a.m. on Saturday 10 May. Actually, the chart was not inaccurate, and Huntford ascribes their error to 'their almost hallucinatory state of mental exhaustion. They had broken the cardinal rule of travel in unknown territory by deserting high ground before being sure of their surroundings.'

CHAPTER XIV

ACROSS SOUTH GEORGIA

THE sun rose with every appearance of a fine day; we were travelling over a gently rising plateau, and at the end of an hour we found ourselves becoming uncomfortably hot. After passing an area of crevasses we paused for our first meal. We dug a hole in the snow about 3 feet deep and put the Primus into it. The hot hoosh was soon eaten, and we plodded on towards a sharp ridge between two of the peaks which lay ahead of us. By 11 a.m. we were almost at the crest.

The slope became precipitous, and we had to cut steps as we advanced. For this purpose the

(Opposite) The landscape cannot have been photographed by Hurley during Shackleton's crossing, but it typifies the lonely wastes of South Georgia with the danger from the crevass. Shackleton's party had no snowshoes or skis and abandoned their sledge as it was too heavy.

Both Shackleton and Crean had plenty of experience of travel across this kind of terrain but Worsley was probably the most experienced, having climbed in the Alps.

(Left) Hurley commented on this picture that it illustrates South Georgia's magnificent 'Alpine' scenery, which 'is subject to sudden furious changes of climate'.

Worsley described how 'every step we took we sank half-way to our knees ... At each quarter of an hour, when we halted for a minute, we threw ourselves spread-eagled on our backs ... drawing in great draughts of air.'

Shackleton insisted on leading as they cut their way down. Then, when he decided to slide, he told Worsley, 'It's a devil of a risk but we've got to take it.' Each man made himself a sort of sledge out of his portion of rope, but nevertheless their trousers were badly torn. They glissaded for about three minutes and Worsley said, 'I was actually enjoying it ... I yelled with excitement.' They had descended 1500 feet at one go.

According to Worsley, this chasm was still bigger, large enough to hold two battleships.

adze proved an excellent instrument. At last I stood upon the razor-back, while the other men held the rope and waited for news. The outlook was disappointing. I looked down a sheer precipice to a chaos of crumpled ice 1,500 feet below. There was no way down for us. The country to the east was a great snow upland, sloping upwards for seven or eight miles to a height of over 4,000 feet. To the north it fell away steeply in glaciers into the bays, and to the south it was broken by huge outfalls from the inland ice-sheet. Our path lay between the glaciers and the outfalls, but first we had to descend from the ridge on which we were standing.

Cutting steps with the adze we moved in a lateral direction round the base of a dolomite, but the same precipice confronted us. Away to the north-east there appeared to be a snow-slope which might give a path to the lower country, and so we retraced our steps down the long slope which had taken us three hours to climb. In an hour we were at the bottom, but we were beginning to feel the strain of unaccustomed marching.

Skirting the base of the mountain above us, we came to a gigantic gully, a mile and a half long and 1,000 feet deep. This gully was semi-circular in form, and ended in a gentle incline. We passed through it, and at the far end we had another meal and short rest. This was at 12.30 p.m. Refreshed by our steaming Bovril ration we started once more for the crest, and after another weary climb we reached the top. The same precipice lay below, and my eyes searched vainly for a way down. The snow, loosened by the hot sun, was now in a treacherous condition, and, looking back, we could see that a fog was rolling up behind us and meeting in the valleys another fog which was coming up from the east. This was a plain warning that we must get down to lower levels before we were enveloped.

The ridge was studded with peaks, which prevented us from getting a clear view either to the right or left, and I had to decide that our course lay back the way which we had come. It was of the utmost importance for us to get down into the next valley before dark. We were up 4,500 feet and the night temperature at the elevation would be very low. The afternoon was wearing on, and the fog was rolling up ominously from the west. We had neither tent nor sleeping-bags, and our clothes were terribly weather-worn.

In the distance, down the valley below us, we could see tussock-grass close to the shore, and if we could get down we might possibly dig out a hole in one of the lower snow-banks, line it with dry grass, and make ourselves fairly comfortable for the night. Back we went, and presently reached the top of another ridge in the fading light. After a glance over the top I turned to the anxious faces of the men behind me and said, "Come on, boys." Within a minute they stood beside me on the ice-ridge, the surface of which fell away at a sharp incline before us but merged into a snow-slope.

We could not see the bottom, and the possibility of the slope ending in a sheer fall occurred to us, but the fog which was creeping up behind us allowed no time for hesitation. At first we descended slowly, cutting steps in the hard snow, then the surface became softer, indicating that the gradient was less severe. There could be no turning back now, so we unroped and slid in the fashion of youthful days. When we stopped on a snow-bank at the foot of the slope we found that we had descended at least 900 feet in two or three minutes. We looked back and saw the grey fingers of the fog appearing on the ridge. But we had escaped.

The country to the east was an ascending snow upland dividing the glaciers of the north coast from the outfalls of the south. From the top we had seen that our course lay between two huge masses of crevasses, and we thought that the road ahead was clear. This belief and the increasing cold made us abandon the idea of camping. At 6 p.m. we had another meal, and then we started up the long, gentle ascent. Night was upon us, and for an hour we plodded on in almost complete darkness, watching warily for signs of crevasses. But about 8 p.m. the full moon rose ahead of us

They had no mugs, so they shared out the meal by taking it in turns to dip their spoons into the saucepan in which Crean had cooked their meal. They had been on the march for fifteen hours.

(Left) Because Hurley was not in the party but returned a year later to obtain stills and film for the fundraising film, it is possible that on this later occasion he photographed areas that Shackleton and party did not cross.

and made a silver pathway for our feet. Onwards and upwards through soft snow we marched, resting occasionally on hard patches. By midnight we were again at an elevation of 4,000 feet. Still we were following the light, for as the moon swung round towards the north-east our path curved in that direction. The friendly moon seemed to pilot our weary feet. We could have had no better guide.

Midnight found us approaching the edge of a great snow-field, and a gentle slope lured our all-too-willing feet in that direction. At the base of the slope we thought that Stromness Bay lay. After we had descended about 300 feet a thin wind began to attack us. We had been on the march for over twenty hours, only halting for occasional meals. After 1 a.m. we cut a pit in the snow, piled up loose snow around it, and again started the Primus. Worsley and Crean sang their old songs when the Primus was going merrily. Laughter was in our hearts, though not on our parched and cracked lips.

Within half an hour we were away again, still downward to the coast. We now felt almost sure that we were above Stromness Bay, and joyfully pointed out various landmarks revealed by the light of the moon, whose friendly face was by this time cloud-swept. Our high hopes were soon shattered. Crevasses warned us that we were on another glacier, and presently we looked down almost to the seaward edge of the great riven ice-mass. I knew that there was no glacier in Stromness and realised that this must be Fortuna Glacier. The disappointment was severe. Back we turned and tramped up the glacier again, working at a tangent to the south-east. We were very tired.

Their boots were in bad shape. Worsley had a spare pair of 'Shackleton boots', which were really copies of those Amundsen had designed for his South Pole expedition, but Shackleton had given his to one of the men in the boat and was wearing leather ski boots. They should have had snow shoes or skis.

They had turned too soon, and had optimistically (for they had been on the march for 24 hours) identified 'various landmarks' which were not there.

Somehow Shackleton kept up a rhythm during the long march, of short regular rests and hot meals every four hours. Nevertheless they were sinking in strength with every step.

At 5 a.m. we were at the foot of the rocky spurs of the range. The wind blowing down from the heights was chilling us, and we decided to get under the lee of a rock and rest. We put our sticks and the adze on the snow, sat down on them as close to one another as possible, and put our arms round each other. I thought that in this way we might keep warm and have half-an-hour's rest. Within a minute my two companions were fast asleep, and I realised how disastrous it would be if we all slumbered together, for sleep under such conditions merges into death. So after five minutes I awoke them and gave the word for a fresh start. So stiff were we that for the first 300 yards or so we marched with our knees bent.

A jagged line of peaks with a gap like a broken tooth confronted us. This was the ridge which runs in a southerly direction from Fortuna Bay, and our course to Stromness lay across it. A very steep slope led up to the ridge and an icy wind burst through the gap. With anxious hearts as well as with weary bodies we went through the gap at 6 a.m. Had the farther slope proved impassable our situation would have been almost desperate; but the worst was turning to the best for us.

The twisted, wave-like rock formations of Husvik Harbour appeared right ahead of us in the opening of dawn. Without a word we shook hands with one another. To our minds the journey was over, though really twelve miles of difficult country had still to be crossed. A gentle snow-slope descended at our feet towards a valley which separated our ridge from the hills immediately behind Husvik, and as we stood gazing Worsley said solemnly, "Boss, it looks too good to be true!"

This was the first time that they could check their position by sight.

Down we went to be checked presently by water 2,500 feet below. We could see the little wave-ripples on the black beach, penguins strutting, and dark objects like seals lolling on the sand. This was an eastern arm of Fortuna Bay, separated by the ridge from the arm we had seen below us during the night.

The slope which we were traversing seemed to end in a precipice above the beach. But our revived spirits were not to be damped by any difficulties on the last stage of our journey, and cheerfully we camped for breakfast. While breakfast was being prepared, I climbed the ridge above us to secure an extended view of the country below; and at 6.30 a.m. I thought I heard the sound of a steam-whistle. I dared not be certain, but I knew that the men at the whaling stations would be called from their beds about that time.

Descending again to the camp I told the others, and in intense excitement we watched the chronometer for seven o'clock, when the whalers would be summoned to work. Right to the minute the steam-whistle came clearly to us, and never had any one of us heard sweeter music. It was the first sound created by outside human agency which had come to our ears since December, 1914. That whistle told us that men were near, that ships were ready, and that very soon we should be on our way back to Elephant Island to rescue the men waiting there. It was a moment hard to describe. Pain and aches, boat journeys, marches, hunger and fatigue, were forgotten, only the perfect contentment which comes from work accomplished remained.

Worsley commented that in normal times Shackleton would be irritable, 'but never when things were going badly and we were up against it'. They had been travelling for twenty-two hours without sleep and, unknown to Shackleton, they had not been taking enough liquid because there was not enough fuel to melt it. This resulted in dehydration and they suffered from its effects, including hallucinations.

My examination of the country before us had not provided definite information, so I put the situation before Worsley and Crean. Our obvious course lay down a snow-slope in the direction of Husvik. "Boys," I said, "this snow-slope seems to end in a precipice, but perhaps there is no precipice. If we don't go down we shall have to make a detour of at least five miles before we reach level going. What shall it be?" They both replied at once, "Try the slope." So again we started downwards.

We abandoned the Primus lamp, now empty, and carried with us one ration and a biscuit each. Deep snow clogged our feet, but after descending about 500 feet we thought that we saw our way clear ahead. A steep gradient of blue ice was the next obstacle. Worsley and Crean got a firm footing in a hole excavated with the adze, and then lowered me as I cut steps until the full 50 feet of our alpine rope was out. Then I made a hole big enough for the three of us, and the other two men came down the steps. In this laborious fashion we spent two hours descending about 500 feet. Half-way down we had to strike away diagonally to the left, for we noticed that the fragments of ice loosened by the adze were taking a leap into space at the bottom of the slope. At last, and very thankfully, we got off the steep ice at the point where some rocks protruded, and then we could see that there was a perilous precipice directly below the point where we had started to cut the steps.

A slide down a slippery slope, with the adze going ahead, completed this descent, and, incidentally, still further damaged our much-tried trousers. When we arrived at the bottom we were not more than 1,500 feet above the sea. The slope was comparatively easy, and presently we came to patches of tussock-grass, and a few minutes later we reached the sandy beach. At our best speed we went along the beach to another rising ridge of tussock, and here we saw the first evidence of the proximity of man. A recently killed seal was lying there, and presently we saw several other bodies bearing the marks of bullet-wounds. Later I heard that men from Stromness go round by boat to Fortuna Bay to shoot seals.

By noon we were well up the slope on the other side of the bay, and half an hour later we were on a flat plateau, with one more ridge to cross before we descended into Husvik. I was leading when I suddenly found myself up to my knees in water and quickly sinking deeper through the snow-crust. I flung myself down and called to the others to do the same, so that our weight should be distributed on the treacherous surface. We were on top of a small lake, snow covered. After lying still for a few moments we rose and walked delicately, like Agag, for 200 yards, until a rise in the surface showed us that we were clear of the lake.

At 1.30 p.m. we climbed round a final ridge and saw a little steamer, a whaling boat, entering the bay, 2,500 feet below. A few moments later the masts of a sailing ship lying at a wharf came in sight. Minute figures moving to and fro caught our gaze, and then we saw the sheds and factory of Stromness Whaling Station. Once more we paused and shook one another warmly by the hand.

Cautiously we started down the slope which led to warmth and comfort, but the last lap of the journey was extraordinarily difficult. Vainly we sought a safe, or reasonably safe, way down the steep ice-clad mountain side. The sole possible pathway seemed to be a channel cut by water running from the upland. Down through icy water we followed the course of this stream. We were wet to the waist, shivering, cold and tired.

Presently our ears detected an unwelcome sound which might under other conditions have been musical. It was the splashing of a waterfall, and we were at the wrong end. When we reached the top of this fall we peered over cautiously and discovered that there was a drop of 25 or 30 feet, with impassable ice-cliffs on both sides. To go up again was, in our utterly wearied condition, scarcely thinkable. The way down was through the waterfall itself.

With some difficulty we made fast one end of our rope to a boulder, and then Worsley and I lowered Crean, who was the heaviest man. He disappeared altogether in the falling water and came out gasping at the bottom. I went next, sliding down the rope, and Worsley, who was the lightest and nimblest of us, followed. At the bottom of the fall we again stood on dry land.

The rope could not be recovered. We had flung down the adze from the top of the fall, and also the log-book wrapped in one of our blouses. That was all we brought, except our wet clothes, from the Antarctic, which a year and a half before we had entered with well-found ship, full equipment and high hopes. That was all of tangible things; but in memories we were rich. We had pierced the veneer of outside things. We had seen God in His splendours, we had heard the text that Nature renders. We had reached the naked soul of man.

Shivering with cold, yet with hearts light and happy, we set off towards the whaling station,

According to Worsley he personally would have preferred the long route, as the screws on their boots were almost worn through. The two others held Shackleton by rope as he cut the footholds, but it was only an illusion of safety, according to Huntford: a single slip would have meant the death of all three.

Worsley describes how he found himself yelling, 'Yoicks! Tally-Ho!'

This was Worsley's log, which they had carried all the way from Elephant Island.

147

They had been travelling continuously for over thirty-six hours, except for stops for meals.

(Right) The Stromness Whaling Station – presumably another picture by Hurley, taken the following year.

This was the manager, a Norwegian, Mr Anderson. Shackleton had made friends with Sorlle when he passed through South Georgia in 1914. Years later a Mr Mansell, who was in the manager's house at the time, described the scene more fully. He said that everyone at Stronness knew Shackleton well and had been very sorry when they heard he was lost, following the rumours from the *Aurora*. They did not recognise the three bearded strangers who walked in that morning. 'Manager say: "Who the hell are you?" and terrible bearded man in the centre of the three say very quietly: "My name is Shackleton." Me – I turn away and weep. I think the manager weep, too.'

now not more than a mile and a half distant. The difficulties of the journey lay behind us. The thought that there might be women at the station made us painfully conscious of our uncivilised appearance, and we tried to straighten ourselves out a bit. Our beards were long and our hair was matted. We were unwashed, and the garments which we had worn for nearly a year without a change were tattered and stained. Three more unpleasant-looking ruffians could scarcely be imagined. Worsley produced several safety-pins from some corner of his garments, and made some temporary repairs which really emphasised his disrepair.

Down we hurried, and when close to the station we met two small boys ten or twelve years old. I asked them where the manager's house was, and they did not answer. They gave us one most informing look and then they ran from us as fast as their legs would carry them.

We reached the outskirts of the station and passed through the "digesting house," which was dark inside. Emerging at the other end we met an old man who gave us no time to ask any question. He hurried away. This greeting was not friendly. Then we came to the wharf, where the man in charge stuck to his station. I asked him if Mr. Sorlle (the manager) was in the house.

"Yes," he said as he stared at us.

"We would like to see him," said I.

"Who are you?" he asked.

"We have lost our ship and come over the island," I replied.

"You have come over the island?" he said, in a tone of entire disbelief.

Then he went towards the manager's house and we followed him. I learned afterwards that he said to Mr. Sorlle: "There are three funny-looking men outside, who say they have come over the island and they know you. I have left them outside." A very necessary precaution from his point of view.

Mr. Sorlle came out to the door and said, "Well?"

"Don't you know me?" I said.

"I know your voice," he replied doubtfully. "You're the mate of the *Daisy*."

"My name is Shackleton," I said.

Immediately he put out his hand and said, "Come in. Come in."

"Tell me, when was the war over?" I asked.

"The war is not over," he answered. "Millions are being killed. Europe is mad. The world is mad."

Mr. Sorlle's hospitality had no bounds. He would scarcely let us wait to remove our freezing boots before he took us into his house, and gave us seats in a warm and comfortable room. We were not fit to sit in any one's house until we had washed and put on clean clothes, but the kindness of the staion manager was proof even against the unpleasantness of being in a room with us. He gave us coffee and cakes in the Norwegian fashion, and then showed us upstairs to the bathroom, where we shed our rags and scrubbed ourselves luxuriously.

Mr. Sorlle's kindness did not end with his personal care to us. While we were washing he gave orders for one of the whaling vessels to be prepared at once, so that it might leave that night to pick up the other three men on the other side of the island. Soon we were clean again, and then we put on delightful new clothes supplied from the station stores and got rid of our superfluous hair. Then came a splendid meal, while Mr. Sorlle told us the arrangements he had made, and we discussed plans for the rescue of the main party on Elephant Island.

I arranged that Worsley should go with the relief ship to show the exact spot where the carpenter and his two companions were camped, while I began to prepare for the relief of the party on Elephant Island. The whaling vessel that was going round to King Haakon Bay was expected

Shackleton asked Sorlle to take their pictures but, alas, he had no film. Worsley said the 'world thus lost a picture of its three most distinguished men'.

Rough Memory Map of Route across South Georgia.

There was no cablehead or radio on South Georgia at this time so, while Shackleton could not send messages, he had the advantage of freedom of action with no interference from home, a situation he preferred.

back on the Monday morning, and was to call at Grytviken Harbour, the port from which we had sailed in December, 1914, in order that the magistrate resident there might be informed of the fate of the *Endurance*. It was also possible that letters were awaiting us there.

Worsley went aboard the whaler at ten o'clock that night; and on the next day the relief ship entered King Haakon Bay and Worsley reached Peggotty Camp in a boat. The three men were delighted beyond measure to be relieved, but they did not recognise Worsley, who had left them a hairy, dirty ruffian and had returned spruce and shaven.

Within a few minutes the whalers had moved our bits of gear into their boat. They towed off the *James Caird* and, having hoisted her to the deck of their ship, they started on the return voyage. They entered Stromness Bay at dusk on Monday afternoon, and the men of the whaling station mustered on the beach to receive the rescued party, and also to examine the boat which we had navigated across 800 miles of the stormy ocean they knew so well.

When I look back at those days I do not doubt that Providence guided us, not only across those snowfields, but also across the stormy white sea which separated Elephant Island from our landing place on South Georgia. I know that during that long march of thirty-six hours over the unnamed mountains and glaciers of Georgia it often seemed to me that we were four, not three. And Worsley and Crean had the same idea. One feels "the dearth of human words, the roughness of mortal speech," in trying to describe intangible things, but a record of our journeys would be incomplete without reference to a subject very near to our hearts.

This was probably a hallucination due to their common dehydration. Fisher suggests that it may have been some time before Shackleton spoke of this experience of the 'fourth man'. This passage did not appear in the working manuscript prepared by Saunders and Shackleton in Australia in 1917, and perhaps Shackleton wrote it after he received Saunders' first version of the book. It was used by T. S. Eliot as the source for a reference in his poem *The Waste Land*.

CHAPTER XV

THE RESCUE

OUR first night at the whaling station was blissful. Crean and I shared a beautiful bedroom in Mr. Sorlle's house, and we were so comfortable that we could not sleep. Outside a dense snow-storm, which started two hours after our arrival and lasted until the following day, was swirling about the mountain-slopes. It would have gone hard with us had we still been on the mountains, and we were thankful indeed to be in a place of safety. Deep snow lay everywhere on the following morning.

After breakfast Mr. Sorlle took us round to Husvik in a motor launch. Avidly we listened to his account of the war. We were like men arisen from the dead to a world gone mad, and it took our minds some time to accustom themselves to the tales of nations in arms, of deathless courage and unimagined slaughter. The reader may not realise quite how difficult it was for us to envisage nearly two years of the most stupendous war of history. I suppose our experience was unique. No other civilised men could have been as blankly ignorant of world-shaking events as we were when we reached Stromness Whaling Station.

I heard the first rumour of the *Aurora's* misadventures in the Ross Sea from Mr. Sorlle. He had heard that the *Aurora* had broken away from winter quarters in McMurdo Sound and had reached New Zealand after a long drift, and that there was no news of the shore party. His information was indefinite as regards details, and not until I reached the Falkland Islands some time later did I get a definite report about the *Aurora*. This rumour, however, made it more important than ever that the rest of the Weddell Sea party should be quickly relieved, so that I should be free for whatever effort was required on the Ross Sea side.

When we reached Husvik on that Sunday morning we were warmly greeted by the magistrate (Mr. Bernsten), who was an old friend of mine, and by the other members of the little community. Moored in the harbour was one of the largest of the whalers, the *Southern Sky*, owned by an English company, but now laid up for the winter. I had no means of communicating immediately with the owners, but, on my accepting all responsibility, Mr. Bernsten made arrangements for me to take this ship down to Elephant Island. I wrote out an agreement with Lloyd's for the insurance of the ship.

Captain Thom, an old friend of the Expedition, happened to be in Husvik with his ship, the *Orwell*, loading oil for use in British munition works, and he at once volunteered to come with us in any capacity. I asked him to come as captain of the *Southern Sky*. There was no difficulty in getting a crew, for the whalers were eager to assist in the rescue of the men in distress. Indeed they started work at once, and willing hands made light labour. I purchased all the stores and equipment

Shackleton did not know until now what had happened at the Ross Sea party in the *Aurora*, but the outside world had picked up its first wireless message from that beleaguered group as early as 24 March 1916 when, released from the ice, it was drifting towards New Zealand (see chapter XVII). The first tentative steps towards a relief party were taken by Lady Shackleton at this time. As for Shackleton's own party, the outside world had no information until the end of May although they reached the whaling station ten days earlier.

The *Southern Sky* was owned by an English company but there was no means of contacting them quickly because there was no telegraph on South Georgia.

Shackleton had met the Norwegian captain Ingvar Thom on his visit to South Georgia in 1914.

151

This was the first of several attempts Shackleton made to rescue the Elephant Island group and it appears that his impatience to get to his men overcame his capacity for careful thought and planning.

When Worsley returned with the three men, they described how, despite the fact that they had lived cheek-by-jowl with Worsley for two years, they did not recognise him after the bath, shave and change of clothing he had been able to have at the whaling station. Shackleton now arranged passages back to England for McNeish and Vincent (without regret, according to Huntford). McCarthy was also sent home, but with Shackleton's and Worsley's warm expressions of gratitude.

It was 23 May, almost exactly a month since leaving Elephant Island in the *James Caird* and only three days since his arrival, exhausted, at the station. Crean and Worsley were with him.

Shackleton made for Port Stanley rather than returning to South Georgia because it was closer to Elephant Island and there were cable facilities there. He had an exclusive contract with the *Daily Chronicle* and one of his first acts was to send them a 2,000-word telegram. He remained incognito until the following day so that the *Daily Chronicle* should have the story first. When he revealed his identity, his reception was far-removed from the enthusiastic welcome he had received at the whaling station. Captain Thom and the *Southern Sky* returned alone to South Georgia and Shackleton set about trying to find a suitable ship.

required, including special comforts for the men we hoped to rescue, from the station stores. And on Tuesday morning the *Southern Sky* was ready to sail.

It is my pleasure as well as duty here to thank the Norwegian whalers of South Georgia for their sympathy and help in our need. Among memories of kindness received in many lands sundered by the seas, the recollection of the hospitality and help given to me in South Georgia ranks high. There is a brotherhood of the sea. The men who go down to the sea in ships, serving and suffering, bring into their own horizons the perils of their brother sailormen.

McCarthy, McNeish and Vincent were landed on the Monday afternoon, and quickly began to show signs of increasing strength under a *régime* of warm quarters and abundant food. McCarthy looked woefully thin after he had emerged from a bath. He was over fifty years of age and the strain had told upon him more than upon the rest of us. The rescue came just in time for him.

At 9 a.m. on Tuesday morning the *Southern Sky* steamed out of the bay, while the whistles of the whaling station sounded a friendly farewell. On the Monday night we had foregathered aboard Captain Thom's ship with several whaling captains who were bringing up their sons to their own profession. They were "old stagers," with lined and seamed faces, and they were even more interested in the story of our voyage from Elephant Island than the younger generation was. It was pleasant to tell the tale to men who knew these sullen and treacherous southern seas, and they congratulated us on having accomplished a remarkable boat journey.

The early part of the voyage down to Elephant Island was uneventful. We made good progress, but the temperature fell very low, and the signs made me anxious about the chances of encountering ice. On the third night out the sea seemed to grow silent. The sea was freezing around us, and presently lumps of old pack began to appear among the new ice.

I realised that an advance through pack-ice was out of the question. The *Southern Sky* was a steel-built steamer and could not endure the blows of masses of ice. So I took the ship north, and at daylight on Friday we were clear of the pack-ice. The morning of the 28th was dull and overcast, with little wind. Again the ship's head was turned to the south-west, but at 3 p.m. a definite line of pack showed up on the horizon. We were about seventy miles from Elephant Island, and we could not take the steamer through the ice which barred the way. Northwest we turned again. We were directly north of the island on the following day, and I made another move south. Heavy pack formed an impenetrable barrier.

To admit failure at this stage was hard, but facts had to be faced. The *Southern Sky* could not enter ice of even moderate thickness, the season was late, and we could not be sure that the ice would open for many months. The *Southern Sky* could only carry coal for ten days, and we had been out six days. We were 500 miles from the Falkland Islands and about 600 miles from South Georgia. So I determined that I would go to the Falklands, get a more suitable vessel either locally or from England, and make a second attempt to reach Elephant Island from that point.

After encountering very bad weather we arrived at Port Stanley, where the cable provided a link with the outer world, in the afternoon of May 31st. The harbour-master came out to meet us, and I went ashore to meet the Governor, Mr. Douglas Young, who offered me his assistance at once. He telephoned to Mr. Harding, the manager of the Falkland Island Station, and to my keen regret I learned that no ship of the required type was available at the islands.

That evening I cabled to His Majesty the King the first account of the loss of the *Endurance* and the subsequent adventures of the Expedition. The next day I received the following message from the King:

"Rejoice to hear of your safe arrival in the Falkland Islands and trust your comrades on Elephant Island may soon be rescued. GEORGE R. I."

I will not attempt to describe in detail the events which followed our arrival at the Falkland Islands. Winter was advancing, and I was bent upon the rescue of my comrades at the earliest possible moment, for I was fully conscious that the lives of some of them might be the price of unnecessary delay.

A proposal to send a relief ship from England had been made, but she could not reach us for several weeks. In the meantime by wireless and cable I asked the Governments of the South American Republics if they had any suitable ship which I could use for rescue. I wanted a wooden ship capable of pushing into loose ice, with fair speed and a reasonable coal capacity.

Messages of congratulations and goodwill were reaching me from all parts of the world, and the kindness of hundreds of friends was a very real comfort in a time of anxiety and stress.

The British Admiralty informed me that no suitable vessel was available in England, and that no relief could be expected before October. I replied that October would be too late. Then the British Minister in Montevideo telegraphed me regarding a trawler named *Instituo de Pesca* No. 1, belonging to the Uruguayan Government. She was a stout little vessel, and the Government had generously offered to equip her fully, and send her across to the Falkland Islands for me to take down to Elephant Island. Gladly I accepted this offer, and the trawler was in Port Stanley on June 10th. We started south at once.

The weather was bad but the trawler made good progress, and in the clear dawn of the third day we sighted the peaks of Elephant Island. Hope ran high; but our ancient enemy the pack was waiting for us, and within twenty miles of the island the trawler was stopped by an impenetrable barrier of ice. All our efforts to dodge or push through it were in vain. The island lay on our starboard quarter, but there was no possibility of approaching it.

The Uruguayan engineer reported to me that he had three days' coal left, and I had to give the order to turn back. A screen of fog hid the lower slopes of the island, and the men watching from the camp on the beach could not have seen the ship. When we reached Port Stanley with bunkers nearly empty and engines almost broken down, H.M.S. *Glasgow* was in the port and the British sailors welcomed us heartily as we steamed in.

The Uruguayan Government offered to send the trawler to Punta Arenas and have her dry-docked there and made ready for another effort. But time was precious, and these preparations would have taken too long. I thanked the Government then for its most generous offer, and want to say now that the kindness of the Uruguayans at this time earned my warmest gratitude. I ought also to mention the assistance given by Lieut. Ryan, a Naval Reserve officer, who navigated the ship to the Falklands, and came south on the attempt at relief. The *Instituto de Pesca* went off to Montevideo, and I looked round for another ship.

Opportunely a British mail-boat, the *Orita*, called at Port Stanley, and I boarded her with Worsley and Crean and crossed to Punta Arenas in the Magellan Straits. There the British Association of Magellanes took us to their hearts. Mr. Allan McDonald was especially prominent in his untiring efforts to assist in the rescue. He worked day and night, and it was mainly due to him that within three days they had raised a sum of £1,500 among themselves, chartered the schooner *Emma* and equipped her for our use. She was a forty-year-old oak schooner, strong and seaworthy, with an auxiliary oil engine.

Out of the complement of ten men all told who were manning the ship, there were eight different nationalities; but they were all good fellows and understood perfectly what was wanted. The Chilian Government lent us a small steamer, the *Yelcho*, to tow us part of the way; but she could not touch ice, being built of steel. However, on July 12th we passed her our tow-rope and proceeded on our way. In bad weather we anchored next day, but, although the wind increased to a

---

Shackleton does not seem to have cabled his wife Emily, who, according to Huntford, learnt the news from the *Daily Chronicle*. Huntford suggests that 'perhaps Emily and her husband, behind the facade, both understood that their marriage could not be revived'.

It was not until 3 June that Shackleton wrote to her saying 'I . . . can tell you that when I get back money will be all right . . . I have had a year and a half of hell, and am older of course, but no lives have been lost, though we have been through what no other Polar expedition has done. It was nature against us all the time. The cable [to the *Daily Chronicle*] but barely describes a little of what it was.'

The captain of *HMS Glasgow* asked the Admiralty to let him take Shackleton on a rescue attempt but their reply was, 'Your telegram not approved.' The feeling in the Admiralty must have been that there was a war on and Shackleton's problems were both self-inflicted and a sideshow.

The Admiralty was now co-ordinating rescue efforts in England. It had obtained Scott's old *Discovery* from the Hudson's Bay Company, but it would not be ready to sail for three months at least. The Foreign Office was therefore asked to request help from the governments of Chile, Argentine and Uruguay.

Punta Arenas was a large, prosperous British colony and the inhabitants were more receptive to Shackleton than those in Port Stanley in the Falklands. They included a number of wealthy sheep farmers, members of the British Club there.

gale, I could delay no longer, so we hove up anchor in the early morning of the 14th. The strain on the tow-rope was too great. With the crack of a gun it broke.

Next day the gale continued, and the *Yelcho*, on my orders, returned to harbour. After three days of continuous bad weather we were left alone once more to try and rescue our comrades, about whom by this time I had very grave fears. At dawn of Friday, July 21st, we were within 100 miles of the island, and we encountered the ice in the half-light. I waited for the full day and then tried to push through. The schooner was tossing like a cork in the swell, and after a few bumps I saw that she was actually lighter than the fragments of ice around her. Progress under such conditions was out of the question.

I worked the schooner out of the pack and stood to the east. We hove to for the night, which was now sixteen hours long. The winter was well advanced and the weather conditions were thoroughly bad. The ice to the southward was moving rapidly north. The motor engine had broken down and we were entirely dependent on the sails. We managed to make a little southing during the next day, but that night we lay off the ice in a gale, hove to, and morning found the schooner iced up. Some members of the scratch crew were played out by the cold and by the violent tossing.

I took the schooner south at every chance, but always the line of ice blocked the way. The engineer tried hard but could not keep the engines running, and the persistent south winds were dead ahead. It was hard to turn back a third time, but it had to be done. So we set a northerly course, and after a tempestuous passage once more reached Port Stanley. This was the third reverse, but I did not abandon my belief that the ice would not remain fast round Elephant Island during the winter, whatever the arm-chair experts at home might say.

We reached Port Stanley on August 8th, and I learned that the ship *Discovery* was to leave England at once and would reach the Falkland Islands about the middle of September. My good friend the Governor said that I could settle down at Port Stanley, and take things easily for a few weeks. But I could not be content to wait for six or seven weeks, knowing that 600 miles away my comrades were in desperate need. So I asked the Chilian Government to send the *Yelcho* to take the schooner across to Punta Arenas, and they consented promptly, as they had to all my requests. So in a north-west gale we went across, narrowly escaping disaster on the way, and reached Punta Arenas on August 14th.

No suitable ship could be obtained, but the weather was improving, and I begged the Chilian Government to let me have the *Yelcho* for a last attempt to reach the island. A small steel-built steamer, she was quite unsuitable for work in the pack, but I promised not to touch the ice. The Government gave me another chance, and on August 25th I started south for the fourth attempt at relief.

This time Providence favoured us. I found as we neared Elephant Island that the ice was open. A southerly gale had sent it northward temporarily, and the *Yelcho* had her chance to slip through. We approached the island in a thick fog, but I did not dare to wait for this to clear. At 10 a.m. on August 30th we passed some stranded bergs, then we saw the sea breaking on a reef, and I knew that we were just outside the island.

It was an anxious moment, for we had still to locate the camp and the pack could not be trusted to allow time for a prolonged search; but presently the fog lifted and revealed the cliffs and glaciers of Elephant Island. I proceeded to the east, and at 11.40 a.m. Worsley's keen eyes detected the camp, almost invisible under its covering of snow. The men ashore saw us at the same time, and we saw tiny black figures hurry to the beach and wave signals to us. We were about a mile and a half away from the camp.

I turned the *Yelcho* in, and within half an hour reached the beach with Crean and some of the Chilian sailors. I saw a little figure on a surf-beaten rock and recognised Wild. As I came nearer I called out, "Are you all well?" and he answered, "We are all well, Boss," and then I heard three cheers.

As I drew close to the rock I flung packets of cigarettes ashore; they fell on them like hungry tigers, for well I knew that for months tobacco had been dreamed and talked about. Some of the hands were in a rather bad way, but Wild had kept hope alive in their hearts. There was no time then to exchange news or congratulations. I did not even go up the beach to see the camp, which Wild assured me had been much improved.

A heavy sea was running, and a change of wind might bring the ice back at any time. I hurried the party aboard with all possible speed, taking also the records of the Expedition and the essential portions of equipment. Everybody was aboard within an hour, and we steamed north at the *Yelcho's* best speed. The ice was still open, and nothing worse than an expanse of stormy ocean separated us from the South American coast.

(Above) This picture appears in more than one form with the rescue boat in different positions. It is usually captioned 'Saved!' Another caption is 'All safe!' All Well!', the news which Shackleton was desperate to hear on 30 August 1916.

The rescued men were unanimous in their praise of the 'Good Old Boss'. Hurley wrote of Shackleton's 'supreme satisfaction in rescuing us by his individual efforts'.

Shackleton was sufficient of a showman to stop at Rio Seco to telephone ahead and then wait a few hours so that a reception could be organised at Punta Arenas. This included a brass-band march for the crew through the town. James described how 'even the Germans and Austrians put their flags out'.

Shackleton went on a mailboat about to sail and wrote hurriedly to Emily, 'I have done it. Damn the Admiralty: I wonder who is responsible for their attitude to me? Not a life lost and we have been through hell. Soon I will be home and then I will rest.' Shackleton ignored any communication with the Falklands, which found out about the rescue second-hand.

In Valparaiso, Shackleton was the guest of the Spanish Consul in Chile. In the Consul's wife's visitor's book he wrote the following lines by Sir John Lucas:
We were the fools who could not rest
In the dull earth we left behind,
And burned with passion for the south,
And drank strange frenzy from its wind.
The world where wise men sit at ease
Fades from our unregretful eyes,
And thus across uncharted seas,
We stagger on our enterprise.

During the run up to Punta Arenas I heard Wild's story, and blessed again the cheerfulness and resource which had served the party so well during four and a half months of privation. The twenty-two men were just at the end of their resources; but I will tell their tale in the succeeding chapter. Let me only say here that Wild had fought a magnificent fight against the demons of despondency and despair, which could but attack a party with only a precarious foothold between the grim ice-fields and the treacherous, ice-strewn sea, and with only the scantiest stock of food.

The *Yelcho* had arrived at the right moment. Two days earlier she could not have reached the island, and a few hours later the pack might have been again impenetrable. We encountered bad weather on the way back to Punta Arenas, and the little ship laboured heavily; but she had light hearts aboard. We entered the Straits of Magellan on September 3rd and reached Rio Secco at 8 a.m. Two or three hours later we were at Punta Arenas, where we were given a welcome which we shall never forget. The Chilian people were no less enthusiastic than the British residents. The whole populace appeared to be in the streets. It was a great reception, and after the long, anxious months of strain we were in a mood to enjoy it.

During the next few weeks I received congratulations and messages of friendship from all over the world, and my heart went out to the good people who had remembered us in the press of terrible events on the battlefields. The Chilian Government placed the *Yelcho* at my disposal to take the men up to Valparaiso and Santiago.

We reached Valparaiso on September 27th. Everything that could swim in the way of a boat was out to meet us, and at least 30,000 people thronged the streets. On the following evening I lectured in Santiago for the British Red Cross and a Chilian Naval charity. The Chilia, flag and the Union Jack were draped together. I saw the President and thanked him for the help he had given to a British Expedition. His Government had spent £4,000 on coal alone. In reply he recalled the part taken by British sailors in the making of the Chilian Navy.

The Chilian Railway department provided a special train to take us across the Andes, and I proceeded to Montevideo in order personally to thank the President and Government of Uruguay for their generous help. We were entertained royally at various spots *en route*. And then, after a brief call at Buenos Ayres, we again crossed the Andes.

By this time I had made arrangements for the men and the staff to go to England, all hands being keen to take their places in the Empire's fighting forces. My own immediate task was the relief of the marooned Ross Sea party, and I decided to take Worsley with me. We hurried northwards *viâ* Panama, and at San Francisco caught a steamer which would get us to New Zealand at the end of November. I had been informed that the New Zealand Government was arranging for the relief of the Ross Sea party, but my information was incomplete, and I was very anxious to be on the spot as quickly as possible.

CHAPTER XVI

ELEPHANT ISLAND

I HAVE obtained an account of the experiences of the twenty-two men left behind on Elephant Island from their various diaries, supplemented by details obtained in conversation on the voyage back to civilisation.

The first consideration, even more important than that of food, was to provide shelter, for several of the men were suffering severely from the ordeals through which they had passed. Rickenson, who bore up gamely to the last, collapsed from heart failure; Blackborrow and Hudson could not move. All were frost-bitten in varying degrees.

The blizzard which sprang up on the day we landed at Cape Wild lasted for a fortnight; the

At first, these three preferred to be on their own in their tent but it was blown to shreds and they moved in with the others.

(Left) Hurley's picture of the Elephant Island party digging a shelter.

157

(Above) The artist Marston was one of those who suggested that by turning the two boats upside down and sealing them with canvas and snow they could make a useful shelter.

This, again, is not an extract from the diary but a shortened form of its text. For example, the following phrase is excluded here, 'Our weakness is best compared with that which one experiences on getting up from a long illness.'

tents, with the exception of the square tent occupied by Hurley, James and Hudson, were torn to ribbons. Sleeping bags and clothes were wringing wet, and the physical discomforts tended to produce acute mental depression. The two remaining boats had been turned upside down with one gunwale resting on the snow, and the other raised about two feet on rocks and cases, and under these the sailors, the invalids and some of the scientists at least found head-cover.

Shelter and warmth to dry their clothes was imperative, so Wild, who was left in command and in whom I had absolute confidence, hastened the excavation of the ice-cave in the slope, which had been started before I had left.

The high temperature, however, caused a continuous stream of water to drip from the roof and sides of the ice-cave, so Wild directed that big flat stones should be collected, and with these, two substantial walls, 4 feet high and 19 feet apart, were made.

"We are all ridiculously weak. . . . stones that we could easily have lifted at other times we found quite beyond our capacity, and it needed two or three of us to carry some that would otherwise have been one man's load.

"The site chosen for the hut was where the stove had been erected on the night of our arrival. It lay between two large boulders, which at least provide valuable protection from the wind, and further protection was provided to the north by Penguin Hill. As soon as the walls were completed and squared off, the two boats were laid upside down on them side by side. Their exact adjustment took some time, but was of paramount importance if our structure was to be the permanent affair

we hoped it would be. Once in place they were securely chocked up and lashed down to the rocks. The few pieces of wood that we had were laid across from keel to keel, and over this the material of one of the torn tents was spread and secured with guys to the rocks. The walls were ingeniously contrived and fixed up by Marston. . . .

"At last all was completed and we were invited to bring in our sodden bags, which had been lying out in the drizzling rain for hours; for the tents and boats that had previously sheltered them had all been requisitioned to form our new residence. We took our places under Wild's direction. There was no squabbling for best places, but it was noticeable that there was rather a rush for the billets up on the thwarts of the boat. Rickenson, who was still very weak and ill, but very cheery, obtained a place in the boat directly above the stove."

The floor was at first covered with snow and ice, frozen in among the pebbles, but this was cleared out, and the remainder of the tents spread out over the stones. Within the shelter of these cramped, but comparatively palatial, quarters, cheerfulness once more reigned among the party. Subsequently, when fine drift-snow forced its way through the crevices between the stones forming the end walls, Jaeger sleeping-bags and coats were spread over the outside of these walls, packed over with snow and securely frozen up, and they effectively kept out the drift.

At first all the cooking was done outside under the lee of some rocks, further protection being provided by a wall of provision cases. There were two blubber-stoves made from old oil-drums, and one day, when the blizzard was unusually severe, an attempt was made to cook inside the hut.

(Above) Marston probably painted this cut-out of their refuge on top of one of Hurley's photographs of the area. Hurley merely describes it as 'an artist's impression', so it may have been another hand. He says that it was lit by two lamps of about half candle power, burning oil rendered down from seal blubber. The lamps themselves were made from old sardine tins.

Marston cut a pair of sea boots into narrow strips with which he bound the tent cloth, as if using a leather binding strip on upholstered chairs, so that it hung down in a valance. The bottom was kept taut by spars and oars. Later a sack-mouth door was made from one of the tents – a tube of canvas sewn on to the tent cloth – through which the men crawled in and out on all fours.

159

The two boats were put side by side to make one 'roof'. The seamen claimed the 'upstairs' thwarts as their own and Hurley came in from his tent and moved in here. Four men were upstairs in the *Dudley Docker*, five in the *Stancomb Wills* and the rest on the floors. Those above showered reindeer hairs on those below with every movement of their moulting bags.

(Below) The party which remained marooned on Elephant Island while Shackleton went off for help. Wordie calculated that their average age was 35 years. He also described how they became increasingly obsessed with food – or the lack of it. At one stage food was stolen from the galley and one afternoon 'three biscuits were stolen from a case inside the boats.'

Pungent blubber-smoke, however, was the result of this first attempt, but a chimney, made by Kerr out of the tin lining of one of the biscuit cases, was soon fitted, and the smoke nuisance inside the hut was a thing of the past.

The cook and his assistant, which latter job was taken by each man in turn, were called about 7 a.m., and breakfast was generally ready about 10 a.m. Provision cases were then arranged in a wide circle round the stove, and those fortunate enough to be next it could dry their gear. So that all should benefit equally each man occupied his place at meal times for one day only, and moved up one on the succeeding day.

The great trouble in the hut was the absence of light. The canvas walls were covered with blubber-soot, and, with the snow-drifts accumulating round the hut, its inhabitants lived in a state of perpetual night. Wild was the first to overcome this difficulty by sewing the glass lid of a chronometer box into the canvas wall. Later on three other windows were added, and this enabled those men who were near enough to them to read and sew, which considerably relieved the monotony of the situation.

"Our reading material at this time consisted of two books of poetry, one book of *Nordenskjöld's Expedition*, one or two volumes of the *Encyclopaedia Britannica*, and a penny cookery book, owned by Marston. Our clothes. . . . had to be continually patched to keep them together at all."

The floor of the hut, having been raised by the addition of loads of clean pebbles, kept fairly dry during the cold weather, but when the temperature rose to just above freezing point the hut

became the drainage-pool of all the surrounding hills. Wild noticed it first, when he found one morning that his sleeping-bag was practically afloat. Other men examined theirs with a like result, so bailing operations began forthwith. Hundreds of gallons of water had to be bailed out from the large hole which was dug in the floor. Eventually this watery problem was completely solved by removing a portion of one wall and digging a long channel nearly down to the sea.

A huge glacier across the bay behind the hut nearly put an end to the party. Enormous blocks of ice would break off and fall into the sea, the disturbance giving rise to great waves. One day Marston was outside the hut when a noise "like an artillery barrage" startled him. Looking up, he saw a tremendous wave, over 30 feet high, advancing rapidly across the bay, and threatening to sweep both the hut and its inhabitants into the sea. Fortunately, however, the loose ice which filled the bay damped the wave down so much that, though it flowed right under the hut, nothing was carried away. But it was a narrow escape, as nothing could have saved the men had they been washed into the sea.

Although they themselves gradually became accustomed to the darkness and dirt, extracts from their diaries show that they could still realise the conditions under which they were living.

"The hut grows more grimy every day. Everything is sooty black. . . . It is at least comforting to feel that we can become no filthier. Our shingle floor will scarcely bear examination by strong light without causing even us to shudder and express our disapprobation at its state. . . . Such is our Home, Sweet Home."

"All joints are aching through being compelled to lie on the hard, rubbly floor which forms our bedsteads."

"Thank heaven man is an adaptable brute! If we dwell sufficiently long in this hut we are likely to alter our method of walking, for our ceiling, which is but 4 feet 6 inches high at its highest part, compels us to walk bent double or on all fours."

"We are as regardless of our grime and dirt as is the Esquimau. We have been unable to wash since we left the ship, nearly ten months ago. For one thing we have no soap or towels; and, again, had we possessed these articles, our supply of fuel would only permit us to melt enough ice for drinking purposes. Had one washed, half a dozen others would have to go without a drink all day. One cannot suck ice to relieve the thirst, as at these low temperatures it cracks the lips and blisters the tongue. Still, we are all very cheerful."

During the whole of their stay on Elephant Island the weather was described by Wild as "simply appalling." On most days the air was full of snow-drift blown from the adjacent heights. On April 25th, the day after I left for South Georgia, the island was beset by heavy pack-ice, with snow and a wet mist. April ended with a terrific wind-storm which nearly destroyed the hut. This lasted well into May, and a typical May day is thus described: "A day of terrific winds, threatening to dislodge our shelter. The wind is a succession of hurricane gusts that sweep down the glacier. Each gust heralds its approach by a low rumbling which increases to a thunderous roar. Snow, stones and gravel are flying about, and any gear left unweighted by very heavy stones is carried away to sea."

Heavy bales of sennegrass and boxes of cooking-gear were lifted bodily in the air and carried away out of sight. These gusts often came without any warning, and on one occasion Hussey, who was outside digging up the day's meat, which had frozen to the ground, was very nearly blown into the sea. On rare occasions there were fine, calm, clear days, when the glow of the dying sun on the mountains and glaciers was incomparably beautiful.

About the middle of May a terrific blizzard sprang up, and Wild entertained grave fears for their hut. In this blizzard huge ice-sheets, as big as window-panes and about a quarter of an inch

The men were bailing out 100-150 gallons a day and one wrote in his diary, 'This is what nice, mild high temperatures mean to us: no wonder we prefer the cold.'

Marston occupied a hammock slung across the entrance. 'As he is large and the entrance is very small, he invariably gets bumped by those passing in and out. His vocabulary at such times is interesting.'

Shackleton remarks of his crew that on these fine days the beauty of the glaciers 'filled even the most materialistic of them with wonder and admiration'.

161

(Above) Clearing up after one of the frequent storms or, as one caption describes them, skinning seals to obtain blubber.

In the original version of *South* three pages were inserted here dealing with food. They begin, 'Wild set all hands to collect as many seals and penguins as possible in case their stay was longer than was at first anticipated.' This was not in fact the case, because Wild would not store large quantities of food as it would give the impression that their stay might be a long one. Orde-Lees urged him to stock up, but he refused and as a result there was 'an estrangement . . . which . . . remains unreconciled'. Orde-Lees said he had 'no use' for Wild's optimistic policy and events were to prove in his favour. The seals disappeared and the number of penguins available declined rapidly. Others, including Hurley, were pessimistic about an early rescue.

thick, were hurled about by the wind, making it as dangerous to walk about outside as if one were in an avalanche of splintered glass. Still, these winds from the south and south-west, though invariably accompanied by snow and low temperatures, were welcome, because they drove the pack-ice from the island, and so on each occasion gave rise to hopes of relief. North-east winds, on the other hand, filled the bay with ice, and made it impossible for any ship to approach the island.

Thus the weather continued, alternating between south-west blizzards, when all hands were confined to the hut, and north-east winds which brought cold, damp, misty weather. Towards the end of July and beginning of August there were a few fine, calm days. Occasional glimpses of the sun were seen after the south-west winds had blown all the ice away, and the party, their spirits raised by Wild's unfailing optimism, again began to look eagerly for the rescue ship.

Unfortunately, however, the first three attempts to relieve the party coincided with the times when the island was beset by ice. From August 16th to August 27th the island was surrounded by pack-ice, but on the latter day a strong south-west wind drove all this ice from the bay, and, except for some stranded bergs, left a clear ice-free sea through which we finally made our way to Elephant Island.

Midwinter's Day, the great Polar festival, was duly observed. A "magnificent breakfast" of sledging ration hoosh, full strength, and well boiled to thicken it, with hot milk, was served. Luncheon consisted of a wonderful pudding, invented by Wild, and made of powdered biscuit boiled with twelve pieces of mouldy nut-food. Supper was a very finely-cut seal hoosh flavoured with sugar. After supper they had a concert, accompanied by Hussey on his "indispensable banjo." The banjo was the last thing saved from the ship before she sank, and it was landed on Elephant Island practically unharmed, and did much to cheer the men. Nearly every Saturday night a concert was held.

The cook who had carried on so well and for so long, was given a rest on August 9th, and as the cook and his "mate" had the privilege of scraping out the saucepans there was anxiety to secure the job. Food was getting terribly short, for the penguins and seals, which had migrated at the beginning of winter, had not yet returned, and old seal bones, which had been once used for a meal and thrown away, were dug up and stewed down with sea-water. Penguin carcasses were likewise treated. One man wrote in his diary: "We had a sumptuous meal today – nearly five ounces of solid food each." No wonder, under the circumstances, that the thoughts and conversation of the party should turn to food.

It was largely due to Wild, and to his energy and resource, that the party kept cheerful all along, and, indeed, came out alive and so well. Assisted by the two surgeons, Drs. McIlroy and Macklin, he kept a watchful eye on the health of each man. His cheery optimism never failed, and each man in his diary speaks with admiration of him. I think without doubt that all the stranded party owe their lives to him. He more than justified the absolute confidence which I placed in him. Hussey, with his cheeriness and banjo, was another vital factor in chasing away symptoms of depression.

Once settled in the hut, the health of the party was, under the conditions, quite good. Every one, of course, was rather weak, some were light-headed, all were frost-bitten, and others, later, had attacks of heart failure. Blackborrow, whose toes were so badly frost-bitten in the boats, had to have all five amputated while on the island. That this operation, under the most difficult conditions, was very successful, speaks volumes for the skill and initiative of the surgeons. Hudson, who developed bronchitis and hip disease, was practically well when relief came. All the men were naturally weak when rescued, but all, thanks to Frank Wild, were alive and very cheerful.

Hurley describes it as 'a catacomb-like scene of objects resembling mummies'.

Fortunately, there was just sufficient chloroform to put Blackborrow out. Macklin was anaesthetist and McIlroy surgeon. The operation took fifty-five minutes to complete. At the end there was some hot water left and Macklin took the opportunity to have his first wash for eight months.

(Below) It is not clear what is happening here – perhaps the Elephant Island team are packing up their stores, though some of the group in the foreground may be extracting blubber.

Wild appears to have been unfailingly cheerful and also able to calm down the inevitable frictions that broke out. He was usually very calm, though he says that he threatened to shoot Orde-Lees unless he kept his mouth shut. Orde-Lees once challenged Macklin to a dawn duel on the beach. The weapons were to be broken oars. The prevailing atmosphere was described by Macklin as one of 'deadly monotony'. They would have disturbed nights, and the cook would start the fires at 6 or 7 a.m. but breakfast was not served till about 9 or 10. Wild then allotted the men various tasks but James said there was 'not much to do as a rule . . . It gets dark too early to do much.' Hurley, with his facility for verbal pictures, describes the scene as making him think 'of a council of brigands'. As for conversation, Hurley says it 'generally wanders back to the civilised world . . . To what we intend doing . . . on returning – Things not likely to be done & orgies physically impossible.'

August 30th, 1916, is described in their diaries as a "day of wonders." Food was very short, only two days' seal and penguin meat being left, and there was no prospect of any more. The whole party had been collecting limpets and seaweed to eat with the stewed seal bones. Lunch was being served by Wild; Hurley and Marston were waiting outside to take a last look at the direction from which they expected the ship to come.

From a fortnight after I had left, Wild had rolled up his sleeping-bag each day with the remark, "Get your things ready, boys, the Boss may come to-day." And sure enough, one day, the mist opened and revealed the ship for which they had been waiting for over four months.

"Marston was the first to notice it, and immediately yelled out 'Ship O!' Those in the hut mistook it for a call of 'Lunch O!' so took no notice at first. Soon, however, we heard him pattering along the snow as fast as he could run, and, in a gasping voice, hoarse with excitement, he shouted, 'Wild, there's a ship! Hadn't we better light a flare?' We all made one dive for our narrow door. Those who could not get through tore down the canvas walls in their hurry and excitement. The hoosh-pot, with our precious limpets and seaweed, was kicked over in the rush. There, just rounding the island which had previously hidden her from our sight, we saw a little ship flying the Chilian flag.

"We tried to cheer, but excitement had gripped our vocal cords. Macklin had made a rush for the flagstaff, previously placed in the most conspicuous position on the ice-slope. The running-gear would not work, and the flag was frozen into a solid mass, so he tied his jersey to the top of the pole for a signal.

(Right) This is another photograph of which some copies show signs of retouching. The ship appears in different places and sometimes a cloud of spray in the centre is inserted. The smoke on the left looks retouched.

(*Left*) Setting off for the little Chilean trawler *Yelcho* which, with the island party on board, became rather overcrowded.

"Wild put a pick through our last remaining tin of petrol, and, soaking coats, mitts and socks with it, carried them to the top of Penguin Hill, and soon they were ablaze.

"Meanwhile, most of us were on the foreshore watching anxiously for any signs that the ship had seen us, or for any answering signals. As we stood and gazed she seemed to turn away as if she had not seen us. Again and again we cheered, though our feeble cries could certainly not have carried so far. Suddenly she stopped, a boat was lowered, and we could recognise Sir Ernest's figure as he climbed down the ladder. Simultaneously we burst into a cheer, and then one said to the other, 'Thank God, the Boss is safe.' For I think that his safety was of more concern to us than our own.

"Soon the boat was near enough for the Boss, who was standing up in the bows, to shout to Wild, 'Are you all well?' To which he replied, 'All safe, all well,' and we could see a smile light up the Boss's face as he said, 'Thank God.'

"Before he could land he threw ashore handfuls of cigarettes and tobacco, and these the smokers, who for two months had been trying to find solace in such substitutes as seaweed, finely chopped pipe-bowls, seal meat, and sennegrass, grasped greedily.

"Blackborrow, who could not walk, had been carried to a high rock and propped up in his sleeping-bag, so that he could view the wonderful scene.

"Soon we were tumbling into the boat, and the Chilian sailors, laughing up at us, seemed as pleased at our rescue as we were. Twice more the boat returned, and within an hour of our first having sighted the boat we were heading northwards to the outer world, from which we had had no news for over twenty-two months.

"We were like men awakened from a long sleep. We are trying to acquire suddenly the perspective which the rest of the world has acquired gradually through two years of war. . . .

"Our first meal, owing to our weakness, proved disastrous to many of us, but we soon recovered. Our beds were shake-downs on cushions and settees, but I think we got very little sleep. It was just heavenly to lie and listen to the throb of the engines, instead of to the crack of the breaking floe, or the howling of the blizzard.

"We intend to keep August 30th as a festival for the rest of our lives."

You can imagine my feelings, as I stood in the little cabin watching my rescued comrades eating the first good meal which had been offered to them for many, many months.

Wild's leadership seems to have been the key to the survival of the party even though, had help arrived later than it did, he might have been responsible for starving them to death by not accumulating food. Even Orde-Lees wrote, 'Wild is a fine fellow to keep one's spirit up. He is as great an optimist as Sir Ernest himself & that is saying a good deal.' But by August pessimism was general and the non-return of Shackleton was discussed. Wild was keeping wood and nails in case the party had to attempt their own boat escape.

Although the rescued men were allowed to eat and sleep as they pleased, they were ordered to keep their hair and beards long enough to satisfy the demands of the publicity photographers on their arrival in port on 3 September.

The Ross Sea. Captain Ross, after whom it was named, wrote, 'We are the first men to burst into this silent sea!' Unseen in this photograph, to the north is a massive mountain and the southern continent's only live volcano, named Mount Erebus along with its dead companion volcano, named Mount Terror after Ross's two little Royal Navy vessels.

166

CHAPTER XVII

THE ROSS SEA PARTY

I NOW turn to the Ross Sea party and the *Aurora*. In spite of extraordinary difficulties, caused by the *Aurora* breaking out from her winter quarters before sufficient stores and equipment had been landed, Captain Æneas Mackintosh and the party under his command achieved the object of this side of the Expedition. The depôt, which was their main object, was laid in the spot indicated by me, and if the Trans-continental party had been able to have crossed they would have found the assistance vital to the success of the undertaking.

Owing to the dearth of stores, clothing, and sledging equipment, the depôt party was forced to travel more slowly and with greater difficulty than otherwise would have been the case. The result was that during this journey the finest qualities were called for, and the call was not in vain, as those who read the following pages will realise.

It is more than regrettable that, after so many months of hardship and toil, Mackintosh and Hayward should have been lost. Spencer-Smith, during those long days, suffering but never complaining, became an example to all men. Mackintosh and Hayward owed their lives on that journey to the care and strenuous endeavours of Joyce, Ernest Wild and Richards, who, also scurvy-stricken, but fitter than their comrades, dragged them on sledges through deep snow and blizzards.

I think that no more remarkable story of human endeavour has been revealed than the tale of that long march which I have collected from various diaries. Unfortunately the diary of the leader of this side of the Expedition was lost with him. The outstanding feature of the Ross Sea side was the journey made by these six men. Mackintosh was fortunate for the long journey, in that he had these three men with him: Ernest Wild, Richards and Joyce.

Before relating the adventures of this party I want to emphasise my gratitude for the assistance I received both in Australia and New Zealand, especially in the latter dominion. And among many friends I wish to lay special stress on the names of Leonard Tripp, whose services to the Expedition are beyond all praise, and of Edward Saunders. If ever a man had cause to be grateful for assistance in dark days, I am he.

The *Aurora*, under the command of Captain Æneas Mackintosh, sailed from Hobart for the Ross Sea on December 24th, 1914. The ship, if necessary, could spend two years in the Antarctic. My instructions, in brief, to Captain Mackintosh were to proceed to the Ross Sea, make a base at some convenient point in or near McMurdo Sound, land stores and equipment, and lay depôts on the Great Ice Barrier in the direction of the Beardmore Glacier for the party I hoped to bring overland from the Weddell Sea coast.

Shackleton's attitude to the other ship and its team is a curious one. The fate of the Ross Sea party must have been in his mind ever since he failed to make a landfall on the South Polar continent, yet he never mentioned them in the earlier part of the book. By pretending, perhaps subconsciously, that this was a separate expedition outside his control he was able to perpetuate the myth that he 'never lost a man'.

To this list of stores and clothing the most recent historian of the Ross Sea party, Bickel, adds, 'Haphazard acquisition, bad planning and lack of money'. Mackintosh was determined to sail before Christmas and so coal was dumped on deck alongside sheep and other livestock. The dogs were not brought on board until Christmas Day. Bickel calls Spencer-Smith 'the worst case of sledging scurvy in history'.

Mackintosh arrived in Australia to find only half the money for *Aurora* that Shackleton had promised. The ship needed a complete refit. By mortgaging the ship and obtaining local loans, Mackintosh managed to leave only six weeks behind schedule. 'The circumstances were disgraceful', said someone on board.

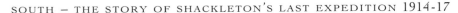

This was ingenuous. Shackleton knew the work would be difficult because it had nearly killed him in 1902-3. He optimistically calculated that he would do the 1,500 miles in 100 days.

It was not particulary uneventful. There was a violent storm and the ship began to leak. Mackintosh accidentally smashed the ship's jib-boom into the cliff, bringing down the top-mast. McMurdo Sound was so-named after an officer on the earlier Ross Sea expedition, and Shackleton gave Mackintosh specific orders not to anchor there as *Aurora* might be frozen in.

(Below) **Penguins were not only used for fuel and food, but their eggs were prized for making pancakes.**

The programme involved some heavy sledging, but I had not anticipated that the work would be extremely difficult. The *Aurora* carried materials for a hut, full equipment for landing and sledging parties, stores and clothing of all the kinds required, and an ample supply of sledges. There were also dog-teams and one of the motor-tractors. I told Captain Mackintosh to lay out depôts to the south immediately after his arrival at his base, and directed him to place a depôt of food and fuel-oil at lat. 80° S. in 1914-15, with cairns and flags as guides to a sledging-party approaching from the direction of the Pole. In the 1915-16 season he would place depôts further south.

The *Aurora* had an uneventful voyage southwards, and on Christmas Day anchored off the sealing-huts at Macquarie Island. The wireless station, erected by Sir Douglas Mawson's Australian Antarctic Expedition, was still occupied, and the *Aurora* had some stores for the party living there. The *Aurora* sailed from the island on December 31st, and three days later they sighted the first iceberg, and on the following day the ship passed through the first belt of pack-ice. On January 7th Mount Sabine, a mighty peak of the Admiralty Range, South Victoria Land, was sighted seventy-five miles distant.

It had been proposed that a party of three men should travel to Cape Crozier from winter quarters during the winter months to secure emperor penguins' eggs. The ship was to call at Cape Crozier, land provisions, and erect a small hut of fibro-concrete sheets for the use of this party. The

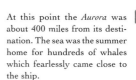

ship was off the Cape on the afternoon of January 9th, and a boat was put off with a party to search for a landing place. But no place to land the hut and stores could be found.

Mackintosh then proceeded into McMurdo Sound, but, owing to heavy pack, it was not until January 16th that the ship reached a point off Cape Evans, where ten tons of coal and ninety-eight cases of oil were landed. During succeeding days the *Aurora* was worked southward, and by January 24th was within nine miles of Hut Point. There Mackintosh made the ship fast to sea-ice then breaking up rapidly, and proceeded to arrange sledging-parties. He intended to direct the laying of the depôts himself and to leave his first officer, Lieut. J. R. Stenhouse, in command of the *Aurora*, with instructions to select a base and land a party.

The first objective was Hut Point, where the hut erected by the *Discovery* Expedition in 1902 stands. An advance party, consisting of Joyce (in charge), Jack and Gaze, with dogs and fully loaded sledges, left the ship on January 24th; Mackintosh, with Wild and Smith, followed the next day, and a supporting party of six men left the ship on January 30th. This last party consisted of Cope (in charge), Stevens, Ninnis, Hayward, Hooke and Richards.

These parties had a strenuous time during the following weeks. The men, fresh from shipboard, were not in the best of training, and the same was true of the dogs. It was unfortunate that the dogs had to be worked while they were still in poor condition and before they had learned to work together as teams. The result was the loss of many dogs, and this proved a most serious matter in the following season.

Captain Mackintosh and his party left the *Aurora* on the evening of January 25th. The dogs were full of eagerness after their long confinement aboard the ship, and Mackintosh hoped to reach Hut Point that night, but luck was against him. The weather broke after he had travelled about five miles, and snow, which completely obscured all landmarks, sent him into camp on the sea-ice. On January 27th, after missing their way in the thick weather, the party reached Hut Point at 4 p.m. There Mackintosh found a note from Joyce who had been at the Hut on the 25th. The Hut contained some stores left there by earlier Expeditions.

The party stayed at the Hut for the night, and Mackintosh left a note for Stenhouse, directing him to place provisions there, in case the sledging parties did not return in time to be taken off by the ship. Early next morning Joyce reached the Hut. He had met bad ice and had returned to consult Mackintosh about the route to be followed. Mackintosh directed him to steer out towards Black Island in crossing the head of the Sound beyond Hut Point.

Mackintosh left Hut Point on January 28th, with a sledge weighing 1,200 lb. This was a heavy load, but the dogs were pulling well, and he thought it practicable. Difficulties from soft snow and the fact that the dogs soon ceased to pull cheerfully began almost at once. The distance covered in the day was under four miles.

A fall of snow held up the party through the following day, and, owing to the soft surface, Mackintosh decided to travel by night. They left the camp before midnight, but difficulties again beset them. "Try as we would, no movement could be produced. Reluctantly we unloaded and began the tedious task of relaying." The work was terrific, and, after struggling for four hours, they camped to wait for evening, when they hoped the surface would be better. "I must say," Mackintosh wrote, "I feel somewhat despondent, as we are not getting on as well as I expected, nor do we find it as easy as one would gather from reading."

The two parties met again that day. Joyce also had been compelled to relay his load, and all hands laboured strenuously and advanced slowly. They reached the edge of the Barrier on the night of January 30th. The dogs were showing signs of fatigue, and when they camped at 6.30 a.m. on January 31st, Mackintosh reckoned that the distance covered in twelve and a half hours was

At this point the *Aurora* was about 400 miles from its destination. The sea was the summer home for hundreds of whales which fearlessly came close to the ship.

Richards joined the party as physicist without making any arrangement about pay. Two years later he received £70.

Alas, Shackleton had also given Joyce written instructions intimating that he was to be in charge of depôt laying, thus causing friction between the two men.

Furthermore, when the stores Shackleton had sent from London were opened, there was barely enough clothing and equipment for half the party.

In fact Joyce and Mackintosh disagreed about how to proceed. Joyce wanted to spend more time acclimatising men and dogs for the difficult journey ahead. Mackintosh made a major error at this point, not only by taking over depôt-laying from the more experienced Joyce but by leaving the ship, on which the safety of all depended, in the hands of officers with no Antarctic experience. He also pushed the unfit dogs beyond their endurance.

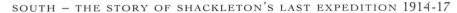

Mackintosh decided at this time that he would himself take charge of all depôt laying, leaving Stenhouse on board the *Aurora* to take command in his absence. This was to prove a fatal decision.

(Right) Hut Point, a picture taken on the Scott expedition, with icebergs and massive clouds in the background. When Mackintosh and Joyce pushed their way into it, they found that since being abandoned in early 1913 it had stayed clean and weatherproof, and the acetylene gas lighting, for winter comfort, was still in order.

about two and a half miles. The experiences of the party during the following day can be shown by extracts from Mackintosh's diary.

"Sunday, January 31st. – Started off this afternoon at 3 p.m. Surface too dreadful for words. We sink into snow at times up to our knees, the dogs struggling out of it, panting and making great efforts. After proceeding about 1,000 yards I spotted some poles. We shaped course for these and found Captain Scott's Safety Camp. After lunching we dug round the poles, and, after getting down about 3 feet, we found a bag of oats and two cases of dog biscuit. A good find. About forty paces away we found a venesta-lid sticking out of the snow. Smith scraped round this with his ice-axe, and presently found one of the motor sledges used by Captain Scott. Everything was just as it had been left, the petrol tank partly filled and apparently unharmed.

The motor sledge was useless. So was the new one brought out by the expedition and abandoned at Hut Point. It had taken the men three days to travel 7 miles from Hut Point.

"February 1st. – After lunch we decided, as the surface was improving, to make a shot at travelling with the whole load. It was a back-breaking job. The great trouble is to get the sledge started after the many unavoidable stops. We managed to cover one mile. Even this is better than relaying. We then camped – the dogs being entirely done up, poor brutes.

"February 2nd. – We were awakened this afternoon by hearing Joyce's dogs barking. They have done well and have caught us up. We issued a challenge to race him to the Bluff, which he accepted. When we turned out at 6.30 p.m. his camp was seen about three miles ahead, and we reached it by 1 a.m. The dogs, seeing the camp ahead, had been pulling well, but when we arrived off it they were not inclined to go on. This starting business is terrible work. If the dogs do not pull together we cannot move. Sledging is real hard work; but we are getting along."

This rearrangement followed an argument with Joyce who was convinced, as a veteran sledger, that Mackintosh was driving the dogs too hard.

During the next few days the surface improved and better progress was made. Joyce was travelling by day and Mackintosh by night, so that the parties passed one another daily on the march. A blizzard on February 10th confined the parties to their tents for twenty-four hours. On the morning of the next day the weather moderated, and Mackintosh camped beside Joyce and proceeded to rearrange the parties.

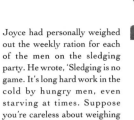

He decided to take the best dogs from the two teams and continue the march with Joyce and Wild, while Smith, Jack and Gaze went back to Hut Point with the remaining dogs. This involved the adjustment of sledge-loads, so that proper supplies might be available for the depôts. Mackintosh had eight dogs and Smith had five. A depôt of oil and fuel was laid at this point and marked by a cairn with a bamboo pole rising 10 feet above it.

The change made for better progress. Smith turned back at once, and the other party went ahead fairly rapidly. They built a cairn of snow after each hour's travelling to serve as guides to the depôt and as marks for the return journey. During succeeding days the party plodded forward, covering from five to twelve miles a day, according to the surface and weather, building cairns regularly, and checking their route by taking bearings of the mountains to the west. On February 21st Mackintosh wrote: "The temperature was very low this morning, and handling the theodolite was not too warm a job for the fingers. My whiskers froze to the metal while I was taking a sight."

They had reached lat. 80° S., and there they laid a depôt. The stores were placed in a cairn built to a height of 8 feet, and on the top they placed a bamboo pole with a flag. Smaller cairns were built at right angles to the depôt as a guide to the overland party. "To-morrow we hope to lay our cairns to the westward, and then to shape our course for the Bluff."

But owing to a blizzard it was not until the afternoon of the 23rd that Mackintosh and Joyce tried to lay out cairns to the west. Two dogs had died during the storm, and after marching a mile and a half to the westward and building a cairn, the weather became so thick that they thought it unwise to proceed further. So they returned to the camp, and on the morning of February 24th, with snow still falling, they started the return march; but they had only gone 400 yards when thick fog compelled them again to pitch their tent.

"We are going back with only ten days' provisions, so it means pushing on for all we are worth. These stoppages are truly annoying. The poor dogs are feeling hungry; they eat their harness or any straps that may be about. If we had not been so delayed we might have been able to give them a good feed at the Bluff depôt, but now that is impossible."

The experiences of the next few days were unhappy. Another blizzard brought heavy snow and held the party up throughout the 25th and 26th.

"Outside is a scene of chaos. We long to be off, but the howl of the wind shows how impossible it is. I am afraid that the dogs will not pull through. We have a week's provisions and 160 miles to travel. It appears that we will have to get another week's provisions from the depôt, but don't wish it. Will see what luck to-morrow. Of course, at Bluff we can replenish."

A day later Mackintosh continued: "We are now reduced to one meal in twenty-four hours It is a rotten, miserable time. It is bad enough to wait, but we have also the wretched thought of having to use the provisions already depôt-ed, for which we have had this hard struggle."

The weather cleared on the 27th, and Mackintosh and Joyce had to return to the depôt and secure some provisions. On the following morning the party resumed the homeward journey, and made good progress. But the dogs had reached almost the limit of their endurance; three of them fell out, unable to work longer, while on the march, and on March 2nd the remaining dogs collapsed. "They are all lying down in our tracks. They have a painless death, for they curl up in the snow and fall into a sleep from which they will never wake."

On March 3rd the party made only three and a half miles. They found the sledge exceedingly heavy to pull, and Mackintosh decided to remove the outer runners and scrape the bottom. He also left behind all spare gear, and found the lighter sledge easier to pull. On the 5th he wrote, "We are struggling along at a mile an hour. It is a very hard pull, the surface being very sticky."

The conditions altered during the next day when a southerly wind made it possible to use a sail.

Joyce had personally weighed out the weekly ration for each of the men on the sledging party. He wrote, 'Sledging is no game. It's long hard work in the cold by hungry men, even starving at times. Suppose you're careless about weighing out the weekly rations . . . ?'

The blizzard's force was close to 100 m.p.h. and more dogs died.

Joyce kept one dog, Pinkey, alive for a few days longer in the hope that he might make it back to the hut.

Joyce's entry in his diary was more laconic still. They had been out a month, he said, and had averaged 5 miles a day.

Despite the fact that both Wild (who had frostbitten feet) and Pinkey travelled on the sledge, the dog died before they could reach the hut. Joyce mourned the loss. 'On polar journeys the dogs seem almost human.'

But the handling of the ropes and sail caused many frost-bites, and occasionally the men were dragged along the surface by the sledge. During the night the wind increased, and by the morning of the 7th was blowing with blizzard force. The party could not move again until the 8th. They were still finding the sledge very heavy and were disappointed at their slow progress, their marches being six to eight miles a day.

On the 10th they got the Bluff Peak in line with Mount Discovery. My instructions had been that the Bluff depôt should be laid on this line, and as the depôt had been placed north of the line on the outward journey, owing to thick weather making it impossible to pick up the land-marks, Mackintosh now meant to move the stores to the proper place. He pitched camp at the new depôt site, and went across, with Joyce and Wild, to the depôt flag, about four miles away, and found the stores as he had left them. These stores were successfully transferred to the correct site, and after a day's blizzard the weather was fine on March 12th, and they built a cairn for the depôt. Early in the afternoon they resumed their march northwards and made three miles before camping.

"Our bags," Mackintosh wrote that night, "are getting into a bad state, as it is some time now since we have had an opportunity to dry them. Getting away in the mornings is our bitterest time. The putting on of the finneskoe is a nightmare, for they are always frozen stiff, and we have a great struggle to force our feet into them. We are miserable until we are actually on the move, then warmth returns with the work."

Wild said each step for him was 'a ball of fire'. The walking trio were headed towards Safety Camp 50 miles to the North.

Owing to blizzards the march could not be resumed until March 15th. By this time food was again short, and both Joyce and Wild had toes frost-bitten while in their bags, and found difficulty in restoring the circulation. Wild suffered particularly in this way.

"March 15th. – The air temperature this morning was −35° Fahr. Last night was one of the worst I have ever experienced. To cap everything I developed toothache and was in positive agony. Joyce and Wild both had a bad night, their feet giving them trouble. We have had to reduce our daily ration. Frost-bites are frequent in consequence. The surface became very rough in the afternoon and the light also was bad. We are continually falling, for we are unable to distinguish the high and low parts of the surface. Our matches, among other things, are running short, and we have given up using them except for lighting the Primus."

The party found the light bad again the next day, and made fairly good progress, and on the evening of March 19th they camped abreast of "Corner Camp," where they had been on February 1st. But on the following day they turned towards Castle Rock and proceeded across the disturbed area where the Barrier impinges upon the land. Joyce put his foot through the snow covering of a fairly large crevasse, and the course had to be changed to avoid this danger. The march for the day was only two miles 900 yards, but, although Mackintosh felt the pace was too slow, the bad surface prevented him from quickening it. The food had been cut down nearly to half rations, and at this reduced rate the supply would be finished in two days. "The first thought this morning was that we must do a good march," Mackintosh wrote on March 22nd. "Once we can get to Safety Camp we are right. We have managed quite a respectable forenoon march. We had lunch at 1 p.m., and then had left over one meal at full rations and a small quantity of biscuits. After lunch we again accomplished a good march, the wind favouring us for two hours. We are anxiously looking out for Safety Camp."

Joyce recorded: 'We are just three old crocks . . . just crawling 3 miles in 10 hours.'

The morning of March 23rd found them prisoners. A blizzard with drift had sprung up, and the weather was appalling. "This weather is rather alarming, for if it continues we are in a bad way. We have just made a meal of cocoa mixed with biscuit crumbs. This has warmed us up a little, but on empty stomachs the cold is penetrating."

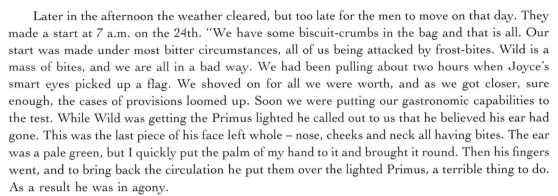

Later in the afternoon the weather cleared, but too late for the men to move on that day. They made a start at 7 a.m. on the 24th. "We have some biscuit-crumbs in the bag and that is all. Our start was made under most bitter circumstances, all of us being attacked by frost-bites. Wild is a mass of bites, and we are all in a bad way. We had been pulling about two hours when Joyce's smart eyes picked up a flag. We shoved on for all we were worth, and as we got closer, sure enough, the cases of provisions loomed up. Soon we were putting our gastronomic capabilities to the test. While Wild was getting the Primus lighted he called out to us that he believed his ear had gone. This was the last piece of his face left whole – nose, cheeks and neck all having bites. The ear was a pale green, but I quickly put the palm of my hand to it and brought it round. Then his fingers went, and to bring back the circulation he put them over the lighted Primus, a terrible thing to do. As a result he was in agony.

"Soon the hot hoosh sent warmth tingling through us. We felt like new beings. We simply ate till we were full, mug after mug. Then we replaced the cases we had pulled down from the depôt, and proceeded towards the Gap. Just before leaving Joyce discovered a note left by Spencer-Smith and Richards. This told us that both the other parties had returned to the Hut, and apparently all was well. So that is good."

By 7 p.m. the party had failed to find a suitable place to descend to the sea-ice, so they camped, hoping to reach Hut Point on the morrow. They broke camp on the morning of March 25th, with the thermometer recording 55° of frost, and a short time later they arrived at Hut Point and reached the door of the Hut. "We shouted. No sound. Shouted again and presently a dark object appeared. This turned out to be Cope, who was by himself. We heard then how the ship had called here on March 11th and picked up Spencer-Smith, Richards, Ninnis, Hooke and Gaze, the present members here being Cope, Hayward and Jack. I got a letter here from Stenhouse giving a summary of his doings since we left him. The ship's party also have not had a very rosy time."

The six men now at Hut Point were cut off from the winter quarters of the Expedition at Cape Evans by the open water of McMurdo Sound. Naturally Mackintosh was anxious to get in touch with the ship and the other members of the shore party; but he could not move until the sea-ice was firm, and, as events occurred, he did not reach Cape Evans until the beginning of June. At the Hut he and his companions lived an uneventful life under primitive conditions. Mackintosh records that the members of the party were contented enough, but, owing largely to the soot and grease from the blubber-stove, unspeakably dirty. The store of seal-blubber ran low early in April, but on April 15th several seals were killed. The operations of killing and skinning them made worse the blackened and greasy clothes of the men.

Before they left on the 24th they had another meal of cocoa mixed with biscuit crumbs.

Joyce knew he should eat sparingly but, as he wrote, 'a starving man has little conscience when the crossroads meet'.

Back at the Hut, Cope (a Cambridge medical graduate) had to amputate the top of Wild's ear and part of a big toe. The large blisters on their faces had to be lanced.

Life in the Hut was not easy. They ran out of fuel and had to dismantle and burn Scott's small observation hut. It was not until 9 May that seals were sighted and slaughtered for fuel and food. It was 30 degrees below.

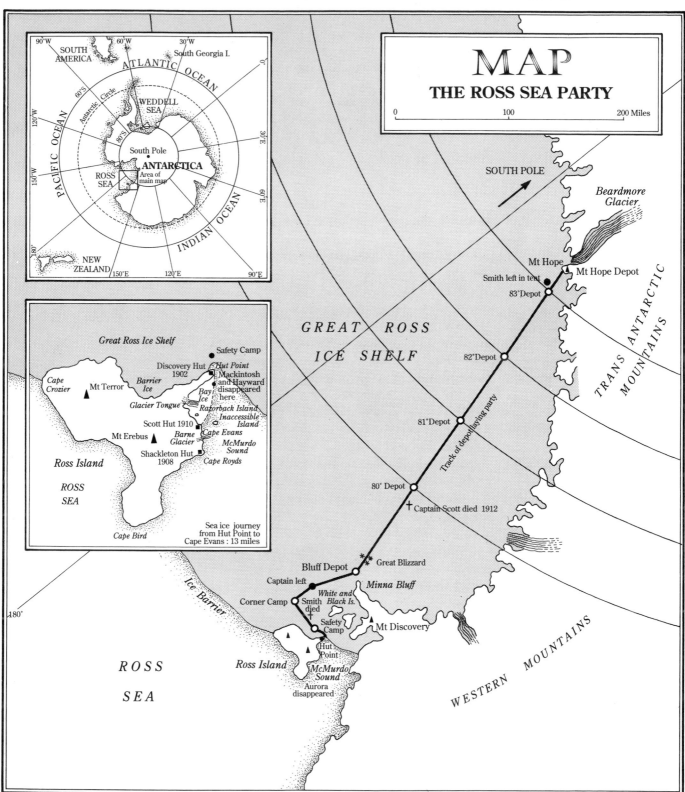

MAP
THE ROSS SEA PARTY

0   100   200 Miles

SOUTH POLE

Beardmore Glacier

Mt Hope
Smith left in tent
Mt Hope Depot
83°Depot

TRANS ANTARCTIC MOUNTAINS

GREAT ROSS ICE SHELF

82°Depot

81°Depot

Track of depot-laying party

80° Depot

† Captain Scott died 1912

✱✱ Great Blizzard

Bluff Depot

Captain left

Minna Bluff

Corner Camp

White and Black Is.

Smith died †

▲ Mt Discovery

Safety Camp

▲ ▲ Hut Point

Aurora disappeared

WESTERN MOUNTAINS

ROSS

SEA

Ice Barrier

Inset — Antarctica overview
90°W   60°W   30°W
SOUTH AMERICA
ATLANTIC OCEAN
South Georgia I.
0°
120°W
WEDDELL SEA
Antarctic Circle
30°E
PACIFIC OCEAN
South Pole
ANTARCTICA
Area of main map
60°E
150°W
ROSS SEA
180°
NEW ZEALAND
150°E   120°E   90°E
INDIAN OCEAN
60°S
80°S

Inset — Ross Island detail
Great Ross Ice Shelf
Safety Camp
Discovery Hut 1902
Hut Point
Barrier Ice
Mackintosh and Hayward disappeared here
Cape Crozier
▲ Mt Terror
Bay Ice
Glacier Tongue
Razorback Island
Inaccessible Island
Scott Hut 1910
Barne Glacier
Cape Evans
Mt Erebus ▲
Shackleton Hut 1908
McMurdo Sound
Cape Royds
Ross Island
ROSS SEA
Sea ice journey from Hut Point to Cape Evans : 13 miles
Cape Bird

180°

ROSS

SEA

CHAPTER XVIII
WINTERING IN McMURDO SOUND

T HE *Aurora*, after picking up six men at Hut Point on March 11th, had gone back to Cape Evans. The position chosen for the winter quarters of the ship was at Cape Evans, immediately off the hut erected by Captain Scott on his last Expedition. The ship on March 14th lay about forty yards off shore, bows seaward. The final moorings were six hawsers and one cable astern, made fast to the shore anchors, and two anchors with about seventy fathoms of cable out forward.

On March 23rd Mr. Stenhouse landed a party consisting of Stevens, Spencer-Smith, Gaze and Richards, and these four men took up their quarters in Captain Scott's hut. They had been instructed to kill seals for meat and blubber, and carry out routine observations. The landing of stores, gear and coal did not proceed at all rapidly, it being assumed that the ship would remain at her moorings through the winter. Some tons of coal were landed during April, but most of it stayed on the beach, and much of it was lost later when the sea-ice went out.

This shore party was in the charge of Stevens, and his report, handed to me much later, gives a succinct account of what occurred, from the point of view of the men at the hut. I quote from it very briefly:-

"CAPE EVANS, ROSS ISLAND,
"*July 30th, 1915*.
"On March 23rd, 1915, a party consisting of Spencer-Smith, Richards and Gaze was landed at Cape Evans Hut in my charge. Spencer-Smith received instructions to devote his time exclusively to photography. I was verbally instructed that the main duty of the party was to obtain a supply of seals for food and fuel. Scientific work was also to be carried on.

"Meteorological instruments were at once installed. . . . The whole of the time of the scientific members of the party was occupied. All seals seen were secured.

"In general the weather was unsettled, blizzards occurring frequently and interrupting communication with the ship across the ice. Only small, indispensable supplies of stores and no clothes were issued to the party on shore. Only part of the scientific equipment was able to be transferred to the shore, and the necessity to obtain that prevented some members of the party landing all their personal gear.

"Though, I believe, it was considered on board that the ship was secure, there was still considerable anxiety felt. The anchors had held badly before, and the power of the ice pressure on the ship was uncomfortably obvious. . . .

"On May 6th the ice was in and people passed freely between the shore and the ship. At

They found discarded clothing, sledging gear and general stores that, Richards wrote, 'were to prove most valuable'.

On 24 March a wireless message from *Aurora* was picked up in Australia. There was difficulty finding anyone in London to whom to deliver it as the offices had been closed. Finally Mrs Shackleton and Mrs Mackintosh met at the solicitor's and decided to try to set up a relief expedition to the Ross Sea. The Royal Geographical Society declined to help, saying that its connection was limited to that of a subscriber. Asquith, the Prime Minister, finally agreed to start a fund.

Shackleton had ordered that *Aurora* was not to winter south of Glacier Tongue, to avoid the fate of Scott who had been ice-bound at Hut Point for two years. Stenhouse and his crew had therefore spent several miserable weeks vainly looking for a berth, with long hours on the bridge with little sleep. They returned, finally to Cape Evans.

(*Right*) The *Aurora* which some 'awesome hand . . . plucked from her moorings' and left to drift.

The drama of the ship's unexpected departure was immense. Stenhouse had said that she was safely tied to the shore. Suddenly, at 3 a.m. on 7 May, Richards found her gone. 'It was as though some awesome hand had plucked her from the moorings and left the steel strands like broken threads of cotton on the shore,' writes Bickel.

11 p.m. the wind was south, backing to south-east, and blew at forty miles an hour. The ship was still in her place. At 3 a.m. on the 7th the wind had not increased to any extent, but ice and ship had gone. As she was not seen to go we are unable to say whether the vessel was damaged. . . . On the afternoon of the 7th the weather cleared somewhat, but nothing was seen of the ship. . . . Nothing has since been seen or heard of the ship, though a look-out was kept.

"Immediately the ship went as accurate an inventory as possible of all stores ashore was made, and the rate of consumption of foodstuffs so regulated that they would last ten men for not less than 100 weeks. Coal and meat were very short, and were therefore used as carefully as possible. "A. STEVENS."

Ice, driven by the gale, carried the *Aurora* away, its cables broken by the force. Stenhouse was unable to raise steam as the furnaces were dead, the boilers cold and the steam feed pipes frozen solid. He wrote in his log, 'We are drifting God knows where! . . . But what of the poor beggars at Cape Evans, and the Southern Party?'

The men ashore did not at once abandon hope of the ship returning before the Sound froze firmly, but when the most violent blizzard yet experienced by the party began on May 10th, hope grew slender. This gale lasted for three days, the wind attaining a velocity of seventy miles an hour. The shore party took a gloomy view of the ship's chances of safety among the ice-floes of the Ross Sea under such conditions.

Stevens and his companions made a careful survey of their position and realised the serious difficulties ahead of them. No general provisions and no clothing required for sledging had been landed. Much of the sledging gear was also aboard. Fortunately the hut contained both food and clothing, left there by Captain Scott's Expedition. As many seals as possible were killed and the meat and blubber were stored.

June 2nd brought a welcome addition to the party in the men who had been forced to remain at Hut Point until the sea-ice was firm. There were now ten men at Cape Evans – namely, Mackintosh, Spencer-Smith, Joyce, Wild, Cope, Stevens, Hayward, Gaze, Jack and Richards. The winter had closed down upon the Antarctic and no move could be made before the beginning of September. Meanwhile they overhauled the available stores and gears, made plans for the future, and lived the severe, but not altogether unhappy, life of the polar explorer in winter quarters.

Mackintosh, writing on June 5th, surveyed his position:-

"The decision of Stenhouse to make this bay the wintering place of the ship was not reached without much thought and consideration of all eventualities. He had already tried the Glacier Tongue and other places, but at each of them the ship had been in an exposed and dangerous position. When this bay was tried the ship withstood several blizzards. . . . Taking everything into account, it was quite a fair judgment on his part to assume that the ship would be secure here. . . . The accident proved again the uncertainty of conditions in these regions."

The *Aurora* could have found safe winter quarters farther up McMurdo Sound, but would have run the risk of being frozen in over the following summer, and I had given instructions to Mackintosh before he went south that this danger must be avoided.

Mackintosh continued: "Meanwhile we are preparing here for a prolonged stay. The shortage of clothing is our principal hardship. The members of the party from Hut Point have the clothes we wore when we left the ship on January 25th. I cannot imagine a dirtier set of people. . . . All is working smoothly here, and every one is taking the situation very philosophically.

"Stevens is in charge of the scientific staff and is now the senior officer ashore. Joyce is in charge of the equipment and has undertaken to improvise clothes from what canvas we can find here. Wild is working with Joyce. He is a cheerful, willing soul. Richards has taken over the keeping of the meteorological log. He is a young Australian, a hard, conscientious worker, and I look for good results from his endeavours. Jack, another young Australian, is his assistant. Hayward is the handy man, and responsible for the supply of blubber. Gaze, another Australian, is working with Hayward. Spencer-Smith, the *padre*, is in charge of photography, and, of course, assists in the general routine work. Cope is the medical officer. . . .

"The day after my arrival I explained the necessity for economy in the use of fuel, light and stores, in view of the possibility that we may have to stay here for two years. . . . We are not going to begin work for the sledging operations until we know more definitely the fate of the *Aurora*. I dare not think any disaster has occurred."

During the remaining days of June the men washed and mended clothes, killed seals, made minor excursions, and discussed plans for the future. They had six dogs, and the animals were well-fed and carefully tended. The party was anxious to visit Cape Royds, north of Cape Evans, but at the end of June open water remained right across the Sound and a crossing was impossible. At Cape Royds is the hut used by the Shackleton Expedition of 1907-1909, and the stores and supplies it contains would have been very useful.

During July Mackintosh made several trips northwards on the sea-ice, but always found that he could not get far. The improving light told of the returning sun, and stores were being weighed out in readiness for the sledging expeditions. Blizzards were frequent and persistent. On August 12th a small fire broke out in the hut. The acetylene-gas lighting plant installed in the hut by Captain Scott had been rigged, and one day it developed a leak. One of the party searched for the leak with a lighted candle, and an explosion fired some woodwork, but fortunately the outbreak was quickly extinguished. The loss of the hut at this stage would have been a tragic incident.

There was no soap or tobacco or luxuries of any kind and only a small emergency box of medical supplies as carried on a sledge. The six men from Hut Point were so excited at reaching Cape Evans that they did not notice that the ship was not there. When Mackintosh was finally told the news he was appalled. The joyful reunion came to a sudden end.

Gaze wrote, 'We won't see her back this year – if ever. We have to face it. We are marooned.'

Shackleton had instructed that the scientific work was to include measurements of wind velocities, temperature readings and observations of wildlife. Ten tons of coal was moved from ship to shore to provide fuel, but it was washed away off the beach. Seal blubber therefore became a necessity.

Mackintosh now faced the gravest challenge of his life. The ship had gone, and with her their vital equipment: sledges, cookers, sleeping bags, clothes and the food they would need for the haul ahead. Footwear, tents, fuel and Primus stoves had all drifted away with the *Aurora*. On 26 June he gathered the men together and warned that they might be stranded for two years.

The Cape Royds hut had been used by Shackleton in 1908. The stores found here were invaluable, and were dog-sledded to Cape Evans.

On August 13th Mackintosh and Stevens paid a visit to Cape Royds. They decided to attempt the journey over the Barne Glacier, and, after crossing a crevassed area, they got to the slopes of Cape Barne and thence down to the sea-ice. This ice was strong enough for their purpose, and they soon reached the Cape Royds hut.

"The outer door of the hut we found to be off," Mackintosh wrote. "A little snow had drifted into the porch, but this was soon cleared away. We then entered, and in the centre of the hut found a pile of snow and ice, which had come through the open ventilator in the roof. We soon closed this. Stevens prepared a meal while I cleared the ice and snow away with a shovel, which we found outside.

"After our meal we began to take an inventory of the stores inside. Tobacco was our first thought. Of this we found one tin of Navy Cut and a box of cigars. Soap, too, which ensures us a wash and clean clothes when we get back. . . . Over the stove in a conspicuous place we found a notice left by Scott's party that parties using the hut should leave the dishes clean."

Mackintosh and Stevens stayed at the hut over the next day and thoroughly examined the stores there. Outside the hut they found a pile of cases containing meats, flour, dried vegetables and sundries, at least a year's supply for a party of six. They found no new clothing, but collected some worn garments which could be made serviceable. On August 15th they set out, carrying their load of spoils, and soon reached Cape Evans. A blizzard raged on the next day, and Mackintosh congratulated himself on having chosen such a fortunate time for the trip.

The record of the remaining part of August is not eventful. All hands were making preparations for the sledging and were rejoicing in the increasing daylight. The sledging of stores to Hut Point, in preparation for the depôt-laying journeys on the Barrier, was to begin on September 1st. Before that date Mackintosh discussed plans fully with the members of his party. Stores, he considered, were sufficient, but the supply of clothes and tents was more difficult. Three tents were

Useful stores abandoned by Scott's men were found in the snow behind the hut at Cape Evans. Wild and Joyce opened up what they called Joyce's Famous Tailoring Shop making clothes for the men out of a large abandoned canvas tent.

(Right) According to the caption in *South* Mackintosh is seated in the centre of this picture, taken by Hurley before the party set off.

available, a sound one landed from the *Aurora*, and two old ones left by Captain Scott. Garments brought from the ship could be supplemented by old clothing found at Hut Point and Cape Evans. Mackintosh had enough sledges, but there were only four useful dogs left. They did not make a full team, and could merely be used as an auxiliary to man-haulage.

The scheme adopted by Mackintosh, after discussion, was that nine men, divided into three parties of three each, should undertake the sledging. One man was to be left at Cape Evans to continue the meteorological observations during the summer. Mackintosh estimated that the provisions required for the consumption of the depôt parties, and for the depôts to be placed southward to the foot of the Beardmore Glacier, would amount to 4,000 lb. The first depôt was to be placed off Minna Bluff, and from there southward a depôt was to be placed on each degree of latitude. The final depôt would be at the foot of the Beardmore Glacier. The initial task would be the haulage of stores from Cape Evans to Hut Point – thirteen miles. All the sledging stores had to be taken across, and Mackintosh proposed to place additional supplies there in case a party, returning late from the Barrier, had to spend winter months at Hut Point.

The first party, consisting of Mackintosh, Richards and Spencer-Smith, left Cape Evans on September 1st with 600 lb. of stores on one sledge, and had an uneventful journey to Hut Point. They pitched a tent half-way across the bay, on the sea-ice, and left it there to be used by various parties during the month. The second trip to Hut Point was made by nine men, with three sledges, and eight men made the third journey. This last party proceeded from Hut Point the next day (September 4th) with loaded sledges to Safety Camp, on the edge of the Barrier. This camp would be the starting-point for the march over the Barrier to the Minna Bluff depôt.

"Everybody is up to his eyes in work," runs the last entry in the journal left by Mackintosh at Cape Evans. "All gear is being overhauled, and personal clothing is having the last stitches. We have been improvising shoes to replace the finniskoe, of which we are badly short. Tomorrow (October 1st) we start for Hut Point. Gaze, who is suffering from bad feet, is remaining behind and will probably be relieved by Stevens after our first trip. With us we take three months' provision to leave at Hut Point."

(Left to right) Ernest Wild, brother of Frank, members of a Yorkshire family who claimed kinship with Captain Cook; Spencer-Smith, the brave padre whose story was one of great heroism; and Joyce, who became the leader of the Ross Sea Party.

Fisher comments that because neither Mackintosh nor Spencer-Smith liked seal meat, they had eaten more than their share of tinned meat and once sledging began they would suffer from the shortage of meat and be unable to regain strength.

September was known to be the most difficult month for sledging, with the soft snows of winter on top of the ice.

179

(*Right*) Mackintosh who volunteered to stay behind on 7 March while the others pushed ahead to find fresh food to combat the scurvy. (*Far right*) Richards (Richy or Ritchie to the others). Joyce said, 'A whiter man never existed'. Wild and Richards were 'worthy of the highest traditions of polar service'.

While all this was going on, the party for whom the supplies were intended was trapped aboard *Endurance* on the other side of the continent. They had missed their landfall, and Shackleton knew there was now every possibility that their ship would be crushed in the ice – as, months later, it was to be.

The nine men reached Hut Point on October 1st. They took the last loads with them. Three sledges and three tents were to be taken on to the Barrier, and the parties were as follows: No. 1: Mackintosh, Spencer-Smith and Wild; No. 2: Joyce, Cope and Richards; No. 3: Jack, Hayward and Gaze. On October 3rd and 4th some stores left at Half-way Camp were brought in, and other stores were moved on to Safety Camp. Bad weather delayed the start of the depôt-laying Expedition until October 9th.

CHAPTER XIX

LAYING THE DEPOTS

$\clubsuit$

MACKINTOSH'S account of the depôt-laying journeys of his parties in the summer of 1915-16 unfortunately is not available. He kept a diary, but he had it with him when he was lost on the sea-ice in the following winter. This short narrative of the journeys is compiled from notes kept by Joyce, Richards and others, and I may say here that it is a record of dogged endeavour in the face of great difficulties and serious dangers.

It is always easy to be wise after the event, and one may realise now that the use of the dogs before they were in condition and trained was a mistake. In consequence hardly any dogs were available for the more important journeys of 1915-16. For six months the men were sledging almost continuously; they suffered from frost-bite, scurvy, snow-blindness, and utter weariness of over-taxed bodies. But they placed the depôts in the required positions, and had the Weddell Sea party been able to cross the Antarctic continent, stores and fuel would have been waiting for us where we expected to find them.

On October 9th the position was that the nine men at Hut Point had with them the stores required for the depôts and for their own maintenance through the summer. The remaining dogs were at Cape Evans. A small quantity of stores had already been conveyed to Safety Camp on the edge of the Barrier beyond Hut Point. Mackintosh intended to form a large depôt off Minna Bluff, seventy miles out from Hut Point, and this would require several trips with heavy loads. Then he would use the Bluff depôt as a base for the journey to Mount Hope, at the foot of the Beardmore Glacier, where the final depôt was to be laid.

The party left Hut Point on the morning of October 9th, the nine men hauling on one rope and trailing three loaded sledges. They reached Safety Camp in the early afternoon, and, after repacking the sledges with a load of about 2,000 lb., they began the journey over the Barrier. Pulling proved very difficult, and next day it was decided to separate the sledges, three men to each sledge. The new arrangement was not a success, owing to differences in hauling capacity and inequalities in the loading of sledges. So on the morning of the 12th, Mackintosh decided to push forward with Wild and Spencer-Smith, hauling one sledge with a relatively light load, and leave Joyce and the remaining five to bring two sledges and the rest of the stores at their best pace. This arrangement was maintained on the later journeys.

Persistent head winds with occasional drift made the conditions unpleasant and caused many frost-bites, but Joyce's party reached the Bluff depôt on the evening of the 21st and found that Mackintosh had been there on the 19th. Mackintosh had left 178 lb. of provisions, and Joyce left one sledge and 273 lb. of stores. The most interesting incident of the return journey was the

Shackleton had no plans for training the dogs, either on *Aurora* or *Endurance*.

It was sheer slavery to ferry thousands of pounds of dried fuel and food across the bay ice to Hut Point and Safety Camp. The men were wearing trousers made out of Scott's old tent that froze like boards. Joyce wrote, 'My nose is one black blister.'

There was a row, with Joyce yelling at Mackintosh to halt 'this farce'. They were being asked to lug 220 pounds each when the maximum agreed at the start of the journey had been 174 pounds. As a result, they were logging 3 miles a day or less. Mackintosh reluctantly agreed to cut the loads and to form these new teams. Richards later recalled this as the point when he realised that the appointment of Mackintosh as leader was a poor choice. He had no natural qualities as a leader and he lacked judgement.

181

Even more valuable than the note was six boxes of dog biscuits impregnated with cod liver oil.

discovery of a note left by Mr Cherry Garrard for Captain Scott on March 19th, 1912, only a few days before Captain Scott perished at his camp farther south. Joyce reached the hut in a blizzard on the night of the 27th, and found that Mackintosh and his party had arrived three days before. Gaze had also arrived with the dogs.

On the second journey to the Bluff depôt Mackintosh decided to use the dogs, and this plan involved sending a party to Cape Evans to get dog-pemmican. Mackintosh himself, with Wild and Spencer-Smith, started south again. Joyce remained in charge at Hut Point with instructions to start south directly the dog food was obtained. Stevens now took Gaze's place at the base, and the party, after being delayed by a blizzard, got away from Hut Point on November 5th. The men pulled in harness with the four dogs, and, as the surface was soft and the loads on the two sledges heavy, the advance was slow. Joyce, however, reached the Bluff depôt on the evening of the 14th and left 624 lb. of provisions. Mackintosh had been there several days earlier and had left 188 lb. of stores.

With the help of the dogs, mileages increased rapidly to 12 and 17, despite the fact that Joyce had blisters on his toes as big as potatoes.

Six days later Joyce was back again after an adventurous finish to his journey. About 10.30 a.m. on this day (November 20th) the party encountered heavy pressure-ice with crevasses, and had many narrow escapes. "After lunch," Joyce wrote, "we came on four crevasses quite suddenly. Jack fell through. We could not alter course, or else we should have been steering among them, so galloped right across. We were going so fast that the dogs which went through were jerked out."

On the 25th the men were again fit enough to start on their third journey to the Bluff. Mackintosh was some distance ahead, but the two parties met on the 28th and discussed plans. Mackintosh was proceeding to the Bluff depôt with the intention of taking stores to the depôt placed on lat. 80° S. in the first season's sledging. Joyce, after depositing his third load at the Bluff was to return to Hut Point for the last load, and the parties then were to join forces for the journey southward to Mount Hope.

The two teams spent Christmas Day apart: had they known it, only 5 miles separated them. Mackintosh's team smoked cigars, and sang 'Adeste Fideles'. Joyce allowed his team less celebrating – it was his eighth Christmas in the Antarctic.

Joyce was back again at Hut Point by December 7th, and, after resting dogs and men, started off once more on December 13th. This was the worst journey the party had made. Crevasses and blizzards caused infinite trouble, but they reached Bluff depôt on December 28th and found that Mackintosh had gone south two days before on his way to the 80° S. depôt, but he had not made much progress and his camp was in sight. He had left instructions to Joyce to follow him.

Joyce left the Bluff depôt on December 29th, and the parties were together two days later. Mackintosh handed Joyce instructions to proceed with his party to lat. 81° S., and place a depôt there. He was then to send three men back to Hut Point, and proceed to lat. 82° S, where he would lay another depôt. Then if provisions permitted he would push south as far as lat. 83°. Mackintosh himself was reinforcing the depôt at lat. 80° S. and would then carry on southward.

The next important incident was the appearance of a defect in one of the two Primus lamps used by Joyce's party, since it was impossible to travel without the means of melting snow and preparing hot hoosh. Joyce, therefore, decided to send three men back from the 80° S. depôt, which he reached on January 6th, 1916. Cope, Gaze and Jack returned and reached Cape Evans on January 16th. Joyce, Richards and Hayward went forward with a load of 1,280 lb., building cairns at short intervals as guides to the depôts. The dogs were being very well fed and Joyce wrote: "It is worth it for the wonderful amount of work they are doing. If we can keep them to 82° S. I can honestly say it is through their work we have got through."

In fact what happened on the 8th was that Mackintosh finally asked Joyce to act as leader of both parties, something which had been inevitable for some time, though it was brought about now by his deteriorating physical condition.

On January 8th Mackintosh joined Joyce, and from that point the parties, six men strong, went forward together. On the evening of the 12th they reached lat. 81° S., and built a large cairn for the depôt. Some of the marching had been done in thick weather, but by means of frequent cairns, with a scrap of black cloth on top of each one, they had managed to keep their course.

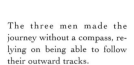

The party moved southwards again on January 13th in bad weather. "It was really surprising to find how we got on in spite of the snow and pie-crust surface. The dogs are doing splendidly. The distance for the day was ten miles 720 yards; a splendid performance considering surface and weather." During succeeding days they advanced rapidly, the daily distances being from ten to twelve miles, and they reached lat. 82° S. on the morning of January 18th. Mackintosh was in trouble with the Primus lamp in his tent, and this made it inadvisable again to divide the party.

It was, therefore, decided that all should proceed and that the last depôt should be placed on the base of Mount Hope, at the foot of the Beardmore Glacier, in lat. 83° 30′ S. The party proceeded at once and advanced five miles beyond the depôt before camping on the evening of the 18th.

The sledge loads, relieved of the stores deposited at the various depôts, were now comparatively light, and on the 19th a good advance was made. But new troubles were developing. Spencer-Smith was suffering from swollen and painful legs and Mackintosh was showing signs of exhaustion. A mountain, believed to be Mount Hope, could be seen ahead, over thirty miles away.

Spencer-Smith, who had struggled on gamely, started next morning and kept going until noon. Then he reported his inability to proceed, and Mackintosh called a halt. Spencer-Smith suggested that he should be left with provisions and a tent while the others pushed on to Mount Hope, and pluckily assured Mackintosh that the rest would put him right. This plan, after consultation, was agreed to, Mackintosh feeling that the depôt must be laid and that delay was dangerous. Spencer-Smith was left with a tent, a sledge and provisions, and told to expect the returning party in about a week. Everything possible to make him comfortable was done. He bade his companions a cheery "Good-bye" after lunch, and before evening the party was six or seven miles away.

Foggy weather hindered the advance, but on the 25th the party did seventeen and three-quarter miles, and camped on the edge of the "biggest ice-pressure" Joyce had ever seen. Of the work done on the 26th Joyce wrote, "Skipper, Richards and myself, roped ourselves together, I taking the lead, to try and find a course through this pressure. We came across very wide crevasses, went down several, came on top of a very high ridge, and such a scene! Imagine thousands of tons of ice churned up to a depth of about 300 feet." But in spite of all difficulties the depôt was laid. On the return journey Joyce was attacked by snow-blindness but "still pulled his whack," and on the 29th they reached Spencer-Smith's camp, and found him in his sleeping-bag and quite unable to walk. Joyce's diary of this date refers rather gloomily to the outlook, for he guessed that Mackintosh also would be unable to make the homeward march. "The dogs," he added, "are still keeping fit. If they will only last to 80° S. we shall then have enough food to take them in, and then if the ship is in I guarantee they will live in comfort the remainder of their lives."

No march, owing to a blizzard, could be made on the 30th, but eight miles were made on the 31st, with Spencer-Smith on one of the sledges in his sleeping-bag. He was quite helpless, but his courage never failed him. Steady advances were made on the next days, but although Joyce, Wild, Richards and Hayward were feeling fit, Mackintosh was lame and weak, and Spencer-Smith's condition was alarming. Helped, however, by strong southerly winds, the daily distances covered were very good, and by February 12th they reached the depôt at 80° S. on their return journey. Spencer-Smith seemed a little better, and all hands were cheered by the rapid advance.

February 14th, 15th and 16th were bad days owing to soft surface, and on the 18th, when the party were within twelve miles of the Bluff depôt, a furious blizzard made travelling impossible. This blizzard raged for five days. Rations were reduced on the second day, and on the third day the party went on half-rations.

"Still blizzarding," Joyce wrote on the 20th. "Things are serious, what with our patient and

The three men made the journey without a compass, relying on being able to follow their outward tracks.

Spencer-Smith was experiencing trouble with more than his leg. He wrote in his diary, 'My heart is rather ricked I fear'. But he did not believe the truth – he had a bad case of scurvy, the killer disease. It was now obvious to the Joyce team that it was utter folly for Mackintosh to have pressed on after the 80° depôt. Amazingly though, Mackintosh and Spencer-Smith continued to march, until Spencer-Smith collapsed. He was never to walk again. The others vainly tried to persuade Mackintosh to stay with him, but the 'Captain' pretended his knee was 'sprained'.

When on 26 June they laid this last depôt at the foot of the Beardmore Glacier (one of the world's biggest frozen rivers) they still thought Shackleton was coming down to it to collect supplies.

Wild nursed the two sick men with what Richards described as a 'devotion that could not be surpassed'. The Padre (as his colleagues called Spencer-Smith) blessed Wild for his kindness over the forty difficult days. He dreamt of food but there was no fresh seal meat that might have relieved his scurvy.

Joyce had now realised that Spencer-Smith and Mackintosh had scurvy.

Joyce, who had taken over from the ailing Mackintosh as leader, insisted that they leave despite the gale. They had little food and no cooking fuel left. 'Our food lies ahead and death stalks behind,' he said.

provisions running short. . . . The most serious of calamities is that our oil is running out. We have plenty of tea, but no fuel to cook it with." The men in Mackintosh's tent were in no better plight and Mackintosh himself was in a bad way.

On the 21st Joyce wrote: "I don't know what we shall do if this does not ease. It has been blowing continuously without a lull. The food for to-day was one cup of pemmican among three of us, one biscuit each, and two cups of tea among the three." Twenty-four hours later he continued: "Same old thing, no ceasing of this blizzard. Hardly any food left except tea and sugar. Richards, Haward and I, after a long talk, decided to start to-morrow in any case, or else we shall be sharing the fate of Captain Scott and his party. The other tent seems to be very quiet, but now and again we hear a burst of song from Wild, so they are in the land of the living. We gave the dogs the last of their food to-night, so we shall have to push, as a great deal depends on them."

When, on February 23rd, they started to dig out their sledge, it took them two hours, for they found themselves terribly weak after lying up with practically no food. Further quotations from Joyce's diary tell their own story:-

"Got under way about 2.20. . . . About 3.20 the Skipper, who had tied himself to the rear of the sledge, found it impossible to proceed. So, after a consultation with Wild and party, decided to pitch their tent, leaving Wild to look after the Skipper and Spencer-Smith, and make the best of our way to the depôt, which is anything up to twelve miles away, So we made them comfortable and went on.

When Mackintosh collapsed crying, 'I'm done for!' there was no alternative but to leave the three men behind and make a rush for the hut.

"I told Wild I should leave as much as possible and get back 26th or 27th, weather permitting, but just as we left them it came on to snow pretty hard, sun going in, and even with the four dogs we could only make half to three-quarters of a mile an hour. Camped in a howling blizzard. I found my left foot badly frost-bitten. Now after this march we came into our banquet — one cup of tea and half a biscuit. Situation does not look very cheerful. This is really the worst surface I have ever come across in all my journeys here."

Mackintosh had stayed on his feet as long as was humanely possible. He had been suffering for several weeks from what he cheerfully called "a sprained leg" owing to scurvy, but the responsibility for the work to be done was primarily his, and he would not give in. Spencer-Smith was sinking. Wild was in fairly good condition. Joyce, Richards and Hayward, who had undertaken the relief journey, were all showing symptoms of scurvy; their legs were weak, and their gums swollen. The decision that the invalids with Wild should stay in camp was fully justified by the circumstances. Joyce and his men had difficulty in reaching the depôt with a nearly empty sledge. Any attempt to make their journey with two helpless men might have involved the loss of the whole party.

"*February 24th, Thursday.* – Up at 4.30; had one cup of tea, half biscuit; under way after 7. Weather, snowing and blowing like yesterday. During forenoon had to stop every quarter of an hour on account of our breath. I wonder if this weather will ever clear up. Camped in an exhausted condition about 12.10. Lunch, half cup of weak tea and quarter biscuit, which took over half an hour to make. . . . This is the second day the dogs have been without food, and if we cannot soon pick up depôt and save the dogs it will be almost impossible to drag our two invalids back the 100 miles we have to go." Bad weather prevented the party from advancing again that day, but, in spite of everything, the men remained very cheerful.

Navigation was uncertain as they had lost sight of the guiding cones and had abandoned their sledge-meter so did not know how far they had travelled. They now had no food left – and the men they had left behind had had no food for five days. Hayward was in a deep depression and 'babbling'.

"*February 25th, Friday.* – Under way at 7; carried on, halting every ten minutes or quarter of an hour. Weather, snowing and blowing same as yesterday. We are in a very weak state, but we cannot give in. We often talk about poor Captain Scott and the blizzard that finished him and party. If we had stayed in our tent another day I don't think we should have got under way at all,

and we should have shared the same fate. But if the worst comes we have made up our minds to carry on and die in harness.

"We camped for our grand lunch at noon. After five hours' struggling I think we did about five miles. Decided to get under way as soon as there is any clearance. Snowing and blowing, force about fifty to sixty miles an hour."

"*February 26th, Saturday.* – We got under way as soon as possible, about 2.10 a.m. About 2.35 Richards sighted depôt. I suppose we camped no more than three-quarters of a mile from it. The dogs sighted it, which seemed to electrify them. They had new life and started to run, but we were so weak that we could not go more than 200 yards at a spell. I think another day would have seen us off. Arrived at depôt at 3.25; I don't suppose a weaker party has ever arrived at any depôt, either north or south. After a hard struggle got our tent up and made camp. Then gave the dogs a good feed of pemmican. If ever dogs saved the lives of any one they have saved ours. Let us hope they will continue in good health so that we can get out to our comrades."

The party found that none of them had any appetite although in the land of plenty, and this Joyce attributed to the reaction, and also that they found no news of the ship, which they had expected to be left there. Consequently they all thought the ship had been lost. Terrible weather followed and Joyce wrote on February 27th: "Wind continued with fury the whole night. Expecting every minute to have the tent blown off us. We are still very weak but think we can do the twelve miles to our comrades in one long march. If only it would clear up for just one day we would not mind. We have not had a travelling day for eleven days, and the amount of snow that has fallen is astonishing. *Later.* – Had a meal 10.30 and decided to get under way in spite of wind and snow. Under way 12 o' clock. We have three weeks' food on sledge, about 160 lb., and one week's dog food, 50 lb. Weight, all told, about 600 lb., and also taking an extra sledge to bring back Captain Mackintosh."

Great difficulties were ahead of them. Hayward was suffering from his knees, the dogs had lost all heart in pulling. The surface was so bad that they could hardly move the sledge at times, and their pace was not more than one-half to three-quarters of a mile per hour. But they struggled on splendidly in spite of blizzards and surface, and on February 29th Joyce wrote: "Up at 5 o'clock;

Richards found that his legs too were showing the telltale signs of scurvy.

On 28 February Mackintosh, convinced that the rescue team could not now return in time, wrote a farewell letter, noting that they had just finished the last of their food (no hot food for nine days). He paid a particular tribute to Wild ('unselfish fellow') and recorded, 'All have done their duty, nobly and well. . . . If it is God's will that we should have given up our lives then we do so in the British manner as our tradition holds us in honour bound to do.'

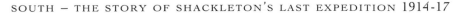

The three men still on their feet were Wild, Joyce and Richards (Wild perhaps the least affected with scurvy). The other three, Mackintosh, Spencer-Smith and Hayward were lashed on the sledges.

still very thick. It cleared a little about 8 o'clock, and, after looking round, sighted camp to the south, so got under way as soon as possible. Got up to the camp about 12.45, when Wild came out to meet us. He told us that they had no food left. The Skipper then came out of the tent, very weak and as much as he could do to talk. He said, 'I want to thank you for saving our lives.' "

Joyce meant to start back at the earliest moment, and after lunch Mackintosh went ahead to get some exercise. Presently the party were ready to get away, and when they lifted Spencer-Smith they found that he was in a great hole which he had melted through. Soon they picked up Mackintosh, who had fallen down, being too weak to walk. They put him on the sledge they had brought out, and camped about 8 o'clock. "I think we did about three miles – rather good with two men on the sledges and Hayward in a very bad way. . . . The dogs seem to have new life since we turned north. We have now to look to southerly winds for help. Hope to try and reach depôt to-morrow, even if we have to march over-time."

On March 1st and 2nd good progress on the return journey was made. "Gives one a bit of heart to carry on like this; only hope we can do this all the way." But the next day brought a raging blizzard, and they found to their disgust that it was impossible to carry on.

"*March 4th, Saturday.* – Up 5.20. Still blizzarding, but have decided to get under way as Hayward is getting worse, and one doesn't know who is the next. No mistake it is scurvy, and the only possible cure is fresh food. Smith is still cheerful; he has hardly moved for weeks and he has to have everything done for him. Got under way 9.35. It took some two hours to dig out dogs and sledges, as they were completely buried. It is the same every morning now. . . . In the afternoon wind eased a bit and drift went down. Found it very hard pulling with the third man on the sledge, as Hayward has been on all the afternoon."

This was a brave attempt to save the others from having to carry them on the sledges, but they only managed a few yards. Spencer-Smith on his sledge was mumbling prayers, sometimes in English, sometimes in Latin.

On March 5th and 6th a fair wind helped the party on their long way, but after lunch on the 6th the wind was not so helpful. "It seems to me," Joyce wrote, "that we shall have to depôt some one if the wind eases at all."

"*March 7th, Tuesday.* – There is double as much work to do now with our invalids. It is very hard going. Hayward and Skipper going on ahead with sticks, very slow pace. If one could only get some fresh food. After a consultation the Skipper decided to stay behind in a tent with three weeks' provisions, while we pushed on with Smith and Hayward. It seems hard, only about thirty miles away, and yet cannot get any help. Our gear is absolutely rotten; no sleep last night, shivering all night in wet bags."

Richards later said, 'We were within a day or two of getting him to the fresh meat that would have saved him.' The bamboo for the cross had been tied behind their knees at night to keep them straight. Bare-headed in the cold wind, they said the Lord's Prayer but Hayward was so affected that he fainted. It was a few days before the Padre's thirty-second birthday.

On the following day they wished the Skipper "Goodbye," and took Smith and Hayward on. Fair progress was made, but a very bad night followed.

"*March 9th, Thursday.* – At 4 a.m. Spencer-Smith called out that he was feeling queer. Wild spoke to him. Then at 5.45 Richards suddenly said, 'I think he has gone.' Poor Smith, for forty days in pain he had been dragged on the sledge, but never grumbled or complained. Sometimes when we lifted him on the sledge he would nearly faint, but he never complained. Wild looked after him from the start. We buried him in his bag at 9 o'clock at the following position: Ereb. 184°-Obs Hill 149°. We made a cross of bamboos and built a mound and cairn, with particulars."

Joyce described 10 March as 'the worst day we have spent'. He was particularly despondent at not knowing what had happened to Shackleton and he feared the *Aurora* had sunk with all hands. Richards was so obsessed with scurvy that he felt an overwhelming desire to drink the blood of the seals that now surrounded them.

Then they got under way again and found the going very hard. "We carried on with Hayward on sledge and camped in the dark about 8 o'clock. Turned in at 10, weary, worn and sad. Hoping to reach depôt tomorrow."

Eventually the party arrived at Hut Point about 3 p.m. on Saturday, March 11th, after a terribly strenuous and anxious time. "It seems strange after our adventures to arrive back at the old hut. This place has been standing since we built it in 1901, and has been the starting point of a few expeditions since. . . . Hut half full of snow through a window being left open and drift getting in;

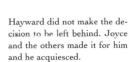

but we soon got it shipshape and Hayward in. . . . As there is no news here of the ship, and we cannot see her, we surmise she has gone down with all hands. I don't know how the Skipper will take it."

The following night all hands suffered from over-eating and all of them were also suffering from more serious trouble. Hayward could hardly move; Joyce's ankles and knees were badly swollen, and his gums prominent; Wild was very black around joints and gums very black. "After digging hut out I prepared food which I think will keep the scurvy down. The dogs have lost their lassitude and are quite frisky."

Seals were plentiful and some were killed and cooked in preparation for their journey to bring in Mackintosh. They started again on March 14th, and soon after lunch on March 16th they sighted the Skipper's camp, and through glasses saw him, to everyone's joy, outside the tent. "Picked him up at 4.15 p.m. Broke the news of Smith's death and no ship. He seems in a bad way. I hope to get him in in three days, and I think fresh food will improve him."

It was a journey of almost 90 miles to find Mackintosh, who had been alone for nine days. He seemed dazed and uncomprehending and was bleeding from the bowels.

A good distance was made on the next day, and the Skipper felt much better after good food. They arrived at Hut Point at 7 p.m. on the following day.

"Found Hayward still about the same. Now we have arrived and got the party in it remains to themselves to get better. Plenty of exercise and fresh food ought to do miracles. We have been out 160 days, and done a distance of 1,561 miles; a good record. Before turning in the Skipper shook us by the hand with great emotion, thanking us for saving his life. I think the irony of fate was poor Smith going under so short a time before we got in."

This account would be incomplete without mentioning the unselfish service rendered by Wild to his two ill tent-mates. From the time he stayed behind at the long blizzard till the death of Spencer-Smith he had two helpless men to attend to, and, despite his own condition, he was ever ready, night or day, to minister to their wants. This, in a temperature of −30° Fahr., at times, was no light task.

The men whiled away the time by cutting each other's hair and reading *Lorna Doone* aloud.

"Without the aid of our faithful friends, Oscar, Con, Gunner and Towser, the party could never have arrived back," Richards wrote. "These dogs from November 5th accompanied the sledging parties, and, although the pace was often very slow, they adapted themselves to it. Their endurance was fine. For three whole days at one time they had not a scrap of food, and this after a period of short rations. Those who returned with them will ever remember the remarkable service they rendered."

The five men who were now at Hut Point quickly found that some of the winter months must be spent there. They had no news of the ship, and were justified in assuming that she had not returned to the Sound, since if she had done so some message would have awaited them at Hut Point, if not farther south. The party must wait until the new ice became firm as far as Cape Evans. With plenty of fresh food and dried vegetables available the patients improved rapidly.

A tally of the stores at the hut showed that on a reasonable allowance the supply would last till the middle of June. Plenty of seals and a few penguins were killed, but the sole means of cooking food was an improvised stove of brick which emitted dense smoke, and covered the men and all their gear with clinging and penetrating soot. Cleanliness was impossible, and this increased the men's desire to get across to Cape Evans. During April the sea froze in calm weather, but winds took the ice out again. A spell of calm weather came during the first week of May and the sea-ice formed rapidly. The men made several short trips over it to the north.

Shackleton's assertion is contested by Richards, who had the benefit of being there. 'I have a positive recollection that there were no provisions at the hut', he recorded. 'There was absolutely nothing in the way of general provisions – no flour, no sugar, no bread. The sole food we had . . . for four whole months . . . was seal meat . . . morning, noon and night.' The blubber fire also depended on a supply of seals. Joyce made salt from seawater.

The disaster that followed is described thus by Richards. "And now a most regrettable incident occurred," he wrote "On the morning of May 8th, before breakfast, Captain Mackintosh asked Joyce what he thought of his going to Cape Evans with Hayward. Captain Mackintosh thought the

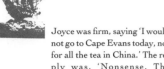

Joyce was firm, saying 'I would not go to Cape Evans today, not for all the tea in China.' The reply was, 'Nonsense. The weather is fine and the ice firm.' Richards said he believed Mackintosh could not stand the primitive conditions in the hut, compared to which Cape Evans was 'palatial'.

Joyce wrote in his diary, 'I fail to understand why these people are so anxious to risk their lives again. They could walk to Cape Evans in less than four hours perhaps . . . but it will be hell to be caught on this ice in a blizzard.' All of them were bitter that, having saved the two men from death, the latter were now acting so rashly. They took no tent, no sleeping bags, nothing for an emergency. Their disappearance coincided with Shackleton's arrival on the coast of South Georgia after his heroic fourteen-day journey in an open boat.

ice quite safe. He was strongly urged at the time not to take the risk, as it was pointed out that the ice, although firm, was very young, and that a blizzard was almost sure to take part of it out to sea."

Mackintosh naturally would be anxious to know if the men at Cape Evans were well and if they had any news of the ship. At 1 p.m., with the weather apparently changing for the worse, he and Hayward left, after promising to turn back if the weather grew worse. At 3 p.m. a moderate blizzard was raging which later on increased in fury, and the hut party had many misgivings for the safety of the absent men.

On May 10th, the first day possible, the three men left behind walked over new ice to the north to try and find some trace of the others. The footmarks were seen clearly enough raised up on the ice, and the track was followed for about two miles towards Cape Evans. Here they ended abruptly, and in the dim light a wide stretch of water, very lightly covered with ice, was seen as far as the eye could reach. It was at once evident that part of the ice over which they had travelled had gone out to sea. That Mackintosh and Hayward were actually lost was learned only on July 15th, when the party from Hut Point reached Cape Evans.

The entry in Joyce's diary shows that he had very strong forebodings of disaster when Mackintosh and Hayward left. Indeed he warned them not to go. The weather during June was persistently bad, and it was not until July 15th that the party could start for Cape Evans. They expected to have the help of a full moon, but by a strange chance they had chosen the period of an eclipse. They, however, reached Cape Evans without difficulty, and found Stevens, Cope, Gaze and Jack at the Cape Evans hut. Nothing had been seen of Captain Mackintosh and Hayward. The conclusion that they had perished was reluctantly accepted.

The men now settled down to wait for relief. When opportunity offered, Joyce led search parties to look for the bodies or any trace of the missing men, but in spite of determined efforts these expeditions were entirely unsuccessful. In September Richards was forced to lay up with a strained heart, and in the same month Joyce, Gaze and Wild went out to Spencer-Smith's grave with a wooden cross, which they erected firmly.

Relief arrived on January 10th, 1917, but it is necessary now to turn back to the events of May, 1915, when the *Aurora* was driven from her moorings.

CHAPTER XX
THE AURORA'S DRIFT

AFTER Mackintosh left the *Aurora* on January 25th, 1915, Stenhouse had considerable difficulties with the ship which were successfully overcome. The break-away from the shore came suddenly and unexpectedly on the evening of May 6th. On that day Stenhouse wrote: "4 p.m. – Wind freshening with blizzardly appearance of sky. 8 p.m. – Heavy strain on after-moorings. 9.45 p.m. – The ice parted from the shore; all moorings parted. . . . In the thick haze I saw the ice astern breaking up and the shore receding. I called all hands and clapped relieving tackles on to the cables on the fore part of the windlass. The bos'n had rushed along with his hurricane lamp, and shouted, 'She's away wi' it!' I ordered steam on main engines, and the engine-room staff, with Hooke and Ninnis, turned to. Grady, fireman, was laid up with a broken rib. As the ship, in the solid floe, set to the north-west, the cables rattled and tore at the hawse-pipes; luckily the anchors, lying as they were on a strip-sloping bottom, came away easily, without damage to windlass or hawse-pipes.

"Slowly as we disappeared into the Sound the light in the hut died away. At 11.30 p.m. the ice around us started to break up, the floes playing tattoo on the ship's sides. We were out in the Sound and catching the full force of the wind. . . . As the pack from the southward came up and closed in on the ship the swell lessened and the banging of floes alongside eased a little."

"*May 7th*. – Moderate gale with thick drift. The ice around is packing up and forming ridges 2 feet high. When steam is raised I have hopes of getting back to the fast ice near the Glacier Tongue."

At first the engineers had great difficulties with the sea connections, but these were overcome, and presently fires were lit in the furnaces, and water began to blow in the boiler. Throughout May 7th the *Aurora* drifted helplessly and on May 8th she was moving northwards with the ice. The wind freshened to a moderate southerly gale, with thick drift, in the night, and this gale continued during the following day.

"Cape Bird is the only land visible, bearing north-east true about eight miles distant," Stenhouse wrote on the afternoon of the 9th, "so this is the end of our attempt to winter in McMurdo Sound. Hard luck after four months' buffeting, for the last seven weeks of which we nursed our moorings. Our present situation calls for increasing vigilance. It is five weeks to the middle of winter. There is no sun, the light is little and uncertain, and we may expect many blizzards. We have no immediate water supply, as only a small quantity of fresh ice was aboard when we broke drift.

"The *Aurora* is fast in the pack and drifting God knows where. We have good spirits and will

It seems surprising that none of the men in the hut heard the noise of the ship being torn from its moorings and carried away. Why did Stenhouse not fire a warning shot? The men left behind at the old hut did not at first understand the full import of the loss of the ship. They thought it was a setback, no more. They made a hot drink and talked about what had happened – and listened for a message over the small radio receiver.

Joyce, back at the hut with the marooned men, was more realistic than Stenhouse. He recalled how, twenty years before, a Belgian ship with some notable men aboard, including Amundsen, had been trapped in the ice for thirteen months before she got free. The crew 'were overcome by a kind of creeping lethargy, which the doctor called "polar anemia" and which you might reckon to be none other than scurvy . . . If the *Aurora* is in a similar plight, then it will be useless to depend on her . . . '

Shackleton does not note here, although it is in the longer version, that in mid-March Stenhouse put the ship in position for winter moorings at Cape Evans, but in early May the ice broke and the ship drifted north with the ice.

get through. But what of the poor beggars at Cape Evans, and the Southern Party. It is a dismal prospect for them. There are enough provisions, but we have the remaining Burberrys, clothing, etc., for next year's sledging still aboard. I see little prospect of getting back to Cape Evans, or anywhere in the Sound. We are short of coal and held firmly in the ice. I hope she drifts quickly to the north-east, then we can try to push through the pack and make for New Zealand, coal and return to the Barrier east of Cape Crozier. This could be done, I think, in the early spring, September. We must get back to aid the depôt-laying next season."

A violent blizzard raged·on May 10th and 11th. "I never remember such wind-force; it was difficult to get along the deck." Stenhouse had had the wireless aerial rigged and tried to communicate with Macquarie Island Wireless Station (1,340 miles away) or the Bluff (New Zealand, 1,860 miles) but had no luck.

The anchors were hove in by dint of much effort on the 13th and 14th. Both anchors were broken, so the ship had only one small kedge-anchor left aboard. The record of the early months of the *Aurora's* long drift in the Ross Sea is not eventful. The ship was quite helpless in the grip of the ice, and after the engine-room bilges had been thawed and pumped out the boilers were blown down. The story of the *Aurora's* drift can be told very briefly by extracts from Stenhouse's log.

"*May 21st*. – Unable to get bearing, but imagine there is little or no alteration in ship's position, as ship's head is same, and Western Mountains appear the same. Hope all is well at Cape Evans and that the other parties have returned safely. Wish we could relieve their anxiety."

Stenhouse's log at this time also reflected his worries. 'Hope all is well at Cape Evans and that other parties have returned safely.'

"*May 24th*. – Blizzard from south-south-east. Quite a lot of havoc has been caused during this blow, and the ship has made much northing. At 2 p.m. felt heavy shock and the ship heeled to port about 70°. Ship badly jammed in."

"*May 25th*. – In middle watch felt pressure occasionally. As far as can be seen there are heavy blocks of ice screwed up on end, and the scene is like a graveyard. So near to Cape Evans, and yet we might as well be anywhere as here. Have made our sledging-ration scales, and crew are busy making harness and getting sledging equipment ready for emergencies."

"*May 26th*. – If the ship is nipped in the ice, the ship's company (eighteen hands) will take to four sledges with one month's rations and make for nearest land. If the ice sets north and takes the ship clear of land we will proceed to New Zealand and return as soon as possible."

"*June 8th*. – Made our latitude 75° 59' S. by altitude of Sirius. This is a very monotonous life, but all hands appear to be happy and contented. Find that we are not too well off for meals and will have to cut rations a little."

"*June 22nd*. – To-day the sun has reached the limit of his northern declination, and now he will start to come south. Observed this day as a holiday."

"*July 1st*. – The 1st of July! Thank God. Through all my waking hours one long thought of the people at Cape Evans, but one must appear to be happy and take interest in the small happenings of shipboard."

The log notes, 'Although worrying does no good, one cannot do otherwise in this present impotent state. 11 p.m. Wind howling and whistling through the rigging. Outside, in glare of moon, flying drift and expanse of ice-field. Desolation!' (21 June)

"*July 6th*. – This morning a lane was distinctly visible and appeared to be 200 or 300 yards wide and two miles along. At 6 p.m. loud pressure-noises were heard from the direction of the open lane and continued through the night. The incessant grinding and grating of the ice to the southward, with seething noises, as of water rushing under the ship's bottom, and ominous sounds, kept me on the *qui vive* all night, and the prospect of a break-up of the ice would have racked my nerves had I not had them numbed by previous experiences."

"*July 9th*. – Ship's position is twenty-eight miles north-north-east of Franklin Island. On the port bow and head of the ship there are some enormous pressure-ridges. Pressure heard from the southward all day."

"*July 13th.* – Very heavy pressure was heard quite close to the ship; the ice could be seen bending upwards, and occasional jars were felt on board. I am inclined to think that we shall now experience the full force of pressure from the south. We have prepared for the worst and can only hope for the best – a release from the ice with a seaworthy vessel under us."

Heavy pressure was frequent during the following days, and on July 21st the rudder was bent over to starboard and smashed, the solid oak and iron going like match-wood. On July 22nd Stenhouse wrote: "Ship in bad position in newly frozen lane, with bow and stern jammed against heavy floes; heavy strain with much creaking and groaning. – 8 a.m. Called all hands to stations for sledges, and made final preparations for abandoning ship. Allotted special duties to several hands to facilitate quickness in getting clear should ship be crushed. Am afraid the ship's back will be broken if the pressure continues, but cannot relieve her. . . . 12 p.m. – Ship is in safer position, lanes opening in every direction."

"*July 23rd.* – The ship's stern is now in a more or less soft bed, formed of recently frozen ice of about 1 foot in thickness. I thank God that we have been spared through this fearful nightmare. I shall never forget the concertina motions of the ship during yesterday's and Wednesday's fore and aft nips."

July 24th was a comparatively quiet day, but very heavy pressure about the ship occurred on the 25th. During the early hours a large field on the port quarter came charging up, and on meeting the *Aurora's* floe tossed up a ridge from 10 to 15 feet high. The blocks of ice as they broke off crumbled and piled over each other to the accompaniment of a thunderous roar. Pressure continued all the day, the floes opening and closing alternately, and the ship creaking and groaning during the nips between the floes.

"*August 4th.* – For nine days we have had southerly winds, and the last four we have experienced howling blizzards. I am sick of the sound of the infernal wind."

"*August 6th.* – After four days of thick weather we find ourselves in sight of Cape Adare in a position about forty-five miles east of Possession Isles. We felt excited this morning in anticipation of seeing the sun. It was a glorious, joyful sight. We drank to something, and with very light hearts gave cheers for the sun."

"*August 9th.* – Donolly got to work on the rudder again. It is a long job cutting through the iron sheathing-plates of the rudder, and not too safe at present, as the ice is treacherous."

"*August 10th.* – The ship's position is lat. 70° 40' S. The distance drifted from August 2nd to 6th was 100 miles, and from the 6th to 10th eighty-eight miles."

"*August 12th.* – By observation and bearings of land we are forty-five miles north-east of Cape Adare. Donolly and Grady are having quite a job with the iron platings on the rudder, but should finish the cutting to-morrow. A jury-rudder is nearly completed. The carpenter has made a good job of the rudder, although he has had to construct it on the quarter-deck in low temperatures and exposed to biting blasts."

"*August 24th.* – We lifted the rudder out of the ice and placed it clear of the stern, athwart the fore-and-aft line of the ship. We had quite a job with it (weight, 4½ tons). I am glad to see the rudder upon the ice and clear of the propeller.

"*August 25th.* – Hooke has just been in with the good news that he has heard Macquarie and the Bluff (New Zealand) sending their weather reports and exchanging signals. Can this mean they have heard the signals which Hooke has been sending, and are trying to get us now?" (It was learned afterwards that no wireless messages from the *Aurora* had been received by any station.)

"*August 31st.* – Very loud pressure-noises to the south-east. I went aloft after breakfast and had the pleasure of seeing many open lanes in all directions. The lanes of yesterday are frozen over,

The log notes on 20 July, 'Shortly after breakfast the raucous voice of the emperor penguin was heard and afterwards two were seen some distance from the ship . . . This is the emperor's hatching season, and here we meet them out in the cheerless desert of ice.'

All the time they were attempting to make radio contact. Stenhouse said of the radio expert Hooke, 'I wish for his sake that he could get through. He is a good sportsman and keeps on trying, although, I am convinced, he has little hope with this inadequate aerial.'

All these quotations from the ship's log are in fact précised from the longer entries quoted in the first edition of *South*.

Although the radio mast came down in a blizzard, it was possible to get the radio working again the following month and efforts to request a relief ship were renewed.

showing what little chance there is of a general and continued break-up of the ice until the temperature rises. We cannot get out of this too quickly."

"*September 5th*. — The mizen wireless mast came down in a raging blizzard to-day. Luckily, as it is dangerous to life to be on deck in this weather, no one was about when the mast carried away."

"*September 8th*. — This is dull, miserable weather. Sometimes it blows in this neighbourhood without snow and sometimes with — this seems to be the only difference."

"*September 9th*. — This is the first day for a long time we have registered a minimum temperature above zero for the twenty-four hours. With the increase of daylight it makes one feel that summer is really approaching."

"*September 17th*. — This is the anniversary of our departure from London. Much has happened since Friday, September 18th, 1914, and I can recall the scene as we passed down the Thames with submarines and cruisers, in commission and bent on business, crossing our course. I can also remember the regret at leaving it all, and the consequent 'fed-upness.' "

"*September 22nd*. — Since breaking away from Cape Evans we have drifted roughly 705 miles around islands and past formidable obstacles, a wonderful drift. It is good to think that it has not been in vain, and that the knowledge of the set and drift of the pack will be a valuable addition to the sum of human knowledge."

By the end of September they were so short of coal that all hope of returning to rescue the men at Ross Island had to be abandoned.

During the month of October the *Aurora* drifted uneventfully, but anxious eyes were strained in vain for indications that the day of the ship's release was near at hand. The floe, however, into which the ship was frozen, remained firm until the early days of November. The temperatures were higher now under the influence of the sun, and the ice was softer. There was a pronounced thaw on the 22nd. Stenhouse thought that a stiff blizzard would break up the pack. His anxiety was increasing with the advance of the season, and his log is a record of deep yearning to be free and active again. But the grip of the pack was inexorable. The jury-rudder was ready to be shipped when the ship was released, but meanwhile it was not being exposed to the attack of the ice. "No appreciable change in our surroundings," was the note for December 17th, and Christmas Day, with its special dinner and mild festivities, came and passed with the ice still firm.

At the end of the first week in January the ship was in lat. 65° 45' S. The pack was well broken a mile from the ship, and the ice was rolling fast. The middle of January passed, however, and the *Aurora* lay still in the ice. The period of continuous day was drawing to a close, and at midnight there was an appreciable twilight. Stenhouse ordered a thorough overhaul of the stores and general preparations for a move. The supply of flour and butter was ample, but other stores were running low, and no chance was lost of capturing seals and penguins.

The break-up of the floe in which the *Aurora* was held came on February 12th. Strong winds put the ice in motion and brought a perceptible swell. The ship was making some water, a foretaste of trouble to come, and all hands spent the day at the pumps. Work had just finished for the night when the ice broke astern and quickly split in all directions. The ship was floating now amid fragments of floe, and bumping considerably in the well. A fresh southerly wind blew during the night, and the ship started to forge ahead gradually without sail. On the morning of the 13th Stenhouse set the foresail and fore-topmast staysail, and the *Aurora* moved northward slowly, being brought up occasionally by large floes.

The log notes that two of the crew were sick, one with frost-bitten toes which were gangrened.

Navigation under such conditions, without steam or rudder, was very difficult, but Stenhouse wished if possible to save his small remaining stock of coal until he cleared the pack, so that a quick run might be made to McMurdo Sound. The jury-rudder could not be rigged in the pack. The ship was making about 3½ feet of water in the twenty-four hours, a quantity easily checked by the pumps.

(Above) Ice being cleared from the deck of the *Aurora* after a blizzard.

During the 14th the *Aurora* worked very slowly northward through heavy pack, but the ship was held up all day on the 15th, heavy floes barring progress in all directions. This state of affairs continued on the 16th, and, with a heavy swell rolling under the ice, the ship had a rough time. "I am afraid," Stenhouse wrote, "our chances of getting south are very small now."

The pack remained close, and on the 21st a heavy swell made the situation dangerous. On the night of the 25th the pack loosened, and a heavy north-west swell caused the ship to bump heavily. This state of affairs recurred at intervals in succeeding days. On the 29th Stenhouse wrote: "The battering and ramming of the floes increased in the early hours until it seemed as if some sharp floe or jagged underfoot must go through the ship's hull. . . . I am anxious about the propeller. This pack is a dangerous place for a ship now; it seems miraculous that the old Barky still floats."

The ice opened out a little on March 1st. Winter was approaching and it was imperative to get the ship out of her dangerous situation, and therefore Stenhouse ordered steam to be raised. But

There was a leak at the propeller-shaft way, and the carpenter filled the space with tar, cement and oakum, although he could not get at the actual leak.

They had been trapped for ten months. She was now 2,000 miles southeast of the southern tip of New Zealand with little coal, no reliable rudder and only wind and sails to take her through very rough waters.

progress was very slow owing to heavy floes and deep underfoots, which necessitated frequent stoppages of the engines. Before noon on the 3rd the ship came to a full stop among heavy floes, and Stenhouse had the fires partially drawn (to save coal) and banked.

No advance was made on March 4th and 5th. A moderate gale closed the ice and set it in motion, and the *Aurora*, with banked fires, rolled and bumped heavily. Seventeen bergs were in sight, and one of them was working southwards into the pack and threatening to approach the ship. "All theories about the well being non-existent in the pack are false," the anxious master wrote. "Here we are with a suggestion only of open water-sky, and the ship rolling her scuppers under and sitting down bodily on the floes." The ice opened when the wind moderated, and on the 6th the *Aurora* moved northward again.

The next three days were full of anxiety. The ship was again held by the ice and severely buffeted, while two bergs approached from the north. On the 10th the nearest berg was within three cables of the ship, but the pack opened and the ship got clear of the danger zone. During the afternoon the pack continued to open, and the *Aurora* passed through wide stretches of small loose floes and brash. She was once more bumped severely during the night.

Early next morning Stenhouse lowered a jury-rudder and moved north to north-west through heavy pack. In the late afternoon of the 13th the ship cleared the main pack but bergs and growlers were a constant menace during the hours of darkness. Anxious work remained to be done, since bergs and scattered ice extended in all directions, but at 2 p.m. on March 14th the *Aurora* cleared the last belt of pack in lat. 62° 27.5' S., long. 157° 32' E. "We 'spliced the main brace,' " says Stenhouse, "and blew three blasts of farewell to the pack with the whistle."

The *Aurora* was not at the end of her troubles, but the voyage to New Zealand need not be described in detail. Any attempt to reach McMurdo Sound was now out of the question. Stenhouse had a battered, rudderless ship, with only a few tons of coal left, and he struggled northward in heavy weather against persistent adverse winds and head seas. The jury-rudder required constant nursing, and the coal shortage made it impossible to get the best service from the engines. At times the ship could make no progress, and fell about helplessly in a confused swell or lay hove to amid mountainous seas. She was short-handed, and one or two of the men created additional difficulties. But Stenhouse displayed throughout fine seamanship and dogged perseverance.

Stenhouse was blamed, unjustly, for the drift of the *Aurora* and the plight of the Ross Sea party was felt to be his fault. However Shackleton continued to support him and in 1917 Stenhouse joined 'The Boss' on his Murmansk venture.

He accomplished successfully one of the most difficult voyages on record, in an ocean area notoriously stormy and treacherous. On March 23rd he established wireless communication with Bluff Station, New Zealand, and the next day was in touch with Wellington and Hobart. The naval officer in New Zealand waters offered assistance, and eventually it was arranged that the Otago Harbour Board's tug *Plucky* should meet the *Aurora* outside Port Chalmers.

There were still bad days to be endured. The jury-rudder partially carried away and had to be unshipped in a heavy sea. Stenhouse carried on, and on April 2nd the *Aurora* picked up the tug and was taken in tow. She reached Port Chalmers on the following morning, and was welcomed with the warm hospitality which New Zealand has always shown towards Antarctic explorers.

CHAPTER XXI
THE LAST RELIEF

W HEN I reached New Zealand at the beginning of December, 1916, I found that arrangements for relief were complete. The New Zealand Government had taken the task in hand before I had got into touch with the outside world. The British and Australian Governments were giving financial assistance. The *Aurora* had been repaired and refitted at Port Chalmers during the year, and had been provisioned and coaled for the voyage to McMurdo Sound.

My old friend, Captain John K. Davis, a member of my first Antarctic Expedition in 1907-1909, and who subsequently commanded Dr. Mawson's ship in the Australian Antarctic Expedition, had been placed in command of the *Aurora* by the Governments, and he had engaged officers, engineers and crew. Captain Davis came to see me on my arrival at Wellington, and I heard his account of the position. Stenhouse also was in Wellington, and I may say again here that his account of his voyage and drift in the *Aurora* filled me with admiration for his pluck, seamanship and resourcefulness.

After discussing the situation with the Minister for Marine, Dr. McNab, who took a deep personal interest in the Expedition, I agreed that all arrangements for the Relief Expedition should stand. Time was precious and there were difficulties about changing plans or control at the last moment. After Captain Davis had been at work for some months the Government agreed to hand the *Aurora* over to me free of liability on her return to New Zealand.

It was decided, therefore, that Captain Davis should take the ship down to McMurdo Sound, and that I should go with him to take charge of any shore operations which might be necessary. I "signed on" at a salary of 1s. a month, and we sailed from Port Chalmers on December 20th, 1916.

After a fairly quick passage Captain Davis brought the *Aurora* alongside the ice-edge off Cape Royds on the morning of January 10th, and I went ashore with a party to look for some record in the hut erected there by my Expedition in 1907. I found a letter stating that the Ross Sea party were at Cape Evans, and was on my way back to the ship when six men, with dogs and sledge, were sighted coming from the direction of Cape Evans. At 1 p.m. this party arrived on board, and they told us of the deaths of Mackintosh, Spencer-Smith and Hayward, and of their own anxious wait for relief. The seven survivors, namely, A. Stevens, E. Joyce, H. E. Wild, J. L. Cope, R. W. Richards, A. K. Jack, I. O. Gaze, were all well, though showing traces of the ordeal through which they had passed.

All that remained to be done was to make a final search for the bodies of Mackintosh and Hayward. There was no possibility whatever of either man being alive. Joyce had already searched south of Glacier Tongue. I thought that further search should be made in the area north of

The financial aid of the two governments, amounting to £20,000, was given most reluctantly.

What actually happened was rather different. Davis, who had been in command of *Nimrod* in 1907-9 and had been asked by Shackleton to command *Endurance* in 1914, was put in charge of the rescue by the Admiralty. When he heard that Shackleton had asserted that he would be in charge of the rescue, Davis offered his resignation, which was not accepted. Shackleton for his part wanted Davis removed. When the two men met, Davis said, 'I found him changed. His sufferings had left him tired: glorious failure had imposed grave worries – personal as well as financial. He had re-emerged into a world with little resemblance to the one he had left.'

Shackleton generously agreed to sign on under Davis, but in fact he had little choice because he had no money to finance a rescue and *Aurora* could have been sold off to pay his debts. 'He had the art of doing things with good grace,' says Huntford.

In the previous July, Joyce had decided that it was safe to cross the ice to Cape Evans. Afterwards Richards broke down and was diagnosed as having heart strain. Cope, the medical officer, was 'quite irrational'.

Glacier Tongue, and the old depôt off Butter Point, and I made a report to Captain Davis to this effect.

On January 12th the ship reached a point five and a half miles east of Butter Point. I took a party across rubbly and water-logged ice to within thirty yards of the piedmont ice, but owing to high cliffs and loose slushy ice we could not make a landing. There was no sign of the depôt or of any person having visited the vicinity. We returned to the ship and proceeded across the Sound to Cape Bernacchi.

The next day I took a party ashore to search the area north of Glacier Tongue, including Razorback Island, but these efforts were in vain. On the 15th a south-east blizzard prevented us from sledging, and we spent the day in putting the hut at Cape Evans in order. On the 16th Joyce and I went to Glacier Tongue, but we could see from the top that there was not the slightest chance of finding any remains owing to the enormous snow-drifts wherever the cliffs were accessible. The base of the steep cliffs had drifts 10 to 15 feet high. I considered that all places likely to hold the bodies of Mackintosh and Hayward had now been searched, and, after reaching the hut that night at 9.40, we left almost immediately for the ship. During our absence from the hut Wild and Jack had erected a cross to the memory of the three men who had lost their lives in the service of the Expedition.

Captain Davis took the ship northward on January 17th, and on February 9th the *Aurora* was berthed at Wellington. We were welcomed like returned brothers by the New Zealand people.

CHAPTER XXII

THE FINAL PHASE

THE foregoing chapters of this book represent the general narrative of our Expedition. That we failed to accomplish the object we set out for was due, I consider, not to any neglect or lack of organisation, but to the overwhelming natural obstacles, especially the unprecedented severe summer conditions on the Weddell Sea side. But, though the Expedition failed in one respect, it was, I think, successful in many others. A large amount of important scientific work was carried out; the meteorological observations in particular have an economic bearing. The hydrographical work in the Weddell Sea has done much to clear up the mystery of this, the least known of all the seas.

To the credit side of the Expedition one can safely say that the comradeship and resource of the members of the Expedition was worthy of the highest traditions of Polar service; and it was a privilege to me to have under my command men who, through dark days and the stress and strain of continuous danger, kept up their spirits and carried out their work regardless of themselves and heedless of the limelight.

The same energy and endurance which they showed in the Antarctic they brought to the Greater War in the Old World. And having followed our fortunes in the South it may interest you to know that practically every member of the Expedition was employed in one or other branches of the active fighting forces during the war. Of the fifty-three men who returned out of the fifty-six who left for the South, three have since been killed and five wounded. McCarthy, the best and most efficient of the sailors, always cheerful under the most trying circumstances, and who for these reasons I chose to accompany me on the boat journey to South Georgia, was killed at his gun in the Channel. Cheetham, the veteran of the Antarctic, who had been more often south of the Antarctic Circle than any man, was drowned when the vessel in which he was serving was torpedoed a few weeks before the Armistice.

Ernest Wild, Frank Wild's brother, was killed while mine-sweeping in the Mediterranean. Mauger, the carpenter on the *Aurora*, was badly wounded while serving with the New Zealand Infantry. The two surgeons, Macklin and McIlroy, served in France and Italy, McIlroy being badly wounded at Ypres. Frank Wild, in view of his unique experience of ice and ice conditions, was at once sent to the North Russian front, where his zeal and ability won him the highest praise. Macklin served first with the Yorks and later transferred as medical officer to the Tanks, where he did much good work. Going to the Italian front with his battalion, he won the Military Cross for bravery in tending wounded under fire.

James joined the Royal Engineers, Sound-Ranging Section, and after much front-line work

Joyce had to remain in hospital for six months and had to wear dark glasses for eighteen months to overcome his snow blindness. Richards, although he lived to be ninety, said he never fully recovered from the ordeal, which had included more days' sledging than either Scott or Shackleton had endured. Joyce lived into his eighties.

Shackleton does not mention the dogs. Three of the four survived the stay at Cape Evans – Oscar, Towser and Gunner. Oscar did not die until 1939.

Wordie was perhaps the most distinguished of the crew. After the expedition and his war service, he returned to Cambridge where he became a Fellow of St John's, then Senior Tutor and, eventually, Master of the College. He chaired the management committee of the Scott Polar Research Institute and, after serving in Naval Intelligence in World War II, he was awarded the CBE and Knighted in 1957. From 1951-54 he was President of the Royal Geographical Society which awarded him its Founder's medals. He died in 1962. His papers on oceanography, geology and the polar ice pack, published in the *Transactions* of the Royal Society of Edinburgh in 1921, constitute the main scientific results of the voyage of the *Endurance*.

Aurora was sold for £10,000, but was later lost with all hands – perhaps blown up by German mines or perhaps because her structure never recovered from the Antarctic battering. Shackleton paid off all his debts in New Zealand and sent Emily £200, the first cash he had given her in four years according to Huntford. Sir Vivian Fuchs' assessment is that, even had Shackleton made the landfall in 1915, he could not have survived the 1,000 mile overland journey to the depot at Beardmore Glacier. 'His chances of success would have been very small indeed . . . The loss of *Endurance* may have saved a worse disaster.'

was given charge of a Sound-Ranging School to teach other officers this latest and most scientific addition to the art of war. Wordie went to France with the Royal Field Artillery and was badly wounded at Armentières.

Hussey was in France for eighteen months with the Royal Garrison Artillery, serving in every big battle from Dixmude to Saint-Quentin. Worsley, known to his intimates as Depth-Charge Bill, owing to his success with that particular method of destroying German submarines, has the D.S.O. and three submarines to his credit.

Stenhouse was with Worsley as his second in command when one of the German submarines was rammed and sunk, and received the D.S.C. for his share in the fight. He was afterwards given command of a Mystery Ship, and fought several actions with enemy submarines.

Clark served on a mine-sweeper. Greenstreet was employed with the barges on the Tigris. Rickenson was commissioned as Engineer-Lieutenant, R.N. Kerr returned to the Merchant Service as an engineer.

Most of the crew of the *Endurance* served on mine-sweepers.

Of the Ross Sea Party, Mackintosh, Hayward and Spencer-Smith died for their country as surely as those who gave up their lives in France or Flanders. Hooke, the wireless operator, became navigator of an airship.

Nearly all the crew of the *Aurora* joined the New Zealand Field Forces and saw active service in one of the many theatres of war.

Four decorations have been won, and several members of the Expedition have been mentioned in dispatches.

On my return, after the rescue of the survivors of the Ross Sea Party, I offered my services to the government, and was sent on a mission to South America. When this was concluded I was commissioned as Major and went to North Russia in charge of Arctic Equipment and Transport, having with me Worsley, Stenhouse, Hussey, Macklin and Brocklehurst, who was to have come South with us, but who, as a regular officer, rejoined his unit on the outbreak of war.

Worsley was sent across to the Archangel front, where he did excellent work, and the others served with me on the Murmansk front. The mobile columns there had exactly the same clothing, equipment and sledging food as we had on the Expedition. No expense was spared to get the best of everything for them, and consequently not a single case of avoidable frost-bite was reported.

Taking the Expedition as a unit, out of fifty-six men, three died in the Antarctic, three were killed in action and five have been wounded, so that our casualties have been fairly high.

Though some have gone, there are enough left to rally round and form a nucleus for the next Expedition; when troublous times are over and scientific exploration can once more be legitimately undertaken.

EPILOGUE

SOUTH was published in November 1919. Shackleton should have started writing it immediately after his return, but according to Huntford he was unenthusiastic. His New Zealand supporter, Tripp, had urged him on, saying that he must complete the vital parts of it 'in case he got killed in the war'. Once again, Edward Saunders was brought from New Zealand to assist, and he travelled to Australia with Shackleton so that the latter could dictate material to him during the journey. There was no money to pay him so Shackleton told Tripp to sell the chronometers brought back by the Ross Sea party and give the proceeds to Saunders.

Shackleton did nothing more on the book until early 1919 when, in London, one of the expedition members, Leonard Hussey, helped him with the final editing. It was a painful process for Shackleton. In the event, the book sold extremely well, being reprinted in the month following publication and twice the following year. Alas, Shackleton gained nothing from it. He had assigned all rights to the estate of Sir Robert Lucas-Toosh, one of his benefactors of 1914, who had been killed in the First World War and whose executors insisted on repayment.

After the rescue, Shackleton was in Australia for some weeks; he returned home via the United States of America, where he gave a lecture tour. On 29 May 1917 he landed back in England, and at once settled down to clearing his debts. Although he soon wrote to Tripp, 'the whole Expedition is now paid off and clear and there are no liabilities', the fact was that Mawson the photographer had not been paid, and there may have been others. At about this time Shackleton obtained the Polar Medal for his men, although he specifically excluded McNeish, Vincent, Stephenson and Holness. Emily had taken a flat in London but Shackleton resumed his friendship with the actress Rosalind Chetwynd and with Janet Stancomb-Wills, who was loaning him money.

Shackleton was anxious to play some part in the war but nothing could be found for him. Eventually, he came under the wing of Sir Edward Carson, the famous Anglo-Irish politician, who sent him to South America – without pay – to improve British propaganda techniques there. He returned to England in April 1918. By the summer he was enrolled in a plan to start a campaign in northern Russia, which was to continue to attack 'the Bolshevik menace' despite the November armistice. Shackleton was in charge of stores for the expeditionary force.

There was an unsuccessful attempt to start up an entrepreneurial development in northern Russia, which included a franchise to develop part of Murmansk. This ended when Russian forces seized the city late in 1919. Back in England, Shackleton had no choice but to resume lecturing, appearing twice daily at the Philharmonic Hall in Great Portland Street. Huntford describes this as 'drudgery and worse'. Various business ventures, including a chemical company, came to nothing and Shackleton took to drinking rather heavily.

Leonard Tripp, a long-time supporter of Shackleton, met him on his return to New Zealand, took his finances in hand, and was present when the explorer dictated parts of the book to Saunders.

Shackleton had also bombarded the War Office with proposals to go to France. He was not actually demobilised until March 1919 on returning from Russia.

John Rowett, the schoolfriend who financed the last expedition, also financed Emily who was once more reliant on her own income of £700 a year.

(Left) On board the Quest: (back row) Green, McIlroy, Jeffrey, Marr, Carr, (front row) Macklin, Visitor, Shackleton, Wild, Worsley, Visitor, (kneeling) Kerr.

By 1920 he was openly expressing a desire to return again to the polar regions. An old school friend from Dulwich offered to finance him, but by the time the offer became firm, Shackleton was left with only three months to plan and man the expedition, half the time taken with the previous two. He sailed on 17 September 1921; having been elected to the Royal Yacht Squadron, he could now fly the White Ensign from the masthead of his ship. He also had an audience with King George V. The expedition's plans were vague: a circumnavigation of the Antarctic continent. The captain of the ship – renamed *Quest* – was his old companion Wild, and the nucleus of the old guard from *Endurance* formed the crew. Some of them thought Shackleton was seeking some mineral discovery that would release him forever from his debts, and all of them found him changed from the previous voyage, as if he had lost his vitality.

He was clearly unwell, and when *Quest* arrived at Rio de Janeiro he had a massive heart attack but, as usual, refused to be examined. He recovered somewhat when they reached South Georgia, and sailed past all the old landmarks. But on 5 January 1922 there was another heart attack, from which he did not recover. At Emily's suggestion he was buried in South Georgia.

PETER KING

GLOSSARY

Although Shackleton explains some of the technical terms in *South* it was felt necessary, in the full edition, to add an Appendix on 'Sea-Ice Nomenclature', written by Wordie. He explained that during the voyage it was noticed that the terms being used to describe the different forms of ice were not always in agreement with those given in Markham and Mill's glossary in *The Antarctic Manual*, published in 1901. An earlier publication in 1820, by Scoresby, had been superseded in some details and Wordie felt 'a restatement of terms is therefore now necessary'. The following terms are those he gives, to which has been added, at the end, a definition of the term *hoosh*, not of course connected with the ice, but vital to ice travellers.

Slush or *Sludge*.   The initial stages in the freezing of sea-water, when its consistency becomes gluey or soupy. The term is also used (but not commonly) for brash-ice still further broken down.

Pancake-ice.   Small circular floes with raised rims; due to the break-up in a gently ruffled sea of the newly formed ice into pieces which strike against each other, and so form turned-up edges.

Young Ice.   Applied to all unhummocked ice up to about a foot in thickness. Owing to the fibrous or platy structure, the floes crack easily, and where the ice is not over thick a ship under steam cuts a passage without much difficulty. Young ice may originate from the coalescence of "pancakes," where the water is slightly ruffled; or else be a sheet of "black ice," covered maybe with "ice-flowers," formed by the freezing of a smooth sheet of sea-water.

In the Arctic it has been the custom to call this form of ice "bay-ice"; in the Antarctic, however, the latter term is wrongly used for land-floes (fast ice, etc.), and has been so misapplied consistently for fifteen years. The term bay-ice should possibly, therefore, be dropped altogether, especially since, even in the Arctic, its meaning is not altogether a rigid one, as it may denote, first, the gluey "slush," which forms when sea-water freezes, and, secondly, the firm level sheet ultimately produced.

Land-floes.   Heavy but not necessarily hummocked ice, with generally a deep snow covering, which has remained held up in the position of growth by the enclosing nature of some feature of the coast, or by grounded bergs throughout the summer season when most of the ice breaks out. Its thickness is, therefore, above the average. Has been called at various times "fast ice," "coast ice," "land-ice," "bay-ice" by Shackleton and David and the Charcot Expedition; and possibly what Drygalski calls *Schelfeis* is not very different.

Floe.   An area of ice, level or hummocked, whose limits are within sight. Includes all sizes between brash on the one hand and fields on the other. "Light floes" are between one and two feet in thickness (anything thinner being "young ice"). Those exceeding two feet in thickness are termed "heavy floes," being generally hummocked, and in the Antarctic, at any rate, covered by fairly deep snow.

Field.   A sheet of ice of such extent that its limits cannot be seen from the masthead.

Hummocking.   Includes all the processes of pressure formation whereby level young ice becomes broken up and built up into

Hummocky Floes. The most suitable term for what has also been called "old pack" and "screwed pack" by David, and *Scholle-neis* by German writers. In contrast to young ice, the structure is no longer fibrous, but becomes spotted or bubbly, a certain percentage of salt drains away, and the ice becomes almost translucent.

The Pack is a term very often used in a wide sense to include any area of sea-ice, no matter what form it takes or how disposed. The French term is *banquise de dérive.*

Pack-ice. A more restricted use than the above, to include hummocky floes or close areas of young ice and light floes. Pack-ice is "close" or "tight" if the floes constituting it are in contact; "open" if, for the most part, they do not touch. In both cases it hinders, but does not necessarily check, navigation; the contrary holds for

Drift-ice. Loose open ice, where the area of water exceeds that of ice. Generally drift-ice is within reach of the swell, and is a stage in the breaking down of pack-ice, the size of the floes being much smaller than in the latter. (Scoresby's use of the term drift-ice for pieces of ice intermediate in size between floes and brash has, however, quite died out). The Antarctic or Arctic pack usually has a girdle or fringe of drift-ice.

Brash. Small fragments and roundish nodules; the wreck of other kinds of ice.

Bergy Bits. Pieces, about the size of a cottage, of glacier-ice or of hummocky pack washed clear of snow.

Growlers. Still smaller pieces of sea-ice than the above, greenish in colour, and barely showing above water-level.

Crack. Any sort of fracture or rift in the sea-ice covering.

Lead or *Lane.* Where a crack opens out to such a width as to be navigable. In the Antarctic it is customary to speak of these as leads, even when frozen over to constitute areas of young ice.

Pools. Any enclosed water areas in the pack, where length and breadth are about equal.

NOTE

HOOSH is the name British polar explorers gave to their sledging food. Its base was pemmican, a concentrate made up of ground, dried meat mixed with fat. This was melted over the Primus stove with a little water to which was added broken biscuit; the biscuit itself was hardened with gluten, a cereal protein. To brighten up a boring hoosh 'soup', chocolate, cheese, sugar, et cetera might be added. Since the mixture was totally devoid of vitamin C, it was inevitable that scurvy would develop if the hoosh was not supplemented by fresh meat or some other source of the vitamin.

INDEX

This index refers to this edition and is not comparable with the short index in the relevant edition of *South*. Illustrations are denoted by italic page numbers and margin notes by page number followed by n.

ACKNOWLEDGEMENTS

Every reader of *South* will benefit from the biographies written by Margery and Jay Fisher (Barrie, 1957, OP) and Roland Huntford (Hodder and Stoughton, 1985) and I am grateful to have been able to use material from these books in the notes, captions, Introduction and Epilogue. A book which has been recently published in Australia has also been valuable. This is Lennard Bickel's *Shackleton's Forgotten Argonauts* (in paperback as *The Last Antarctic Heroes*, Allen & Unwin, Australia), which deals with the Ross Sea party. For reasons explained in my notes, Shackleton treats this group as a separate expedition from the 'main' party and Bickell provides much additional material from interviews with Dick Richards, a survivor, and from the newly-discovered diaries of Spencer-Smith. I am glad to have been able to use this in my notes.

Mr Richard Kossow first drew my attention to the Hurley photographs which had been exhibited in Australia and which appear to have been captioned by him, and these are reproduced with Mr Kossow's kind permission. Plates by Hurley are available in the Royal Geographical Society's picture library and I am grateful to the Society and to Miss Rachel Duncan, the picture librarian, for being able to reproduce from them. The Society has presentation albums of Hurley prints, possibly gathered together by Hurley himself, which have been a useful source, and the Scott Polar Research Institute also has two similar albums from which they have kindly allowed me to reproduce pictures. I am most obliged to Mr Robert Headland, the Institute's archivist, and to Mr David Rootes for their assistance. The captions, apart from those specifically noted as being by Hurley, and thus from the exhibition mentioned above, are my own and any errors therefore my responsibility. There is scope for error since, for reasons explained in the text, many of Hurley's plates were lost, others were obtained after the expedition returned, and for significant sections of the expedition neither Hurley nor his cameras were available. In particular, although Spencer-Smith is said to have been appointed photographer for the Ross Sea party, it is not known what happened to his pictures. In 1929, Ernest Joyce published a book based on his journal, illustrated with a number of photographs, including one captioned to indicate that the Ross party's photographer was A. O. Stevens. Possibly many members of both parties had cameras and managed to save some of their exposed film. The only pictures in the book which I am sure were not contemporary with the expedition are a few in the Ross Party chapters which are from the Royal Geographical Society's albums and taken by the earlier Scott expedition at Hut Point where the Ross Party based themselves. The map of Elephant Island was kindly lent to me by Mrs Alison Stancer, daughter of Sir James Wordie and I am very grateful to her for her assistance.

Hurley, a most distinguished photographer, seems to have worked on his prints over the years, introducing elements of drama where these were lacking, and as a result some of them have been published in different forms over the years.

My thanks also to David Fordham, whose contribution has been far more than that of designer, and to Mary Scott and Angie Hipkin for their editorial and transcription work.

PETER KING

PICTURE CREDITS

In the following page references *T*: top, *B*: bottom, *L*: left, *R*: right, *M*: middle

Australian Antarctic Division: 179*R*

Hulton Picture Library: 22

Richard Kossow: 26, 49, 61, *74*, 82, 86, 88*BL*, 94, 97, 98, 102, 112, 131, 126, 132, 133, 135, 143, 159

Mawson Institute, Adelaide: 193

Royal Geographical Society: 35, 63, 68, *70R*, 76, 77, 83, 85, 89, 90, 91, 100, 113, 119*T*, 120, 129, 141, 142, 145, 162, 163, 165, 166, 168, 170

Scott Polar Research Institute: 2, 6, 23, 27, 28, 29, 30, 31, 32, 33, 34, 36, 37, 38, 39, 40, 41, 42, 43, 44, 45, 46, 47, 48, 49*M,R*, 50, 51, 52, 53, 54, 55, 56, 57, 58, 59, 60, 62, 64, 65, 66, 69, *70L*, 71, 73, 75, 78, 79, 80, 81, 84, 88*TL*, 88*TR*, 88*BR*, 92, 103, 105, 107, 108, 109, 111, 116, 118, 119*B*, 123, 124, 137, 138, 139, 148, 149, 155, 156, 157, 158, 160, 164, 179*L*, 179*M*

Syndication International: 18

Pictures were reproduced from the following books:

Margery and James Fisher, *Shackleton* (Barrie, 1957): 8, 9, 10, 12 (*South Polar Times*), 13, 15, 17, 21, 72, 200 (*F. L. Horton*)

Sir Ernest Shackleton, *South, The Story of Shackleton's 1914-17 Expedition,* (William Heinemann Ltd, 1919): 65, 109, 134, 178, 185

Maps
First Edition (*Caroline Simpson*): 24-5, 174

Every effort has been made to contact the copyright holders of the material reproduced; but if any has been inadvertently overlooked the necessary correction will be made in any future edition of this book.

Picture research by Peter King and David Fordham